REDISTRIBUTIVE EFFECTS OF GOVERNMENT PROGRAMMES:

The Chilean Case

Other Titles of Interest

BALASSA, B.
Policy Reform in Developing Countries
COLE, S.
Global Models and the International Economic Order
JOLLY, R.
Disarmament and World Development
LASZLO, E.
The Inner Limits of Mankind:
Heretical Reflections on the Predicament of Mankind
LASZLO, E. & BIERMAN, J.
Goals in a Global Community, Volume 1
Goals in a Global Community, Volume 2
MENON, B. P.
Global Dialogue:
The New International Economic Order
PECCEI, A.
The Human Quality
TICKELL, C.
Climatic Change and World Affairs
WENK, E.
Margins for Survival:
Political Limits in Steering Technology

The World Employment Programme (WEP) was launched by the International Labour Organisation in 1969, as the ILO's main contribution to the International Development Strategy for the Second United Nations Development Decade.

The means of action adopted by the WEP have included the following:

—short-term high-level advisory missions;

—longer-term national or regional employment teams; and

—a wide-ranging research programme.

A landmark in the development of the WEP was the World Employment Conference of 1976, which proclaimed inter alia that "strategies and national development plans should include as a priority objective the promotion of employment and the satisfaction of the basic needs of each country's population". The Declaration of Principles and Programme of Action adopted by the Conference have become the cornerstone of WEP technical assistance and research activities during the closing years of the Second Development Decade.

This publication is the outcome of a WEP project.

REDISTRIBUTIVE EFFECTS OF GOVERNMENT PROGRAMMES
The Chilean Case

by

ALEJANDRO FOXLEY
Corporation for Latin American Economic Research (CIEPLAN), Santiago, Chile

in collaboration with

EDUARDO ANINAT
Boston University, Boston, USA

J. P. ARELLANO
Corporation for Latin American Economic Research (CIEPLAN), Santiago, Chile

A study prepared for the International Labour office within the framework of the World Employment Programme

PERGAMON PRESS

Oxford · New York · Toronto · Sydney · Paris · Frankfurt

U.K. Pergamon Press Ltd., Headington Hill Hall, Oxford OX3 0BW, England

U.S.A. Pergamon Press Inc., Maxwell House, Fairview Park, Elmsford, New York 10523, U.S.A.

CANADA Pergamon of Canada, Suite 104, 150 Consumers Road, Willowdale, Ontario, M2J 1P9, Canada

AUSTRALIA Pergamon Press (Aust.) Pty. Ltd., P.O. Box 544, Potts Point, N.S.W. 2011, Australia

FRANCE Pergamon Press SARL, 24 rue des Ecoles, 75240 Paris, Cedex 05, France

FEDERAL REPUBLIC OF GERMANY Pergamon Press GmbH, 6242 Kronberg-Taunus, Pferdstrasse 1, Federal Republic of Germany

---

First Edition 1979

British Library Cataloguing in Publication Data

Foxley, Alejandro
Redistributive effects of government programmes.
1. Income distribution – Chile
2. Chile – Economic policy
I. Title II. Aninat, Eduardo III. Arellano, J P
IV. International Labour Office.
World Employment programme
339.2.0983 HC195.15 78–41098

ISBN 0–08–023130–6

The responsibility for opinions expressed in signed articles, studies and other contributions rests solely with their authors, and publication does not constitute an endorsement by the International Labour Office of the opinions expressed in them.

The designation employed and the presentation of material do not imply the expression of any opinion whatsoever on the part of the International Labour Office concerning the legal status of any country or territory or of its authorities, or concerning the delimitation of its frontiers.

Printed in Great Britain by
Biddles Ltd, Guildford, Surrey

Contents

Preface

The most striking feature of economics today is the increasingly dominant position of distributional aspects in the discussion of almost any issue. Concern with income distribution in developing countries, which started in the 1960s, represented a reaction to the growth-oriented development theory of earlier days. The present upsurge of interest in distributional problems in industrialised countries has started a little later – perhaps as a consequence of the decline in the rate of economic growth which began in the early 1970s. But it is an upsurge almost without precedent – as witnessed by the flow of reports emanating, e.g. from the Royal Commission on the Distribution of Income and Wealth, or from the Australian Commission of Inquiry into Poverty (the Henderson Commission), and by the numerous studies appearing in the United States, France, Scandinavia, etc. For developing countries most studies of income distribution are due mainly to the work of the World Bank and of the International Labour Organisation's Programme on Income Distribution and Employment, but purely national studies are also becoming more frequent.

Within the broad field of income distribution one particular area has so far not received the attention it deserves – the area of redistributive effects of fiscal policy. There are a number of such studies for developed countries, beginning with the classical study of Tibor Barna on redistribution in Great Britain in 1937 and leading to the present appearance of a number of studies on redistribution in the United States and some other industrialised countries. Systematic attempts to examine redistributive effects of government expenditure and taxation in developing countries are, however, very few. The present study by Alejandro Foxley and his collaborators should take pride of place as one of the most systematic and comprehensive examinations of redistribution in a developing country.

The authors of this book make a thorough examination of government redistributive policy in Chile over the period 1964 until 1973. They examine the incidence of taxation, government expenditure and social security operations on different income groups and note the critical factors which limited vertical redistribution effects of fiscal policy. Their analysis, however, is not confined to evaluation of the distributional effects of the traditional fiscal instruments. They conclude their study by examination of the redistributive effectiveness of two non-traditional policy instruments, of the land-reform programme and of nationalisation of industrial enterprises. Their work is a pioneering exercise in an important field of economic policy and can be recommended not only to those interested in Chile but to the wider audience concerned with economic development in general.

FELIX PAUKERT
Chief Income Distribution
and International Employment
Policies Branch,
International Labour Office

Geneva, November 1978

CHAPTER 1

State and Redistribution

The intervention of the State in economic life is a topic of permanent controversy. In every modern society the State is a fundamental agent in the functioning of the economy. A growing proportion of national income is channelled through the State or is generated in state-controlled productive units. Particularly since the so-called Keynesian revolution in economic thought, the State has come to control and manage a broad set of economic policy instruments, by means of which it intervenes, defines and modifies the rules of the economic game and the relations between the various productive and consuming agents. These mechanisms in turn invest the State with the ability to generate benefits for and impose losses on the various social groups. The State is not a neutral entity from the point of view of distribution. It extracts and reorients resources in various directions, strongly influenced by the economic and political forces which provide its support and basis of action. The outcome could be to accentuate spontaneous tendencies originating in the free play of the market, or to correct distortions, even to radically change the distributive content of the process of economic growth. This is one of the characteristics that renders the role of the State a controversial one and explains why the discussion about its action in the economy is already quite old and charged with ideological content.

The topic takes on special relevance in developing economies. The low levels of *per capita* income in these economies and its unequal distribution are conducive to greater dissatisfaction with the functioning of the economic system in these societies. The State, then, takes on a greater importance as the centre of power and as the point at which these problems can be solved.

In a mixed economy, the State controls or directly participates in the process of capital accumulation. The nature and interests of the groups with access to the State may influence the form that capital accumulation takes (public, private or collective), therefore indirectly conditioning the development pattern.[1] The development pattern, in turn, provides the framework within which the economic policies and the instruments to carry them out are specified. Policies may be exclusively growth-oriented or they may have a redistributive character, according to the development strategy chosen.

Recent attention in economic thinking has shifted towards redistribution-oriented development, and one of the topics that clearly emerge from this new concern is how can the government influence the way income and welfare is distributed in society? The study of this topic necessarily involves the identification of the beneficiaries of state action and of those who have paid its cost, of the pattern of income distribution that results from state action and of the relation between the pattern of distribution and the type of development being applied.

A thorough analysis of these matters would probably require an interdisciplinary approach and the incorporation of a large number of variables. Economists have provided partial contributions in the form of studies of public finance and fiscal incidence.[2] In this book, we intend to take up the incidence approach and place it in the broader perspective of the problem described above. Our effort is partial and tentative. It does not go beyond the undisciplinary framework, but we hope it will serve to provide some clarifying insights and open the way for future studies of an interdisciplinary nature.

The empirical part of this study is focused on several features of state action in Chile between the years 1964 and 1973. In particular, we will

[1]For a discussion of this relation, see F. H. Cardoso, *Estado y sociedad en América Latina,* Ediciones Nueva Visión, Buenos Aires, 1972.

[2]For Latin American countries, see Urrutia and Sandoval, ''Fiscal policy and income distribution in Colombia'', in A. Foxley (ed.), *Income Distribution in Latin America*, Cambridge University Press, 1976; R. Webb, ''Government policy and the distribution of income in Peru'', Princeton University Discussion Papers No. 39, 1973; and a survey in L. de Wulf, ''Fiscal incidence studies in developing countries: Survey and Critique'', IMF Staff Papers, March 1975.

examine the impact on various socio-economic groups of economic policy instruments with redistributive potential. The empirical analysis should lead to tentative conclusions about the interrelations between the nature of the State and the pattern of development chosen.

STATE REDISTRIBUTIVE ACTIVITY IN CHILE

The Chilean economy offers an interesting opportunity to study the use of redistributive instruments and to analyse their potential and limitation in advancing toward a more egalitarian growth process. This country was one of the pioneers in Latin America in the search for greater equality of incomes and opportunities. State intervention, which has been quite significant during the past 50 years, has not been neutral from the point of view of income distribution.

At the beginning of the 1970s, Chile had the highest level of state participation in the economy of any of the Latin American countries. The coefficient of public spending to GNP in Chile was higher than the Latin American average.[3]

The Chilean state apparatus consists of a centralized or fiscal sector and a decentralised sector composed of agencies that are autonomous but administrative and usually financially dependent on the central government. By 1970 fiscal expenditures represented 24 per cent of GNP, whereas the public sector as a whole – the sum of centralised and autonomous institutions – totalled 46 per cent.[4] The present study covers the entire public sector.

The situation observed at the beginning of the 1970s is the result of a long, growing process of state intervention. The process had its roots in the changes occurring in Chile in the nineteenth century, but did not achieve breadth until the first decades of the present century. Perhaps the

[3] For country figures, see ECLA, *Economic Survey of Latin America, 1970,* Santiago, 1971.

[4] These coefficients are provided only as an illustration. Strictly speaking, the numerator and the denominator are not comparable. The definition of public expenditure in the numerator includes transfers which are consolidated in the definition of GNP. Thus the measure overestimates the real participation of the government in economic activity. The State was directly responsible for somewhat more than 14 per cent of domestic production and 16 per cent of employment.

first initiatives of a purely redistributive nature took place in the 1920s, as will be described below. The following period, from 1938 to 1955, was one of consolidation and extension of the policies envisaged in the previous years, with significant advances for the middle sectors. After an intervening decade in which egalitarian efforts were restricted in order to pursue price stabilization, the period of greatest emphasis on redistribution in the country's history was begun in 1965. Not only is the sector to be benefited more numerous – encompassing now the peasants and the marginal urban groups – but the quantity of resources to be transferred and the gamut of instruments used is also greater. It is this period that is the object of the analysis in the following chapters.

The background of the process begun in the 1920s is to be found in the prior trajectory of the Chilean economy. During the nineteenth century and up to the great crisis of 1930, the "engine" of national development was external demand. The dynamic sectors of the economy until the last third of the nineteenth century were the mining of high-grade metals – copper, silver and gold – and agricultural exports. Social structure was dominated by an oligarchy whose control was unchallenged and whose use of the state apparatus was oriented to the building of infrastructure for export activity.

Nitrate mining assumed the central role in the economy in the last two decades of the nineteenth century and lasted until shortly after the First World War. The nature of the nitrate mining and the foreign control of mine ownership had much to do with what happened later on. The labour needs in the mines were met by a heavy migration from the central zone of the country and created a worker proletariat hitherto unknown in Chile. This generated the groundwork for an organised workers' movement that soon became an important factor in the social process.

The foreign ownership of the nitrate mines encouraged the growth of the State in response to the need to develop mechanisms to capture part of the export earnings and channel them into internal economic development. The construction of the first railways was speeded up and additional infrastructure works were financed with taxes levied on the export sector. Policies to increase the participation of non-oligarchical groups in the fruits of development continued to be absent. The government budget barely provided for scant funds for education and for charitable works organised by the Church.

The kind of state intervention, together with the diversification of the economy and the expansion of services as a result of urbanisation, set the stage for the rise of a middle sector whose influence in subsequent periods of social development would be significant.[5]

This process of rapid urbanisation accompanied by the rise of a strong proletariat and the emergence of the middle sectors has its only parallel in Argentina among the Latin American countries of the era.

The emerging groups made their presence felt in the social sphere by organising themselves in labour unions[6] and expressing their demands in various ways, including violent strikes.[7] The degree of social tension brought about by this process caused the State to be more receptive to social demands. Significant changes occurred in the administration of Arturo Alessandri in the first half of the 1920s. The new attitude toward urban workers led to the adoption of the first genuinely redistributive measures. The group of "social laws" promulgated in this period is an example of these measures. The most important were the creation of social-security programmes for blue-collar workers (1924) and non-government white-collar employees (1925), the implementation of the income tax (1924) and of the progressively scaled Global Complementary Tax (1925), and the adoption of the Labour Code (1931).

The policies were oriented to the defence of wage earners in the process of collective bargaining and provided for a system of free medical attention, sick pay and disability and old-age pensions. The programmes were financed by the State but were of limited coverage. Only a small portion of workers actually had access to their benefits, which in some cases, such as retirement pensions, involved extremely small amounts of money.

While the tax measures of the period were not of great significance in terms of providing additional revenues for the public budget, they introduced progressivity for the first time into Chilean tax levies.

The process of state intervention for redistributive motives was in large measure interrupted by the 1930 crisis, which severely affected the

[5]See A. Pinto, "Desarrollo económica y relaciones sociales en Chile", *Un Caso de desarrollo frustrado,* Ed. Universitario, Santiago, 1973.

[6]By 1920 there were more than 100,000 workers affiliated to labour unions.

[7]See C. Pizarro, "Hacia una interpretación global de la evolución de la huelga y del sindicato en Chile, 1890–1970", CEPLAN, 1975.

Chilean economy. State action was redirected to face the emergency. The crisis did serious damage to the economy because of its extreme dependency on foreign trade. At the same time, a new style of development, based on import substitution with strong state support, was adopted in response to the crisis.

During the 1938–55 period, most of which was under Radical Party governments, the import substitution process was promoted by protectionist policies for domestic industry and direct state intervention to stimulate the development of the manufacturing sector. Public funds were chanelled through the Development Corporation (CORFO), which was established for that purpose in 1939. During those years the State undertook major direct investments in energy (electricity, oil), iron and steel works, which were indispensable for industrial development. The development of private industry was also backed by state financing. It was thought that these measures would benefit all social sectors and constituted, therefore, an effective measure to improve the standards of living of the middle- and low-income groups.

Nevertheless, the governments had to respond to the pressures from the middle sectors, which constituted the bulk of their support. The result was the establishment of more directly redistributive measures encompassing wage and social-security policies, public spending and subsidisation of basic consumer products.

The wages policy, aimed at defending the purchasing power or workers' earnings against inflation, provided for obligatory wage readjustments. In order to protect workers with less bargaining power, minimum wages were established first for white-collar workers (1937) and later for farm workers (1953) and urban workers (1956). Although wage statistics for this period are of doubtful reliability, they indicate a relative improvement for the white-collar sector.

Social-security changes were designed to increase the coverage of the system and to improve its benefits. This also brought about a relative advance for white-collar workers.

Price policy was a widely used instrument to protect the buying power of the urban consumers. Controlled prices were applied to basic consumption agricultural products, to rents, and to other products considered to be essential. By means of exchange policy, certain consumer items such as gasoline were subsidised. The public budget provided subsidies for urban mass transit and for transportation in general.

State revenues and expenditures showed a continuous growth trend. The collection of revenues had to depend increasingly on internal sources due to the reduced weight of foreign trade in the economy and the new commitments assumed by the State. Tax rates were raised and coverage was extended, with emphasis on indirect taxes. The new expenditures were oriented to financing works of development promotion and social programmes. Outlays for education and social security were increased while at the same time new government-financed programmes appeared in the fields of public health and housing construction.

The demands made on the State by the principal pressure groups were so strong that they led to the acceleration of inflation. On the one hand, the middle sectors strongly pushed their demands for higher real wages (wage readjustments and price controls) and public benefits (social security, housing, health and education). On the other hand, the entrepreneurial sector exerted no less pressure to increase real profits (through price readjustments, wage controls, and resistance to tax increases) and to expand the volume of credits – subsidised as a rule – channelled to the private sector by the State.

Since the power of the various pressure groups was relatively equivalent, and because their demands contradicted one another, the State was unable to resolve the conflicts satisfactorily on a permanent basis. The course taken by the State frequently was to provide temporary satisfaction to the demands of the various groups by going beyond the limits imposed by available resources, thus building up inflationary pressure.

The years after 1955 are characterised by the persistence of what came to be known as the "social draw" among the various groups and by the attempts of a state apparatus representing various power coalitions to resolve the impasse.

In summary, the years 1938–55 were for the middle sectors – white collar and skilled workers – a period of extension of benefits channelled through the public budget and of improvement of wage levels. The decade after 1955 saw redistributive policies relegated to a very secondary plane as the emphasis of the economic programme shifted to price stability.[8]

[8] For an analysis of the decades of the 1950s and 1960s, see R. Ffrench-Davis, *Políticas económicas en Chile, 1952–70*. Ediciones Nueva Universidad, Santiago, 1973.

The anti-inflationary measures imposed often implied wage readjustments below inflation rates and attempts to reduce government spending. The main source of improvement of poorer groups income was considered to be the economic growth that would be achieved as one of the natural effects of halting inflation. Meanwhile, the stimulation of growth – which depended fundamentally on private initiative – was undertaken by granting privileges and tax exemptions to attract private investment from national and foreign capital.

A plan for construction of low-cost housing supported by state funds was an exception to the general policy. The programme was developed in the years 1959–62 as an attempt to stimulate the depressed level of economic activity of the previous years.

The failure of the stabilisation programmes and the losses in real wage levels suffered by wage earners led the great majority of the electorate to support programmes offering a more egalitarian distribution of the fruits of development. From 1965 on, the idea that the improvement of living standards of low-income groups was based exclusively on economic growth gave way to renewed emphasis on redistributive policies. Indeed, it was now postulated that the reduction of inequalities constitutes a requisite for economic growth.

The redistribution process thus emerged again with even greater intensity than in prior periods. The volume of resources to be transferred and the number of instruments to be employed for this purpose were greater than in previous years. Non-traditional mechanisms such as land reform were included. Moreover, the policies adopted reached all social groups. Groups such as peasants and certain urban sectors that previously had been on the fringe of state action began in this period to be involved as beneficiaries of important public programmes.

The economic programme carried out during the last 6 years of the 1960s had among its explicit objectives the redistribution of income in favour of workers, and in particular in favour of the peasants. The traditional wage readjustment policy was used for this purpose. In addition, a tax reform was carried out to introduce greater progressivity in the system and provide revenue to finance the increased spending. Tax revenues increased 140 per cent during the 6 years, from both direct and indirect levies. The new direct taxes, especially the property tax and the readjustability of previous year taxes, contributed to the progressivity of the system. Public expenditures registered increases in practically all government departments during the period, with the greatest rises in educational programmes, housing and agrarian reform. Government spending rose 125 per cent in real terms between 1964 and 1970.

A programme of agrarian reform which included the expropriation of 15 per cent of agricultural land was started. At the same time, unionisation was promoted, especially among farm workers, and neighbourhood organisations were set up among popular urban sectors in order to redistribute power towards the weaker groups.

A triennium of even greater redistributive emphasis began in 1970. Along with redistribution, the government's highest priority was the transformation of economic and social structure. Worker and peasant sectors were the principal beneficiaries of state action, which was carried out mainly through changes in the system of ownership. The agrarian reform was speeded up until large land holdings were eliminated. In 2 years, expropriations reached 35 per cent of total agricultural land. Parallel to the agrarian reform was the creation of the area of social property, which came to encompass 360 manufacturing enterprises under state ownership. In this way, the State obtained the control of over 60 per cent of the capital in the industrial sector. The purpose of the nationalisations was to lay the foundation for a socialist economy that would allow the State to secure control of resources in order to channel them to the priority social sectors.

Wage policy, which provided readjustments higher than inflation rates, and the sharp increase in public spending were also oriented to benefit workers while at the same time seeking to expand employment. Prices of essential products and many inputs were subsidised and/or controlled, in an attempt to alter the structure of relative prices in favour of increasing consumption among low-income sectors.

The mechanics of the process of changes undertaken in these 9 years required a broadening of low-income groups' organisational base and of their participation in the state apparatus. The political activation and increase in real power among the poorer groups led them to intensify their demands on the State. Since the State could not in the short term abandon its traditional commitments, it was confronted with demands that exceeded by far its possibilities of action. The result was acute inflation.

The disproportion between response capability and demands that characterised the situation of the State and the struggle for power at all institutional levels were particularly acute in the 1972–73 biennium. The political-social tension and the loss of efficiency in the economy that were the result of these distortions explain at least in part the institutional crisis that led to the end of the Allende government and to the establishment of an authoritarian military régime.

In the new economic scheme defined at the end of 1973, improvements for low-income sectors are basically made dependent on the benefits received from growth – based on private initiative – expected once high inflation was reduced.

As can be seen in this brief overview, the Chilean experience in redistribution is rich in intensity and in the variety of mechanisms utilised.

CRITERIA FOR EVALUATING STATE ACTION IN CHILE

In order to judge the action of the State in Chile it is necessary to propose – explicitly or implicitly – some objective or goal of economic activity. Likewise it becomes necessary to evaluate the relative efficiency of the various economic agents in the accomplishment of the goal. Within the context of the capitalist market economies the predominant position in this respect has been an explicit preference for the "non-intervention" by the State.

This view assumes that the free play of private interests through the market leads to the best allocation of resources and maximum growth. Thus state intervention is justified only in very specific areas and in exceptional situations. It encompasses the function of distribution of public goods (defence, justice, etc.) which cannot be efficiently produced in private form and consequently should be provided by the public sector. It also includes intervention in the presence of distorted market prices due to the absence of competitive conditions (monopoly, oligopoly, etc.). These in turn could be derived from inadequate information, the existence of various externalities, and of economies of scale. Some of the latter have been called "natural monopolies", as is the case with public services such as railway transportation, telecommunications, etc.

The basic assumptions behind this model are that the productive structure is homogenous, that resources and factors are perfectly mobile, that information flows without restrictions and that the decision-making units (families, enterprises) enjoy symmetrical positions in the socio-political system so that accumulation of power is effectively prevented. Under these assumptions, no distortions occur in resource allocation. Moreover, the efficiency of the latter is measured in terms of the maximisation of national income.

The validity of the approach is obviously influenced by the reliability of its assumptions. If distortions in the economic structure are the rule rather than the exception – an empirically verifiable question – then the potential for broader state action is much greater. In the Latin American economies in particular, there are two characteristics that seem to directly contradict the assumptions of the competitive model. One is the tendency toward concentration of income and therefore of power, with all the detrimental consequences for resource allocation and maximisation of collective welfare. The other is the heterogeneity of the productive apparatus and its pronounced monopolistic and oligopolistic nature. In such circumstances, it is difficult to speak solely in terms of small corrections or doing away with distortions.

Nor is it likely that the same conclusions will be reached about the role of the State if the principal objective posited for economic activity is not only the maximisation of national income but encompasses, for example, an improved distribution of income and opportunities. In that case the action of the State must be logically judged according to the objectives really being pursued by society and not only in terms of national income and output levels.

The strongly redistributive orientation of social demands in Chile conditioned the type and intensity of public action in Chile. The measurement of results in terms of efficiency, then, should not only encompass the achievement of traditional goals such as output and price stability but also take into account a redistributive objective which was the result of the pressure for greater social equality exerted by social forces on the State.

CONTENTS OF THE BOOK

What type of state intervention is required to implement a redistributive objective? There is a wide gamut of instruments that in theory are capable of achieving redistribution. The instruments range from traditional mechanisms such as the public budget, wage policy and social security to more radical measures that imply changes in the ownership of the means of production or direct alterations of the productive structure.

The purpose of this book has been to examine the behaviour of the State when redistribution has been given high priority. A comparative analysis will also be carried out as to the various redistribution instruments in order to determine which of them is most efficient in accomplishing the goals established by the governments.

With this in mind, four redistributive instruments have been examined: the tax system, government expenditures, the social-security system and redistribution of property. The study is based on the Chilean experience of the past decade. Data for the measurement of the distributive effects of fiscal policy and social security are from 1969. The analysis of the effects of ownership redistribution programmes is based on the 1964–70 period in the case of the Agrarian Reform, and 1970–73 for the study of the distributive effects of the expropriation of industrial enterprise.

The first chapter in the book is the present one. It has discussed the role of the State as an economic agent and particularly with respect to its potentiality and limitations for implementing redistributive objectives. The chapter has also given an historical background to state intervention in Chile and criteria to evaluate government performance when redistribution is a high priority target.

The second chapter of the book will examine the tax system. One of the purposes of the tax system is to capture resources that could be oriented to redistribution. Thus, at least theoretically, a greater volume of tax revenues can generate higher capacity for redistribution. It is of interest, then, to determine the margin of available economic surplus that can be extracted by means of the tax system and to ascertain the most effective use of this capability.

The quantity of resources that is extracted, however, is not the only determinant of redistributive potential. The kind of levies chosen and the form in which they are applied are also important. The same quantity of resources can be obtained by levying tax burdens on distinct socio-economic groups and thus produce different effects on the welfare of each group and on the equity of the system of the whole. In order to measure the effect of the tax system on the welfare of each group a ''tax incidence'' study is carried out.[9] Such incidence studies have had a long trajectory in economic literature.[10] The chapter will go beyond the so-called legal incidence to determine the real economic incidence of the assumptions. A tax burden destined legally for a particular economic agent can follow three possible paths: it may fall on that agent, it may be shifted to other agents with whom the first conducts transactions, or it may be evaded.

The distribution of the burden depends on the economic base upon which it is imposed – personal income, property, profits, sales, etc. – and on the kind of transaction affected by the tax-goods and services, payrolls, labour, etc. The fundamental factors determining the destination of the tax burden are the structure of the market, the behaviour of the economic agents and the macroeconomic context.

The structure of the market indicates the relative power of the various economic agents and their capability to impose decisions in their favour. Under certain conditions, an oligopolistic market, for example, the producers are better able to shift the tax burden to consumers than is the case under competitive conditions. Market structure also includes the characteristics of demand for goods and factors. For example, a levy applied to a product that is difficult to substitute and for which, therefore, demand is very inelastic falls in greater proportion on the consumer than would be the case if the taxable item had a large number of substitutes.

[9]The incidence of a tax indicates the economic agents bearing the tax burden and the magnitude of the burden on each agent. The law itself may determine that the burden falls on a particular agent (legal incidence). But this agent may be able to pass on the burden to other agents and ultimately bear only a portion of it or even evade its effects entirely. The net effect on an agent after partial, total or no transfer to other agents is what is normally called economic incidence (in contradistinction to legal incidence).

[10]The first calculations go back to the beginning of the century: H. Samuel, ''The taxation of the various classes of people'', *Journal of the Royal Statistical Society,* March 1919. A review of these studies for underdeveloped countries is found in L. de Wulf, *op. cit.,* and in R. M. Bird and L. de Wulf, ''Taxation and income distribution in Latin America: a critical review of empirical studies'', mimeo, IMF, 1973.

The behaviour of economic agents in the determination of price is another indispensable element in understanding the process of tax shifting. the producer's action with regard to tax shifting will vary according to whether he bases his prices on marginal costs or on net profit margins over average costs. In the latter case, a tax on profits will probably be transferred completely to the consumer.

Finally, the macroeconomic context, especially an inflationary situation, will allow the tax burden on a productive unit to be shifted to a greater or lesser extent via prices.

This study of incidence proposes first of all to identify the economic agents upon which each tax levy falls. Then the socio-economic characteristics of the members of the tax-paying group will be described. This description is based on family income. In this way we can establish the magnitude of the tax burden borne by the families at the various income levels. We can then use these findings to analyse the conditions under which the tax system could better fulfil its redistributive role. These are some of the topics we will take up in the second chapter.

The next two chapters (third and fourth) will examine the distributive effects of public expenditures and will identify the real beneficiaries of state-financed programmes. Like taxes, these benefits can be shifted to agents other than the direct recipient. This is the case, for example, with most subsidies and loans granted to enterprises. This situation presents an additional difficulty for our analysis, since it is necessary to calculate the value of the benefits. The problem has not been adequately resolved in the literature on the subject. The present work is no exception to traditional methods in considering state expenditures as an approximation of the value of benefits. A more detailed discussion of these and other methodological problems is contained in Chapters 3 and 4.

The method of setting values according to costs is useful, despite its deficiencies, for identifying beneficiaries of expenditure programmes. How can the distributive impact be assessed? The criterion is to compare the distribution of expenditures with family income. Public expenditures are said to be progressive if they make the distribution more equal neutral, if they do not change; or regressive, if they make it worse.

The chapters focus special attention on the effect of expenditure programmes on low-income groups. We will examine in particular the possibilities of reallocating expenditures toward programmes that have greater impact on the poorer groups. This reallocation faces certain obvious limitations: general expenditures essential for the functioning of the State (justice, police, foreign relations, defence, etc.) can be reduced only partially. Moreover, a major portion of spending on productive infrastructure and promotion of development is fairly rigid.[11] Second, expenditures of a specifically redistributive nature, as are the majority of social programmes and certain development expenditures, involve leakage of benefits towards non-priority groups. The varied nature of these programmes and the differentiated demands made on the State by the various social groups prevent the totality of these expenditures from being directed exclusively to the most needy families. All above observations show that the margin of reallocation of spending is necessarily restricted. This margin can be broadened by capturing new resources through the tax system or by gradually reducing over time the relative importance of non-redistributive expenditures, and controlling the leakage in the redistributive programmes as such.

From another point of view, not only the behaviour of the State in one moment of time but also the dynamic effects produced by its activity are important in achieving efficient state action. For this reason expenditures whose effects are long range deserve special treatment. On the one hand are those expenditures in programmes which constitute investments in human capital – education, nutrition and health. On the other hand are those oriented to augment physical capital, which include direct state investment in transportation, irrigation and communications, in public utilities and energy. In our work, we distinguish between this kind of programme and those whose main effect is to increase present consumption of the beneficiaries. Public expenditures also include credits to the private sector. Finally, cursory treatment of these aspects is undertaken by the present study, but we have indicated their principal distributive effects.

Given the wide variety of topics included in the study of public expenditures we divided the presentation of the subject in two chapters as we have mentioned before. Chapter 3 concentrates on a discussion of the

[11] Expenditures in productive sectors are destined in large part to public workers and – especially when the State is promoting industrialisation – to investment in energy. Among these activities there are few projects whose benefits reach poorer groups preferentially.

determinants of government expenditures, on international comparisons and on a global analysis of the impact of the programmes over poverty groups.

Chapter 4, on the other hand, deals in detail with sectoral programmes (it covers the analysis of 140 different expenditure programmes) and identifies the beneficiaries of those programmes by means of the incidence study. In the last two sections, the incidence results are summarised. This is followed by a discussion of policy issues arising from the previous results.

Chapter 5 examines the system of social security. This type of programme can be considered as part of the public budget since it involves public financing. Despite the affinity to the state budget we chose to analyse the social-security system separately, in view of certain characteristics that distinguish it from other public programmes.

The social-security system is one of the oldest widespread redistributive mechanisms. The income and expenditures of the system are normally linked together and are less flexible than other public funds. Programmes may range from systems of common funds to those of capitalisation. Each produces different distributive effects. In the former, for example, the beneficiaries are not only those who finance the system, but the entire population. In the latter programmes there is strict identity between contribution and beneficiaries. It thus resembles a system of obligatory private insurance.

The system in Chile is an intermediate scheme. A rather complex analysis is needed in order to determine who ultimately finances the contributions in the Chilean system and who benefits from it.

Special attention in this chapter is devoted to the employment effects of the social-security system. Depending on the financing mechanisms used, the employment and therefore distributive consequences are entirely different.

In Chapter 6 the net incidence of the public budget is calculated. By considering together the tax burden borne by each socio-economic stratum and the benefits accruing to each, it is possible to determine their net effect. These findings are assessed in terms of progressivity (benefits to the poorest sectors) or regressivity. The results are compared to the nature, direction and magnitude of similar effects in other countries. Another frame of reference is the comparison of the manner in which public resources are distributed with respect to the magnitude of unsatisfied needs for each stratum, in particular that of lowest incomes. The chapter also measures the net effects of fiscal programmes on social groups (low, middle and upper groups). It concludes with a discussion of the fiscal policy options that are compatible with the objectives of economic redistribution.

In Chapter 7 we will examine a non-traditional redistributive instrument, that designed to redistribute the ownership of the means of production. This mechanism could be considered necessary for use within a strategy of redistribution for two reasons, first, the resources able to be extracted for the purpose of redistribution from traditional taxation channels and from social security might be inadequate in comparison to the magnitude of the basic needs that go unsatisfied. Secondly, an excessive concentration of property and wealth undoubtedly makes the redistribution process more difficult. Freedom of action is restricted by the economic and political opposition of those whose power is based on their wealth. In that case the alteration of the scheme of ownership seems to be a necessary step for changes in the pattern of development.

In either of these situations, it is interesting to determine how expropriation of manufacturing enterprises and changes in land tenancy affect the distribution of the surplus generated in the productive process. These surpluses could be transferred by way of improved wages to workers of the manufacturing or farm enterprises themselves, they could accrue to new groups of workers by means of expanded employment, or they could benefit consumers if the policy is to set prices below production costs. Finally, the State could theoretically appropriate all of the surplus from the nationalised enterprises and destine it to purposes with highest priority from the point of view of redistribution.

In addition, the type of organisation implemented in the redistributed property – state, community or private – will influence the use to which the surplus is put. Likewise, the characteristics of the groups that support the nationalisation process, their relative power, ideological orientation and economic demands will be of influence.

Our examination in Chapter 7 of the process of redistribution of property will focus on economic aspects, but it will also take these other factors into account.

CHAPTER 2

The Incidence of Taxation

1. INTRODUCTION

Taxation and public expenditures are important policy tools in the hands of the government in order to influence the way income is distributed in the economy. Examining the net effects of both types of instruments over income distribution is the subject-matter of incidence studies.

Modern public finance studies have de-emphasized the analysis of the normative considerations of theory and focused on the very basic question of incidence: who pays and who benefits from government action? Before worrying about whether or not the State should cope with a larger share of the economic activity in the nation, an idea of who are the actual beneficiaries and the burdened groups from existing government programmes is essential. Thus we can say that focus has shifted from the question of "what should the State do?" to the question of knowing "what in fact it has been doing".

There seems to be no escape from normative consideration and value judgements when evaluating government action. Divergences on individual opinions with respect to preferences for public action and to feelings about income distribution are unavoidable. Advancing knowledge on the incidence pattern shown by taxes and expenditures may be of great help in order to provide a more scientific ground to such evaluations.

This chapter deals with the incidence of the tax system.[1] We studied

[1] For a good survey of incidence studies in Latin America, see R. M. Bird and L. DeWulf, *op. cit.*

what the Chilean tax burden was in the year considered (1969), analysed some of the factors determining average tax effort in Chile and measured the effects of Chilean taxation over the distribution of income. This is done, in detail, for each and every type of tax with the use of the appropriate combination of shifting assumptions. An economic analysis which explicitly considers Chilean market structure is performed for justifying the assumptions when appropriate.

The chapter ends with an over-all incidence picture, where the redistributive character of the Chilean tax system is assessed, in terms of its progressiveness of regressiveness. Degrees of freedom for various tax-policies are evaluated. Some of the implications of the previous analysis for the design of a more redistributive tax system are drawn in the final section of this chapter.

2. AVERAGE TAX BURDEN IN CHILE

2.1. The determinants of tax effort

The literature on taxation points to the following elements affecting the country's "taxable capacity": the absolute level of aggregate income, the degree of economic development, the size of the foreign sector, the size of the distribution of income, the share of total production originating in the industrial sector, and the composition of government expenditures.

Higher levels of economic development bring in higher degrees of literacy, increased monetisation and urbanisation, stricter law enforcement, all factors which make potentially easier the process of tax collection. A proxy which is normally used for indicating the "level of economic development" is *per capita* income. It is often assumed that as *per capita* income rises in a country, the proportion of total income required for subsistence needs is lowered, thereby leaving an extra margin of taxable income.

Another important determinant, is the degree of openness in the economy. Both the size of the foreign sector, as well as the form in which a country regulates its exports and imports, are factors which influence tax collection. There is no doubt that in a small, developing economy, the external sector will tend to play an important role as a source of tax revenue, although this will vary in relation to the composition of the external sector itself.

The size distribution of income in a country also influences the potential taxable base. In theory, the higher the degree of concentration of incomes and wealth is, the greater the scope for the use of the tax instrument in fiscal-policy programmes. In actual practice, the inverse relationship may hold, since higher concentration implies more power in the hands of the rich, and consequently a more effective resistance to government actions destined to increase tax revenues.

On the one hand, it is certainly easier to collect taxes in a country where the industrial origin of output dominates over other sources (i.e. agriculture, services, etc.) due to the common link between industrialisation and urbanisation, the greater reliability of the figures of production and of the accounting procedures, the characteristics of stability and continuity of such activity, etc. In fact, some taxes are the direct result of the process of industrialisation itself, like the corporation income tax, the payroll taxes, etc.

Finally, public expenditures may indirectly exert a considerable influence over tax-efforts. The level of government expenditures clearly imposes a limit on the resources which are to rest in private hands, hence, on the taxable base of the economy.[2]

On the other hand, as long as the economy is not working at full employment, government expenditures will have direct and indirect effects over the size of aggregate demand and income. If the latter is taken as a proxy for the tax base, it is obvious that actual tax effort will be strongly influenced by the magnitude of the effect of public spending on the general level of economic activity.

2.2. The tax burden in Chile: a comparison with international patterns

Average tax burden in Chile fluctuated around one-fifth of GNP during the 1960s, a figure which is raised to almost a third of aggregate income, if social-security contributions are included. The first element evaluating the relative importance of these figures is provided by international comparisons.

[2] The nationalisation of industry in Chile is a clear example of this effect. See Chapter 7.

It may be noted that whatever the criteria used for drawing the line on fiscal accounts, an indispensable prerequisite for relevant international comparisons is consistency in treatment of data for the countries studied. This is why we preferred to contrast the Chilean case with OECD countries, as presented in B. Hansen's study[3] where a considerable effort of homogenisation of accounts was undertaken. We applied the same definitions used by Hansen to the appropriate Chilean data.

Figures in Table 1 show average tax ratios – including social security contributions – with respect to GNP at market prices. Chile ranks well under either France or the Federal Republic of Germany, and relatively close to Belgian and American standards. If one excludes the high share

TABLE 1

Average rates of taxation with respect to GNP at market prices
Selected countries – 1965(1)
(Per cent)

Country/Item	(1) Social-security contributions	(3) Direct taxes on corporations	(2) Other direct taxes on households	Indirect taxes	Total taxes
Chile					
(1965)	9.0	4.2(3)	2.0–3.4(2)	12.0	27.2
(1969)	9.7	4.7	2.3–3.1	13.1	29.8–30.6
France	14.2	2.1	4.6	17.6	38.5
Federal Republic of Germany	9.8	2.5	7.9	14.2	34.4
United Kingdom	4.8	1.9	9.2	14.1	30.0
Belgium	8.6	1.9	7.1	12.2	29.8
United States	4.2	4.5	9.3	9.3	27.3

Notes: (1) All data are for General Government. The data for European countries and the USA were obtained from OECD, National Accounts Statistics, as classified in Bent Hansen and W. Snyder, *Fiscal Policy in Seven Countries, 1955–1965*, OECD, March 1969. Data for Chile were computed with the same classification as in Hansen, from National Accounts.

(2) When property taxes are assigned as direct taxes on households, the ratio rises to 3.4% of GNP in 1965 and to 3.1% in 1969.

(3) Includes the taxation on copper, collections which represented 2.2% of GNP in 1965 and 3.2% in 1969.

[3] B. Hansen and W. Snyder, *Fiscal Policy in Seven Countries, 1955–1965,* OECD, March 1969.

represented by social-security contributions, then Chile ranks the lowest in terms of "tax effort".

Another important feature is the fact that Chile shows a relatively low rate (between 2 and 3.4 per cent) in direct taxes on households (apart from social security) as a percentage of GNP. This might be contrasted with the higher shares shown by all other countries, a factor which from the equity point of view worsens the relative position of Chile, since direct taxes are generally progressive in their effect on income distribution.

One way of judging "tax-effort" is to evaluate what a particular country has been able to do on its own terms – in a historical sense – and compare it with "potential" tax revenues. A comparison for some of the main taxes was carried out, contrasting for each case the time-pattern of actual tax receipts with the time-pattern shown by the corresponding potential base.[4] In this way, a disaggregate picture of "tax-effort" in a dynamic perspective was obtained.

The conclusions that emerged from the study of "tax-effort" through time showed the rapid growth profile experimented by taxation in the last decade (1960–70). Discretionary changes brought forth by governments in this period had a positive payoff in terms of rapidly increasing resources available to the government. This effort, however, was not homogenous, since it was concentrated on the transactions-front, rather than on incomes or property.

In terms of particular taxes, the Sales Tax was by far the one that showed the highest increase, since revenues augmented at a much faster rate than did aggregate production.[5]

The "pay as you go" tax on wages and salaries showed that its share remained almost constant, since tax collections rose in proportion with the taxable base. This is consistent with the inexistence of discretionary changes for this kind of tax, throughout the period considered.

Next, direct taxes on enterprises showed an irregular behaviour, and property-taxes had the worst performance of all, due to a problem of subvaluation of assessments. In particular, agricultural property experienced a lowered tax burden, since rural property assessments lagged behind the general price index, and even behind the assessments

[4]Tax collections for each year were obtained from Internal Revenue Service statistics, and the tax-basis were constructed with the appropriate National Account concepts.

[5]With the appropriate adjustments as described in a separate mimeo, *op. cit.*

values of urban property. Agricultural property assessments were devalued by almost 30 per cent in real terms between 1965 and 1972, whereas urban real-estate assessments lost about 20 per cent of their value in the same period.

Thus, "tax effort" was concentrated on indirect tax policies. This explains at least in part why in the 1970s almost three-fifths of public revenues came from indirect taxation, whereas direct taxes on households, enterprises and property do not represent more than two-fifths of the tax mix. Obviously, such elements are influencing average performance of the fiscal system and its pattern through time.

Finally, a missing element in tax-incidence studies, which affects the final distribution of incomes and which also affects government revenues – hence influences "tax effort" – is the incidence of the so-called "inflation tax".[6] In a country like Chile, having a long history of inflation and certain customary reliance on deficit-financing, it is certain that this source of government finance exerts a powerful influence on the capacity to tax, and on the actual tax effort displayed by governments.

3. REDISTRIBUTIVE INCIDENCE OF TAXATION

The essence of tax-incidence studies is to measure the reduction in real incomes that results from the imposition of a certain set of taxes. This reduction in real incomes may operate by affecting the incomes of individuals or families in their role as producers, or by increasing the prices of consumer goods and by reducing the purchasing power of a given amount of money income.

The reallocation of resources and the effects on incentives that may be caused by the different tax schemes are aspects which are normally left out from incidence studies. These studies consider as given the allocation of resources, the levels of employment, output and economic activity. They concentrate on the distribution of tax burdens, showing how the distribution of disposable income under a given tax system differs from what the distribution would have been if all tax revenues had come from a proportional income tax with the same yield.

[6] We shall analyse this matter in a specialised study on the subject.

We have adopted essentially the same procedure, the so-called "differential incidence" approach, which is currently being used in most modern public finance studies.[7]

In this section, we analyse the fiscal year of 1969, and present the results for the allocation of burdens from direct and indirect taxes to the various groups of families classified by income brackets. This is done in detail for each and every tax in the government budget (forty tax items in all).

The information on the original distribution of family incomes was obtained from a survey done for 1968–69 by the National Institute of Statistics (INE), on a nationwide basis. The survey included a comprehensive definition of family incomes, and consisted of a sample of 10,625 family units.[8]

We defined income brackets on the same terms as the survey did, that is, on the basis of "minimum annual income units" (s.v.a.), a concept

TABLE 2

Original income distribution. Survey on family incomes, 1969[(a)]

Family income bracket (annual)	Bracket limits (in minimum annual income units)	Bracket limits (in US $ of 1969)	Distribution of households (%)	Distribution of family incomes (%)
I	0 – 1	0 – 670	29.8	7.6
II	1 – 2	670 – 1,340	31.6	20.1
III	2 – 3	1,340 – 2,010	17.6	18.9
IV	3 – 4	2,010 – 2,680	7.4	11.2
V	4 – 5	2,680 – 3,350	4.5	8.7
VI	5 – 6	3,350 – 4,020	2.9	7.1
VII	6 – 8	4,020 – 5,360	2.7	8.0
VIII	8 – 10	5,360 – 6,700	1.5	5.9
IX	– 10+	– 6,700+	2.0	12.5
			100.0	100.0

(a) Average income per household was equivalent to US $2,890, which means an income *per capita* of US $580 (annual) considering an average of 5 persons per household.

Source: Encuesta Nacional sobre Ingresos Familiares, Instituto Nacional de Estadísticas.

[7] For a discussion of its advantages and disadvantages, see R. Musgrave and P. Musgrave, *Public Finance in Theory and Practice,* McGraw Hill, 1973.

[8] The definition of family income consisted of the sum of all gross incomes received by each family member (with no deduction of social-security contributions or personal income taxes), inclusive of income in kind and self-consumption.

which is used in Chile as a standard for identifying units of constant purchasing power in terms of a predefined set of goods. Table 2 presents the distribution of family incomes and households throughout the income scale, and expresses the equivalence of "minimum annual income units" in US dollars of 1969. This distribution and equivalences should be kept in mind when assessing the incidence results presented throughout this book.[9]

3.1. Legal and economic impact of the Chilean tax system

We start by presenting the legal characteristics of Chilean taxes. Table 3 provides a disaggregated representation of legal incidence, legal tax rates, taxable base, exemptions contemplated, form of payment and estimated degree of evasion, for the various tax items. No time will be spent describing the legal characteristics of these taxes, in the assumption that this summary view can give a fairly good idea on the matter, sufficient for our limited purposes.

It is important now to provide detailed information on the 1969 receipts of taxes levied on persons, enterprises, property and indirect tax components. We present estimates for the composition of the various tax items in the next pages. These magnitudes were used to allocate burdens and estimate incidence.[10]

Besides legal considerations, it is important to observe some of the essential features of the Chilean tax system in 1969, analysing the different stages of the process of income-generation and goods-production, where taxes are levied.

In principle, taxes may be levied at the sources side or the uses-of-income side. On the other hand, any particular transaction may be taxes at either the household or the firm side of the market counter. Under competitive conditions, taxing on either side would be similar in terms of economic incidence. We shall see, however, that in reality the effective pattern of incidence depends very crucially on the specific side of the counter considered. Moreover, we shall see how taxes are shifted away

[9] A caution on these figures appears below on Section 3.4.
[10] For a detailed description of the nature and coverage of these taxes, see Table 4.

from their legal point of impact and how this affects income distribution.[11]

In this sense, some of the more remarkable characteristics of tax legislation in Chile which are worth noticing are summarised in the following facts:

(i) A relative predominance of indirect taxes falling on income on the "uses" side, and nominally placed on the firms' side. Among them the very important Sales Tax which accounts for more than a fifth of receipts collected.

(ii) The relatively lower quantitative importance of taxation levied over income flows generated in the capital market, a feature which contrasts with the cumulative impact of taxation (and social security) over labour-income flows.

(iii) The general dispersion of the tax system into various relatively small taxes, and the double taxation resulting thereof. An important example of this sort is the accumulation of taxes in the labour-earning side.

(iv) The concentration of direct taxation on levies collected near the sources of earnings, either through retained income taxes on payrolls (or retained social security contributions) and the importance of taxes which reach profits prior to their distribution.

(v) The very low taxation over independent economic activity.

(vi) The relatively low taxation over households and business savings, and over capital goods' transactions (these tend to be exempted from the sales tax). Also, the escape-avenue from personal income taxes, which is available for capital incomes through the retained-earnings mechanism used by enterprises.

(vii) The reliance of property taxation on urban real-estate taxes, rather than on more general wealth levies.

(viii) The existence of a comprehensive direct levy over household income – The Global Income Tax – having moderate influence in terms of tax collections.

In general, we shall see that this picture of nominal tax impacts will change considerably, once we take into account the actual market structure in Chile. In fact, considerable tax-shifting will occur, changes

[11] Analysed in Chapter 5.

which will tend to diminish or even reverse a certain degree of progressivity which the legislator might have intended. A major force underlying the divergence of legal and effective incidence, apart from market-structure *per se*, is the basis of the tax-mix towards indirect levies, and specially, the relative importance of taxes on consumption expenditures.

3.2. The incidence of direct taxation

Having identified actual amounts collected from each and every tax, and having assessed legal responsibilities for these taxes, we proceed to assign burdens in line with the ultimate bearer of each tax. For this purpose, we analyse the underlying economic structure, and choose a distribution series which corresponds as closely as possible with the economic concept of incidence.

Table 8 describes in summarised form the set of tax-burden assumptions and the distribution-series used for each and every one of the tax-items we are concerned with. We analyse in some detail here, the cases of profit-taxation, wealth-taxation and some of the personal income taxes.

(a) *Taxation on enterprises.* Direct business-taxation is mainly composed of taxation over corporate profits which represents some 60 per cent of the total and taxation over profits of unincorporated enterprises, with 40 per cent of total receipts under this category.[12]

For a more disaggregated picture we have looked at the Internal Revenue Service's statistics, and constructed a table which decomposes the sources of profit-tax receipts, both according to the economic sector of origin as well as to the legal form of the contributor. This is done in the next chart which shows that both in terms of the number of contributors declarating, as well as according to the relative importance of taxes paid, the industrial sector is of great significance (Table 5).

Taking a weighted average of receipts generated by different forms of organisation (corporations, collective enterprises or "sociedades

[12] This includes the appropriate shares of the CORVI 5 per cent Obligatory Housing Provision.

TABLE 4

Tax receipts, classified by different types of tax items, 1969.
(Millions of escudos)

I. *Direct taxation*	5,143.9
1. *On persons*	1,345.0
1.1. On income of professionals[1]	72.0
1.2. 3.5% tax on employees	331.8
1.3. 3.5% tax on blue-collar workers	169.0
1.4. Taxation on corporate-directors' incomes[2]	10.6
1.5. Comprehensive, global income tax	749.4
1.6. Other direct taxes on persons (lottery income tax, tax on foreign trips, etc.)	12.2
2. *On enterprises*	3,105.9
2.1. On capital incomes	
2.1.1. On corporate profits[3]	464.7
2.1.2. On profits of unincorporated enterprises and banks[4]	278.4
2.1.3. On rentier income and income derived from financial assets	26.6
2.2. Capital gains tax	10.2
2.3. Taxation of foreign-owned income (additional tax)	310.0*
2.4. Taxation on copper sector	2,016.0*
3. *On property*	693.0
3.1. Net wealth tax	55.5
3.2. Real-estate taxes	
3.2.1. On agricultural property[5]	79.2
3.2.2. On non-agricultural property[6]	436.6
3.2.3. Other property taxes[7]	25.0
3.3. Vehicle licences	77.0
3.4. Inheritance and gift tax	19.7
II. *Indirect taxation*	7,295.8
4. *Sales tax*	3,125.0
4.1. Commodities subject to general tax rate[8]	2,387.9
4.2. Tax on luxury goods	68.2
4.3. Tax on leisure-sector goods[9]	90.7
4.4. Tax on automobiles' transfers	28.5
4.5. Tax on basic necessities[10]	60.6
4.6. Tax on alcoholic beverages	78.5
4.7. Tax on special semi-durable goods[11]	176.9
4.8. Tax on wine and liquors	103.5
4.9. Heavily taxed items[12]	130.2
5. *Excise taxes*	533.3
5.1. Tax on the production of alcoholic beverages	83.4
5.2. Tax on the tobacco industry[13]	443.8
5.3. Other excise taxes	6.1*

TABLE 4 – *continued*

6. *Energy taxes*	516.2
6.1. Gas and electricity	89.4
6.2. Liquefied gas(14)	29.2
6.3. Petroleum	288.0
6.4. Kerosene	12.6
6.5. Oil and lubricants	97.0
7. *Service tax*	951.5
7.1. Services subject to general tax rate(15)	419.0
7.2. Banking services	20.9
7.3. Insurance	52.1
7.4. Transport and other(16)	14.7
7.5. Hospital and laundry services	35.4
7.6. Entertainment services	28.7
7.7. Tax on bank interest on loans	295.7
7.8. Other services(17)	85.0*
8. *Import duties*	1,451.5*
8.1. Taxation on imported goods	1,646.0
8.2. Other levies on imports	543.0
8.3. (Adjustment for nominal import taxes on fiscal sector)(18)	(−737.4)
9. *Stamp and legal documents*(19)	693.1
10. *Other indirect taxation*	25.1*
11. *Miscellaneous taxes, surcharges and delayed payments, and accounting adjustments in the budget*	48.3
Total consolidated tax receipts of the public sector	12,487.6

*Not accounted for in the incidence study at this stage.

Notes to Table 4

(1) Includes all "second-category" income taxation on professionals comprising: monthly retentions, annual reliquidation, patents paid by professionals, and the corresponding share of delayed payments derived from tax liabilities of preceding years figuring also in the 1969 Budget, as second-category tax receipts (Morosos).

(2) Includes the share of "delayed payments" received this year, from this group of taxpayers.

(3) Includes not only the normal 30 per cent profit tax but also a tax levied on asset revalorisation (indexation to correct for the effect of inflation on balance sheets), "delayed payments" received, and first-category taxation on income generated in the mining sector as well as that accruing from real-estate property (agricultural and non-agricultural) owned by corporations. Finally, some 24.8 million escudos paid in the form of obligatory housing contributions (CORVI) by corporations were also included.

(4) Includes the 17 per cent tax rate on profits of unincorporated enterprises the 3.75 per cent rate on small industry and artisan-activity, as well as the rest of the tax items mentioned in (3). Some 15 million escudos of obligatory housing contributions (CORVI) by this sector were also distributed at this level.

TABLE 4 – *continued*

(5) These are the so-called "Contribuciones" or territorial taxes on land and improvements ("Bienes Raíces Agrícolas"). Agricultural taxes of this sort amount to some 14.6 per cent of the total receipts from all real-estate taxes.

(6) The "Contribuciones" or Property taxes on houses, urban land and other real estate of this sort, levied on non-agricultural property ("Bienes Raíces No Agrícolas"). This source represented some 80.7 per cent of total receipts from real-estate taxes.

(7) This corresponds to taxes on "unimproved urban land", urban sites apparently not being utilised for housing or business purposes, the so-called "*sitios eriasos*". Receipts from this source were 2.7 per cent of total real-estate taxation. Also included at this level is taxation levied on "Líneas y Postaciones", which includes physical items attached to land such as telephone lines, water pipelines, etc. This represented the remaining 2 per cent of real-estate taxation.

(8) Here we have tax receipts from the sales tax, on that part of goods' transactions or transfers which are taxed at the modal ("general") 8 per cent tax rate. Hence, it includes the normal 8 per cent tax levied at the fabrication-process for first transfer, as well as all other classes of good-transfers taxed with the 8 per cent basic rate (follows the grouping done by the Internal Revenue Service).

(9) Basically, sales tax on good transactions performed by bars, canteens, restaurants, cafés and the like (modal legal tax rate of 14 per cent).

(10) Articles such as semi-processed agricultural goods and foodstuffs are considered "necessities", and taxed at a 1.4 per cent rate.

(11) This includes taxation over a group of goods comprising items such as record-players, records, toilet goods, etc.

(12) Here the classification includes goods which in general support higher than average tax rates, while not being necessarily considered "luxury goods". Tyres support a 21 per cent legal tax rate, special kinds of liquors a 29 per cent rate, and playing cards a 70 per cent tax rate (the heaviest taxed item).

(13) This is an excise tax levied on tobacco, cigars and cigarettes. This item also includes taxation on matches and cigarette-lighters.

(14) We refer here to the tax levied on compressed gas balloons which are sold for purposes of lighting gas-heating appliances, as well as for kitchens functioning on liquefied gas. This is a widely spread form of heating, utilized in Chilean households.

(15) Receipts from services subject to the modal 17 per cent tax rate (ex. most commercial and distribution services).

(16) Mostly maritime (exported cargo's share of tax has been deducted).

(17) In this account, there is a whole range of special taxes levied at the central, regional or municipal level. Examples: licences for the operation of radios, TV-stations and cinemas, fees charged on municipal parking lots, tax on telegraph foreign services, levies on tourism, etc.

(18) This adjustment is due to the fact that although nominally, fiscal entities are liable to import duties on the goods and services they bring from abroad, effectively, this is only an account-type operation, since no real new receipts are generated for the public sector as a whole.

(19) Basically, stamp tax receipts, as well as legal fees established on notary documents and the like (birth certificates, marriage licences, residence certificates, legal contracts, property titles, etc.). Also includes fees on the inscription of commercial brand names and other patents.

TABLE 5

Profit-tax receipts. Sectoral origin by different legal forms, 1969.
(In percentage)

	Service	Commerce	Industry[a]	Total
A. *Unincorporated business*				
1. Individual enterprises				
(a) Taxes paid	19	59	22	100
(b) Number of contributors	35	57	8	100
2. Collective enterprises				
(a) Taxes paid	11	47	42	100
(b) Number of contributors	16	59	25	100
B. *Corporate business*				
3. Corporations				
(a) Taxes paid	6	34	60	100
(b) Number of contributors	5	44	51	100

[a] Includes the construction sector, which is of minor importance for tax collections, in view of the significant franchises which it enjoys.

Source: Constructed on the base of Internal Revenue Service Statistics.

individuales'') it turns out that over half of these taxes come from the industrial sector alone. This in part is explained by the relative ease in administration, assessment and control of taxes having urban origin.

Another interesting feature is the fact that there appears to be a correlation between organisational form and economic sector: corporations are relatively more concentrated in industry, unincorporated collective business in the commerce sector, and ''individual societies'' in both commerce and services. Hence, these three classes of legal entities for organising production tend to specialise in terms of the type of economic activity undertaken (type of goods produced, production techniques used, etc.). This is important as an indicator of segmentation of the economic structure. It is also important because each type of enterprise is subjected to differential rates of taxation (30 per cent on corporate profits, 17 per cent on unincorporated enterprises, 3.75 per cent on small industry and handicrafts).[13]

The annotated differentials can also be observed to some extent within the industrial sector proper, which as we said is the main tax-generating sector in the economy.

[13] All of these rates are proportional, and independent of the absolute size of profits.

If we analyse the information available in the *Census of Manufacturers (1967)*, we observe that big industry tends to be organised in the corporate fashion facing therefore a legal tax rate of 30 per cent, medium-size industry is usually organised as unincorporate enterprise subject to the 17 per cent rate, and small industry and handicrafts face a preferential tax rate of 3.75 per cent.

From the point of view of the amounts of tax collections, it is meaningful to distinguish only in terms of corporate business on one side and forms of unincorporated business (including collective business, small industry and handicrafts) on the other. Different incidence models will be applied to each of those two categories.

Two main reasons underline this differential treatment.

First, the fact that corporations are the largest economic units and they have traditionally faced a well-protected market (due to the effects of tariffs and other foreign trade restrictions on imports).

Secondly, oligopoly seems to be the prevailing form of organisations for this type of firm. In contrast, individual and collective business of the unincorporated type consist of medium and small size industries and of enterprises in ''sector libre'' Commerce and Services. In these cases we find a relatively large number of producers and market conditions allow for a relatively higher degree of competition.

In sum, the narrow and limited channels for capital mobility that prevail throughout the different sectors and organisations in the economy imply that the standard postulate of homogeneity commonly advanced in incidence studies will not do for the Chilean case and that a differentiated treatment is required when the economic incidence of taxes falling on enterprises is going to be measured.

(b) *Incidence of the profits tax.* The analysis of incidence of the profits tax must necessarily include three kinds of considerations: (a) the pricing behaviour of firms, (b) their market power, (c) institutional factors. In relation to the first aspect, a reasonable hypothesis would be that the typical pricing rule followed by Chilean enterprises is based on the practice of mark-up pricing. Under this practice, costs are ''marked up'' to allow for a given ratio of profits to costs, and normally ''costs'' are defined inclusive of taxes so as to deal with a net-of-tax margin.[14]

[14] For a similar discussion of the hypothesis applied in incidence studies for other realities, see R. Musgrave and P. Musgrave, *op. cit.*, and J. Pechman and B. Okner, *Who Bears the Tax Burden?*, The Brookings Institution, 1974.

The preceding comments refer to a pricing behaviour which "intends" to pass taxes on to higher prices. Whether or not the firm actually succeeds in this depends on its actual market power and on the degree to which this is exploited. Here we find important differences between different classes of business organisations which must be considered in the analysis.

Big firms are usually those organised under more modern and sophisticated legal forms (corporations). They are bound to have relatively strong institutional power, and they generally obtain various kinds of "institutional advantages" (tax-franchises, favourable depreciation schemes, easier access to credit and information, etc.) which added to the effect of their size and levels of production over a relatively small and protected market, leaves little or no margin for small, unorganised rivals to dispute their share of the market. The data of the *Census of Manufacturers* (1967), showing the number of establishments operating in the industrial sector in corporate form and the share of total industrial production represented by corporate-supply, are indicators of the clear supremacy that corporate firms have over their unincorporated rivals, in terms of market-shares.

If one also considers the fact that corporations are concentrated in the industrial sector – which is the most protected and oligopolistic sector of all – a hypothesis of forward shifting to consumers on the part of corporations seems reasonable.

Finally, there are two extra elements which must be mentioned. The first is that the actual success of forward-shifting also depends on the extent to which enterprises have already exercised their market power in the pretax situation.

It is worthwhile to consider this point in the context of persistent inflation for the economy as a whole. Annual inflation rates were around 30 per cent on average for 1960–70, and in 1969 – the year of reference – inflation reached 29 per cent.[15] In such an inflationary milieu, prices are changing continuously throughout the year and enterprises are frequently changing their prices in order to keep pace with, or even anticipate, the inflationary process. In this setting, the degree of exploitation of market power may be considered to be a positive function of inflation. It is easier for enterprises to shift to consumers and increased

[15] As measured by the official Consumer Price Index (December to December variations).

share of their financial and tax burdens in the context of inflation than it is in conditions of stability.

However, forward-shifting in the case of the profits tax cannot be complete, not only due to constraint coming from the demand side of the market (demand price-elasticities are different from zero), but also due to the institutional ceilings represented by price-controls. Chilean industry has frequently been subjected to one or another form of regulation by government, and many products or sectors have been under price-control. Still, it is true that large-scale firms have been able to pressure government officials for the validation of their own cost margins, but in any case, these regulatory practices represent an inhibiting factor for the tax-shifting process.

This is why, in spite of allowing for considerable forward-shifting of the profits tax, we have still assumed that a part of it would rest on the firm.[16]

That part of the profits tax which is assumed to fall directly on the firm must be distributed according to income brackets. In the case of corporate business, we distributed the tax burden according to the observed income distribution of employers (Survey of Family Incomes). For the unincorporated business, the assumption was that the burden of the profit tax on the firm is distributed through the income scale in direct relationship with the way income from capital in the Commerce and Services sector is distributed by income brackets.

(c) *Personal income tax.* Chilean tax laws rely on one comprehensive kind of personal taxation, the Global Complementario or Global Income Tax. The tax rates are progressive and affect incomes generated from different sources. This accounted for some 56 per cent of receipts of direct personal taxes in 1969.

From the point of view of the total number of taxpayers, it was the tax with by far the highest coverage[17]: 80 per cent of all taxpayers declaring for direct taxes were filling Global Income Tax returns, 6 per cent were filling for the Net-wealth Tax, 10 per cent for Profit Taxes and 3 per cent for the Tax on Professionals.

[16] We assumed that one-half of total taxes on corporations were shifted forward to consumers in general, and one-quarter of total taxation levied on unincorporated business was similarly shifted.

[17] Excluding the payroll taxes which operate on a retention basis, at the firm level.

In spite of it being one of the most important individual sources of tax revenues (second only to the Sales Tax), its high potentiality as an income redistributor was reduced by the interplay of three main factors: the abundant credit-provisions and tax deductions contemplated, the importance of legal erosions in its tax base and the high degree of evasion and fraud (estimated as 40 per cent of the potential tax base).

Legally, the income base subject to tax obeys the following formula, and is taxed at a progressive scheme of rates ranging from 10 to 60 per cent:

Taxable Income = Gross Income − Cedular Income Taxes Paid[18] − Real Estate Property Taxes Paid

whereas

Gross Income = All Taxable Labour Income[19] + All Taxable Capital Income + Incomes which had been exempted from Cedular Income Taxes.

The tax scheme contemplated an exemption for those earning the "minimum income" or less (s.v.a.),[20] so that persons with a taxable income included in this range would pay zero tax. Also, various tax credits and deductions based on family dependants were contemplated in the Law. Hence, these two elements made an important weight in lowering the effective tax burden borne by low-income families.

The distribution of burdens among the various occupational categories shows that these seem to be concentrated on employees (54 per cent of total tax collected), employers (31 per cent of total) and professionals (8 per cent), in that order. The interbracket distribution of burdens within each of these occupational categories is one factor that explains the redistributive character of the Global Income Tax. We summarise this pattern on the next incidence table, where the relative distribution of burdens is contrasted with the pre-tax distribution of family incomes.

(d) *Property taxes.* The bulk of property taxation in Chile derives from real-estate taxes on urban property, the so-called "Contribuciones de

[18] "Cedular" refers here to (first category) taxation on non-corporate profits and incomes, and (second category) taxation on wages, salaries and the incomes of professionals.

[19] Taxable refers here to the actual cedular tax base of first category and second-category taxes, excluding any exemptions contemplated in these taxes.

[20] See the definition of this "minimum income" above.

TABLE 6

Distribution of the tax burden from the Global Income Tax (Global Complementario), 1969

Family income scale	Total burden (thousands of escudos, 1969)	Relative distribution of burden (%)	Pre-tax distribution of family incomes (nationwide) (%)
0 – 1	–	–	7.6
1 – 2	56,700	7.57	20.1
2 – 3	85,600	11.42	18.9
3 – 4	61,500	8.20	11.2
4 – 5	58,300	7.78	8.7
5 – 6	62,500	8.34	7.1
6 – 8	72,200	9.64	8.0
8 – 10	52,200	6.96	5.9
10 +	300,400	40.09	12.5
Total	749,400	100.00	100.00

Source: See our incidence results in Table 9.

Bienes Raíces'', which accounted for 63 per cent of all property-tax receipts. Next comes the Real Estate Tax on agriculture (rural real estates), then the fees on vehicle licences and the Net-wealth Tax (Patrimonial). The Inheritance and Gift Tax produced as little as 2.8 per cent of property taxation.

Focusing on the Net-wealth Tax, or Patrimonial,[21] we note that in theory this could have been an important instrument for correcting the unequal distribution of wealth. Like other taxes, it was created as a source of new revenue needed by government, with the advantage that it could conceivably collect it in an equitable way, with little interference in the allocation of resources.[22]

The tax base of the Net-wealth Tax was composed of the gross value of assets minus liabilities, with an important margin of personal net wealth being exempted (from 15 up to 120 annual minimum incomes) and deductible from this base. An examination of the formula for computing the taxable base shows that this tax was a levy concentrated mainly on physical assets, and that valuation was done by looking at legal assessments.

[21] This tax has been abolished (1974) by the new government.

[22] This is explained by the fact that it consisted of a general personal tax, with no differential treatment for specific economic activities.

Another element which reduced the scope or coverage of this tax (apart from the legal deduction, the uncovered forms of wealth and assessment problems) was that taxpayers were allowed a tax credit, equivalent to 50 per cent of the value of the Global Income Tax paid. This had the effect of strongly reducing tax collections from the tax, although it represented an incentive for a more accurate declaration of incomes at the personal income-tax stage. This also means that actual tax payments coming from this source would tend to be concentrated in the upper echelons of the income scale, a matter to be considered when assessing its redistributive effects.

With respect to the rest of property-taxation, the bulk of it consists of real estate taxes over individual urban landlords, taxes which are hard to shift[23] and which due to the concentration in the distribution of property ended up having a favourable redistributive content. Table 7 summarises the real-estate tax structure in terms of sector of location (rural/urban) and nature of taxpayer.

The main problem of real-estate taxes lies on the assessment side rather than on shifting or evasion. Throughout the last years in Chile, real-estate assessments have been underestimated and experienced lags in relation to the inflation rates. This has clearly eroded the property tax-base (with negative implications for the Net-wealth and Global Income Taxes as well) and lowered the effectiveness of this policy instrument, for income redistribution purposes.

(e) *Other direct taxes*. The rest of direct taxes are more readily interpretable and straightforward in their economic effects. None of them are shifted away from its legal bearer.

They include the (second category) Income Tax on Payrolls, which taxed wages and salaries at a proportional 3.5 per cent rate, with a monthly retention mechanism at the firm's level.[24] Due to the amplitude of the base, this tax on earned-income generated some 10 per cent of direct tax receipts, or 3.4 per cent of all fiscal income.

Another direct tax on personal incomes is the tax on the Income of Professionals which produced only 1.4 per cent of direct tax receipts, a

[23] In the context of house-rent controls, as in the Chilean experience.

[24] After deducting from gross wages and salaries, the employee part of social security contributions.

TABLE 7

*Real-estate taxes by sector and nature of taxpayer**
(Millions of escudos, 1969)

	Amounts	%
1. *Real estate taxes on agriculture*	79,162	14.6
1.1. Paid by individual landlords	77,801	14.4
1.2. Paid by enterprises		
1.2.1. Corporations	1,314	0.2
1.2.2. Other enterprises	47	
2. *Real-estate taxes on urban property*	461,562	85.4
2.1. Paid by individual landlords	346,537	64.1
2.2. Paid by enterprises		
2.2.1. Corporations	91,228	16.9
2.2.2. Other enterprises	23,797	4.4
Total	540,724	100.0

*Includes taxation on (*sitios eriazos*) ''vacant sites'' (14,325 million escudos) and other immovables (*líneas y postaciones*), 10,672 million escudos; the first assigned entirely to individual (urban) landlords.

fact in part due to the high degree of evasion present in this source of earned income (tax evasion here has been estimated as high as 70 per cent of the potential base),[25]

Finally, there are other minor taxes such as a tax on corporate-directors' income, a Capital Gains tax, a tax on rentier income, taxes on lottery income and foreign trips, etc., details on which may be found in the summary and incidence tables presented next.

(f) *Summary of tax-burden assumptions and incidence results.* We proceed to list all the assumptions used for estimating direct tax-burden incidence, along with the particular distribution series used. Summary Table 8 provides an orderly description for each tax item. This listing in turn corresponds with the listing of tax burdens by income class in table A-1 in the Annex.

For some of the tax items, there are different alternatives in terms of incidence assumptions and distribution of burdens. They arise mainly in situations where there is a possibility of shifting. Other alternatives arise

[25] H. Allende, Ministerio de Hacienda, 1969.

TABLE 8
Description of tax-burden assumptions

Tax item		Burden assumed to fall on	Distribution series used (all relate to family income brackets, predefined)
I. Direct taxes			
A. *On personal incomes*			
1.1.	Second-category tax on professionals	Families having members with completed university education	Gross incomes of population with completed university education (adjusted)
1.2.	Second-category tax on employees	White-collar workers	Income distribution of employees
1.3.	Second-category tax on blue-collar workers	Blue-collar workers	Income distribution of wage earners
1.4.	Second-category tax on corporate directors' participation	Families with corporate-directors members	All burden assigned to the highest family-income bracket
1.5.	Global Income Tax	All types of income-earners in the economy	Adjusted declared taxable incomes by occupational category (IRS sources) crossed with corresponding family-income distributions (survey)
1.6.	Other personal taxes	White-collar workers	Income distribution of employees
B. *On capital incomes (Enterprises)*			
2.1.1.	On corporation profits	11a* – Employers	(a) Adjusted income distribution of employers
		11b* – Consumers	(b) Distribution of household expenditures by income brackets
		(B) 11c – ½ on employers, ½ on consumers	(c) Distributions (a) and (b) combined with equal weights
2.1.2.	On profits of unincorporated enterprises	12a – Capital incomes	(a) Distribution of income to capital in the commerce and services sector (Survey on Family Incomes)
		12b – Consumers	(b) Distribution of household expenditures by income brackets

TABLE 8 – *continued*

Description of tax-burden assumptions

Tax item		Burden assumed to fall on	Distribution series used (all relate to family income brackets, predefined)
		(B) 12c – ¾ on capital incomes, ¼ on consumers	(c) Distribution of income to capital in the commerce and services sector (Survey on Family Incomes) Distribution of household expenditures by income brackets
2.1.3.	On rentier income and other capital incomes	Shareowners	Distribution of family incomes of shareowners (crossed information on wealth-tax declarations; Internal Revenue Service, and family incomes by occupational category of owners, Survey on Family Incomes)
2.2.0.	Capital gains tax	Employers	Income distribution of employers
C.	*On property*		
3.1.	Patrimony or net wealth tax	Owners of physical and financial assets	Ownership of property by occupational category (Internal Revenue Service), crossed with family incomes (Survey) by occupational category, adjusted for exemptions and Global Income Tax rebated effect
3.2.1.	Real-estate tax on agricultural property		
3.2.1.1.	Portion falling on individual landowners	Owners of agricultural real estate	Onwership of real estates in agriculture, by occupational category (Internal Revenue statistics), crossed with family incomes (Survey) by occupational category adjusted for exemptions
3.2.1.2.	Agricultural property owned by business corporations	(B) – Employers	Adjusted income distribution of employers
3.2.2.	Real-estate tax on non-agricultural property		

TABLE 8 – *continued*

Description of tax-burden assumptions

Tax item	Burden assumed to fall on	Distribution series used (all relate to family income bracket, predefined)
3.2.2.1. Portion falling on individual landowners	Owners of urban real estates	Ownership of non-agricultural property by occupational category of landlord (Internal Revenue statistics) crossed with family incomes (Survey) by occupational category, adjusted for exemptions
3.2.2.2. Business portion corporate and unincorporated firms	(B) (a) Employers (b) Consumers (c) ½ on consumers, ½ on employers	(a) Adjusted income distribution of employers (b) Distribution of household expenditures by income brackets (c) Distributions (a) and (b) combined with equal weights
3.2.3. Other property taxes		
3.2.3.1. Portion on individual owners	Owners of urban property and other realty	Ownership of urban property and other realty by occupational category of landlord, crossed with family incomes
3.2.3.2. Business portion	(B) (a) Employers (b) Consumers (c) ½ on consumers, ½ on employers	(a) Adjusted income distributions of employers (b) Distribution of household expenditures by income brackets (c) Distributions (a) and (b) combined with equal weights
3.3. Vehicle licences	Vehicle owners	Distribution of vehicles' ownership in Net-wealth Declarations, including first two income brackets
3.4. Inheritance and gift tax	Owners of physical and financial assets	Property ownership by occupational category (IRS) crossed with family incomes, by occupational category (Survey)

*These numbers refer to column numbers in 8.
(B) = Benchmark assumption.

simply from the choice one can make about the particular income-distribution series which best approaches the actual income positions of particular bearers.

These alternatives will inevitably produce more or less progressiveness in the final incidence; and they can be regarded as reasonable ways of providing some sensitivity analysis on results which sometimes are based on hypothetical models or educated assumptions. In particular, one may combine the "most progressive" set of assumptions and calculate the resulting incidence over family incomes, and perform the same exercises with the "least progressive" combination of assumptions. These two incidence profiles would then probably define the range where effective incidence lies. A "benchmark" combination of assumptions and its results should therefore be compared with these two incidence limits, in order to have a more accurate picture.

This is done in Table 9, where three incidence exercises are performed: one for the "most progressive", one for the "most regressive" and one for the "benchmark" combination.

If we use the combination of assumptions which excludes the possibility of shifting, the incidence pattern that emerges is as indicated by the "most progressive" set of rates.[26] A comparison of these with effective tax rates distribution by incomes, computed on the basis of taxable incomes reported by the Internal Revenue Service for Global Income Tax taxpayers, shows that our results are consistent with the general pattern followed by tax returns.

The overall conclusion of direct-tax incidence is that the pattern of such levies is progressive, with upper-income families bearing a higher burden than the poor. This favourable result in terms of redistributive effects will become impaired by the influence of indirect taxation, as we see next.

3.3. Incidence of indirect taxation

A major component of indirect taxes was the Sales Tax; traditionally, the individual tax item with the largest amount of collections in the

[26] This is equivalent to exclude the influence of distributions based on consumption or family expenditures, distributions which in general work toward regressiveness.

TABLE 9
Sensitivity analysis of direct tax incidence

Income bracket	Total family income (millions of escudos)	Tax burdens (millions of escudos)			Tax burdens divided by family incomes (%)		
		Bench-mark case	Most progres-sive case	Most regres-sive case	Bench-mark case	Most progres-sive case	Most regres-sive case
0–1	3,536.0	52.7	6.2	115.8	1.5	0.2	3.3
1–2	9,351.7	327.4	241.8	438.3	3.5	2.6	4.7
2–3	8,793.4	361.05	306.95	427.75	4.1	3.5	4.9
3–4	5,211.0	227.94	204.14	254.34	4.4	3.9	4.9
4–5	4,047.8	226.49	226.19	222.89	5.6	5.6	5.5
5–6	3,303.3	232.24	244.34	216.54	7.0	7.4	6.6
6–8	3,722.1	282.34	297.44	258.54	7.6	8.0	6.9
8–10	2,745.0	205.31	219.71	182.01	7.5	8.0	6.6
10+	5,815.7	902.14	1,070.84	701.44	15.5	18.4	12.1
Total	46,526.0	2,817.61	2,817.61	2,817.61	6.1	6.1	6.1

Budget.[27] It represented some 25 per cent of all fiscal receipts, and explained by itself around 45 per cent of total indirect taxation in 1969. Along with the Services Tax, Production Taxes (a series of excise levies) and the Stamp Tax, it has had a major impact over the real purchasing power of households. On average, we shall see that it reduced household incomes by more than 10 per cent.

The Sales Tax was an indirect tax on all industrial and commercial transactions, affecting not only the purchase of final goods by consumers, but also all intermediate transactions by firms. Hence, one of the great disadvantages of this multiphase tax was encouraging an excessive vertical integration of enterprises and raising in a compound way the price mark-up implicit in goods.

The Sales Tax had been structured on the basis of a nominally "semi-progressive" scheme of rates. With a whole group of goods exempted from the tax (mainly agricultural products such as milk, eggs, cereals, bread, etc.),[28] the rest were taxed at rates ranging from 1 per cent to 70 per cent, depending on the character of the goods ("normal" or

[27] This tax was replaced by a Value Added Tax in 1975.

[28] This is because the legislator assumed that these were mainly mass-consumption goods, that bear heavily on the family budgets of low-income people. Recently the Value Added Tax has been also extended to these products.

"luxury", "intermediate" or "final"), with a model rate of 8 per cent covering a vast list of commodities.

A simple crude method in order to tackle the problem of tax incidence would be to use the distribution of total family consumption, by income brackets, assigning the burden of the Sales Tax – which we suppose is completely shifted forward to consumers – according to the share on total consumption. Results obtained by using this method based on information of a National Survey on Household Budgets performed in 1968–69 are reported in Table 10.

TABLE 10

Distribution of the indirect-tax burden in line with aggregate consumption

Income bracket (annual minimum income units)	% distribution of family incomes[a]	% distribution of aggregate consumption[b]
0 – 1	7.6	13.2
1 – 2	20.1	25.2
2 – 3	18.9	20.0
3 – 4	11.2	10.5
4 – 5	8.7	7.3
5 – 6	7.1	6.1
6 – 8	8.0	6.0
8 – 10	5.9	4.6
10 +	12.5	7.3
Total	100.0	100.0

Sources: [a] National Survey on Family Incomes, 1969.
[b] National Survey on Household Expenditures, 1968–69 (unpublished).
Note: The income basis of both surveys had been made compatible.

Figures in Table 10 show that if the crude method of assigning burdens in line with the per cent distribution of total expenditure (column 2) were applied, the incidence picture would end up being strongly regressive (column 1 vs. column 2). But this method would tend to overestimate the actual regressiveness of the Sales Tax, since it does not allow for the effect of tax-rate differentials for various kinds of goods.

That is the reason why we used a slightly more sophisticated method which allowed us to capture some of the effects of the tax-rate structure by groups of commodities. We grouped expenditure items according to the main observable tax rates affecting them, then we classified consumption data in the Survey in a corresponding way, and crossed this new "expenditure classes" with household incomes.[29] Finally, we distributed the actual tax receipts generated by each of these groups, in exact correspondence with the relative importance of family consumption by income brackets, for each of these "goods".

This method has the advantage of starting from officially tabulated, reliable data, on tax receipts by groups of commodities affected. However, it has the disadvantage of showing incidence only at a final stage of the expenditure process. This "hides" the compound effect arising when goods experience several transfers in the distribution process and the consequently higher mark-ups and higher net effective tax rates that result. However, the incidence pattern does not appear to be highly sensitive to this, as explained later on in this chapter.

Incidence results (defined as the ratio of "tax-burden" over total "family income" in each bracket) are regressive, as Table 11 indicates.[30]

If we analyse the relative distribution of tax burdens, we observe that the pattern is remarkably similar to figures on the relative importance of consumption of goods taxed at the general tax rate (8 per cent), distributed throughout the income scale, as can be seen on Table 11.

It may be observed that figures in columns 2 and 4 in Table 11 tend to match quite closely.[31] This is not surprising, since on the one hand, 74.5 per cent of all tax receipts from the sales and energy tax were generated by this class of expenditure – goods taxed at the general tax rate of 8 per cent – and on the other hand, the composition of household expenditures in terms of so-called "necessities", "normal goods", "sumptuaries" and "luxuries" does not seem to be extremely differentiated by income brackets,[32] and tax-rate differentials for these goods do not seem

[29] For a description of the fourteen groups of commodities considered in the Sales and Energy Taxes, and their basic legal tax rates, see Table in section 3 and the notes following Table 3.

[30] For a detailed analysis see Table A-2, presented in the Annex at the end of this chapter.

[31] Similarly, the relative distribution of aggregate consumption (see Table 10) lies very close to that shown for the "8 per cent class" of commodities.

[32] This is subject, however, to three kinds of qualifications: (i) it is difficult to detect appropriately the differences in "quality" of similar goods consumed by families of different incomes; (ii) there are problems in the measurement of the expenditure on durable goods (the flow of services consumed in a given year, the financement of these purchases); (iii) in the case of services, expenditure patterns seem more differentiated.

TABLE 11

Incidence of indirect taxation, 1969

Family income (s.v.)	Indirect taxes[a] (millions of escudos) (1)	Per cent distribution of indirect taxes (2)	Tax incidence on family incomes (3)	Distribution of expenditures on goods taxed at general rate (8% sales taxes) (4)
0–1	601.0	10.5	17.0	13.1
1–2	1,221.3	21.3	13.1	24.0
2–3	1,121.1	19.6	12.7	23.5
3–4	596.6	10.4	11.4	10.6
4–5	430.8	7.5	10.8	7.3
5–6	369.4	6.4	11.2	6.6
6–8	387.2	6.8	10.4	5.7
8–10	349.4	6.1	12.7	4.2
10+	651.2	11.4	11.2	6.0
Total or average	5,728.0	100.0	12.3	100.0

[a] Including the sales taxes, the services tax, production and energy taxes, the stamp tax and the tax on loans interests.

powerful enough to effectively discriminate in the burden falling over distinct income groups. This, we think, is a basic element which has either been ignored or overlooked in the design of taxation policy.

Before exploring some of the tentative policy conclusions that arise from our study, it is useful to report briefly on the sensitivity analysis which was done on the incidence results for indirect taxation, we experimented with data reported for the Gran Santiago area in the Survey of Household Budgets. This area includes some 50 per cent of all national population and roughly accounts for half of production in the country. It has the advantage that it represents the more "reliable" set of information reported by households included in the Survey, and that it allows for a reclassification of expenditure groups. This time, we focused on the Sales Tax, excluding energy or services' taxations. We distinguished five family-income categories (0–2, 2–4, 4–6, 6–8, 8–+ in minimum annual income units), which we crossed with six well-defined expenditure categories. This time, explicit consideration was given to a category for "exempted goods" in order to test for the existence of consumption biases between different income classes.

Even with the reclassification of commodity groups and income brackets, results were relatively insensitive to the existence of a differentiated tax-rate structure, confirming therefore our previous findings.[33]

Finally, we carried out a short-cut estimate for "theoretical incidence" where we took explicit account of the reasonable number of transfers that different commodity groups were experimenting, in the process of distribution of goods. Through this method we tried to capture the compound effect of accumulated taxation brought forth by the tax, as it is levied over transactions.[34] Again, results confirmed the regressive incidence pattern.

It is also important to point out that with these data, the ratios for "theoretical incidence" doubled those obtained for "effective incidence" (computed in both cases, for each and every income bracket in the scale). This implies that – on average – there was an evasion factor of 50 per cent in the Sales Tax. Other authors – in alternative calculations – had estimated a degree of evasion over 80 per cent.[35]

In sum, the main conclusion reached after the analysis of indirect taxation in Chile (1969) is its regressivity. Furthermore, our calculations show that the indirect tax burden seemed to impinge very heavily on the welfare of the poorest families of society.

3.4. **The overall incidence of taxation**

The picture that emerges from the incidence of direct and indirect taxes is shown in Table 12. The analysis of the combined effect of direct and

[33] Among the important facts that showed up were the following:

(i) For all income brackets, it was true that about 30 per cent of total expenditures per bracket were concentrated on the list of exempted goods. Also, around 80 per cent of total family expenditures in each income bracket was accounted for by consumption of exempt goods and goods taxed at the 8 per cent (general) rate.

(ii) Tax-burden ratios calculated using total family expenditures instead of income per bracket as the base appear to follow a rather proportional pattern. This might be one element which accounts for the misleading incidence assumptions of legislators, policy-makers and some academicians.

[34] The formula used in the computation of "theoretical incidence" rates was: $(1 + \text{legal tax rate applicable})^{i} - 1$, where i = number of estimated transfers in the distribution process of the relevant commodity.

[35] R. Beca, T. Galvez and E. Imperatore, *Análisis Cuantitativo de los Impuestos a las Compraventas y a las Importaciones,* Centro de Estudios de Estadísticas y Matemáticas, Facultad de Ciencias Económicas, Universidad de Chile, 1969.

TABLE 12
Redistributive effects of taxation
(in percentages)

Family income brackets (annual minimum incomes)	Relative distribution of families (1)	Relative distribution of direct and indirect tax burdens (2)	Relative distribution of pre-tax family income (3)	Incidence of taxation (*total burden*) (family income) (4)
0 – 1	29.8	7.6	7.6	18.5
1 – 2	31.6	18.1	20.1	16.6
2 – 3	17.6	17.3	18.9	16.9
3 – 4	7.4	9.6	11.2	15.8
4 – 5	4.5	7.7	8.7	16.2
5 – 6	2.9	7.0	7.1	18.2
6 – 8	2.7	7.8	8.0	18.0
8 – 10	1.7	6.5	5.9	20.2
10 +	2.0	18.2	12.5	26.7
Total or average	100.0	100.0	100.0	18.4

indirect taxes over family incomes shows that taxation is of a semi-proportional nature.

Our findings indicate that the high degree of progressiveness reported in the case of direct taxation is almost completely compensated for by the regressiveness of indirect taxes, and that this is especially so in the case of the lower- and middle-income classes.[36]

The figures in the last column of Table 12 show that incidence ratios for different family-income brackets tend to lie close to the average rate of 18.4 per cent. The exception is the figure shown for the top-income bracket, a fact which is subject to important qualifications.[37]

[36] As we explained before, this is strongly due to the fact that indirect taxation represents a very large share of total government finance in Chile. If we consider, for example, the range of countries with a similar GNP *per capita* like Chile (those belonging to the range of US $500–850) we observe that Chile depends on indirect levies as a source of taxation, in a share which exceeds the average proportion computed for the group of these countries (60 per cent in comparison with 50 per cent). See John Due, *Indirect Taxation in Developing Economies,* 1970.

[37] See E. Aninat, "Ajuste de los ingresos familiares de la Encuesta I.N.E. a los datos de ingresos de Cuentas Nacionales", mimeo CEPLAN, 1975.

Although the income-base used for calculating the average tax-incidence ratio was adjusted to make it consistent with income data from national accounts, it was not possible to perform a detailed adjustment for each and every income-bracket considered. This was simply done on a proportional basis.[38]

The preceding comments are particularly important for the top-income bracket. First, this is an open-ended one, which means that the tax-burden rate represents only the "average" situation experienced in the whole bracket, thereby hiding the effective relative burdens falling on the various subgroups belonging to this class. It is reasonable to expect considerable variability in the effective tax rates borne by different categories such as employers, rentiers and professional workers.

Second, complementary evidence on individual taxable incomes tends to show that average income levels in this bracket[39] are probably quite a bit higher than what our adjusted survey's data shows. It is quite common that surveys on family incomes tend to underestimate the income levels of rich families. The composition of their incomes (rents, interests, other capital incomes, etc.) is of such a nature that makes it harder to assess and control.

Tentative corrections for the income-share of families belonging to the top bracket indicate that – in its upper bound – it could even reach one-fourth of total income, a figure which doubles the income-share considered in the Survey and in our study. This fact would imply that the tax-incidence ratio computed for these families would fall to a figure below that of the national average (i.e. below 18.4 per cent).

In any case, what we may surely conclude is that tax-incidence rates are disappointingly undifferentiated throughout the income scale, a fact which obviously contrasts with the normative goal of progressivity, commonly advanced for any tax system.

For example, if we compare incidence rates of personal income taxation in Chile and the USA for 1969, we confirm that the pattern of

[38] See E. Aninat, "Ajuste de los ingresos familiares . . .", *op. cit.*

[39] If we study the individual taxable income declared to the Internal Revenue Service we observe that average income levels for different occupational categories which belong to this open-ended bracket have a significant variance. In the case of professionals the average income level (in 1969) was the equivalent of US $9,400; for employers in general, US $11,500; for rentiers it was US $17,000, whereas for employers in the mining sector the average income was twice this level.

progressivity for direct taxes in Chile could probably be improved (see Table 13).

First, US families belonging to the upper-income brackets make a greater tax effort in comparison with similar Chilean families (incidence rates of 11.7 per cent versus 7.2 per cent). Second, the degree of progressiveness throughout income brackets appears to be fairer in the USA than in Chile, given that Chilean tax rates show a more rapid increase between low-income and middle-income brackets, and a much

TABLE 13

Comparative incidence rates of personal income taxation: Chile–USA (1969)

Country	Family income bracket (min. family income) 0–6	6–10	10–+
1. USA[(a)]	2%	2.9%	11.7%
2. Chile[(b)]	2%	3.2%	7.2%

[(a)] Includes the tax burdens under the Individual Income Tax at the federal, State and local levels. Incidence rates were computed on the basis of the study by R. Musgrave, K. Case and H. Leonard, "The distribution of fiscal burdens and benefits", Harvard Institute of Economic Research, Discussion Paper No. 319, September 1973.

[(b)] Includes the tax burdens arising from the Global Tax, the second-category tax on wage and salary earners, and the taxation on the income of professionals. Incidence rates are based on our results of Section 2.

milder increase between middle- and high-income brackets. In sum, personal income taxes in Chile show an "early" degree of progressiveness which is soon tempered off, in comparison with the USA situation.

An obvious inequitable fact of the Chilean system is the excessive taxation that is observed at the bottom income levels. The Chilean tax system wipes-off 18.5 per cent of the gross incomes of poor families (those earning less than US $670 a year).

An urgent policy target is to seek ways of reducing the tax burden of these families. One possibility is to reduce the average rates of indirect taxation, and particularly, those levies which affect most heavily the goods consumed by the poor.[40]

The reduction in the tax burden of the poor should be accompanied by an effort to close loopholes, reduce evasion and in general increase the taxes paid by high-income groups.

Tax-reform in Chile should work in the direction of increasing the "vertical efficiency" of the Government Budget. This means that the tax system should be tailored so as to permit the positive effects brought forth by pro-poor public expenditures are not impaired by the negative effects that tax levies have over the real purchasing power of the lower-income groups. In many countries, the tax system has represented a check to the positive effects of transfers received by poverty groups, thereby reducing the effectiveness of state action.[41] Chile is no exception to this phenomenon.

Reasons for this fact are principally encountered on the historical trend experimented by taxation in Chile. In spite of the fact that overall tax-effort has – on average – proved acceptable in Chile, it has concentrated on the "wrong" side: on the transactions front and the utilisation of indirect levies. Given the characteristics of low-income families consumption, and given the undue weight of indirect taxation in the tax-mix, the potential redistributive character of the Chilean fiscal system is significantly diminished. Different areas subject to new taxation should be explored in the future, if the welfare position of poverty groups is not to be worsened.

Two examples which illustrate the importance of fiscal measures which redress inequities are explained below.

First, if stricter law enforcement were established so that present rates of tax erosion on the earnings of professionals – estimated as 70 per cent

[40] One incidence analysis is useful for identifying these levies with precision (see Section 2). In order to compensate for the reduction in tax collections, indirect levies such as the gasoline tax, the tax on bank interests and some types of taxes on services, could conceivably be reinforced in the indirect tax-mix, given that they impinge mainly on middle- and high-income groups.

[41] In the United States, for example (1968), the group earning less than US $2,000 was receiving the highest amount of government transfers as a proportion of incomes (106.5 per cent) but at the same time it was burdened with the highest tax-incidence ratio (50 per cent). See C. Hsieh, "Fiscal measures to combat poverty in the United States", *International Labour Review,* ILO, vol. 91, 5, May 1975.

of their potential income base – were eliminated, tax collections would increase by the amount necessary to compensate for one-fourth of the actual tax burdens borne by the poor (families in the first bracket).

Secondly, if effort were concentrated on the elimination of avenues which presently erode government receipts from the Global Income Tax[42] (estimated as 40 per cent of the relevant income base), the tax system would generate some 75 per cent of the resources needed in order to compensate for present tax burdens of the poor.

These are some of the priority areas to concentrate on, if mobilising new tax-resources is required for the State to achieve its redistributive goal.

CONCLUSIONS

Having examined the basic characteristics of the Chilean tax system and the redistributive incidence, we should now examine what could be general features to consider in a future tax system, that were more equitable and efficient. Here we will present some of the relevant elements, as they are derived from the central points in our previous analysis.

From the point of view of equity, an ideal tax system would contain a single and progressive scheme of levies on a tax base that is broad and homogeneous and which includes each and every increase of real wealth of natural persons, without distinctions as to the sources of such increases. What is important in the final analysis is the net total effect of taxes on the level of real income of the inhabitants of the country. This final result can be better known and defined if the various tax schemes are grouped together in a common and unique type of tax.[43]

This standard constitutes the "optimum" framework for achieving a goal of vertical and horizontal equity which every tax system should aim for.

From another point of view, a tax system should cause the smallest number of distortions in the allocation of resources and at the same time

[42] By closing loopholes such as those represented by undistributed profits, and eliminating unjustified deductions and exemptions, etc.

[43] H. Simons, *Personal Income Taxation,* University of Chicago Press, 1938.

contain incentives for maximum utilisation of existing resources. It should also help in promoting employment, intensifying the use of available capital and raising the levels of savings and investment in the country.

These are "ideal" features for a tax system, from the theoretical point of view. Now we will examine some of the restrictions imposed on the scheme by the practical realities of a developing country like Chile.

First, we should examine tax levels. Compared to international levels, the level of tax burden in Chile is, on average, acceptable. The overall level of taxation depends, among other factors, on the levels of public expenditure that must be financed and ultimately on the role assigned to the State.

Chile is a country of intermediate development, with a mixed economy, growing at a rather low rate but which historically has maintained very definite redistributive and social goals. It is, therefore, reasonable to think that the role of the government in the process of development and redistribution should be important.

Moreover, since the margin of resources that can be collected from foreign sources through taxation and foreign aid is relatively small, the inevitable conclusion is that the level of general taxation should not be reduced in the future. It could in fact be incremented if some of the measures suggested in the next chapters were implemented.

A different, but equally important question is how to restructure the present tax burden in order to approach a more optimum framework. Probably a first step would be to change the relative proportion between direct and indirect levies. The direct levies should be reinforced in order to take advantage of their progressivity. The indirect taxes should be lowered to reduce the inequities introduced by their regressive character.

Secondly, the changes should help in the direction of creating a single system of direct taxation levied on incomes homogeneously and comprehensibly. This can be done by means of a system of single progressive rates. Thus, fragmented or cedular taxation schemes could be avoided in favour of universal direct income taxation, such as the previously described "Global Complementary Income Tax".

Nevertheless, the proposed new structure faces three kinds of difficulties: administrative restrictions, restrictions created by the structural characteristics of the economy and political restrictions.

In the first group, the problems are related to assessment and supervision of the flows of tax receipts. Traditionally tax evasion has reached considerable proportion in countries such as Chile, as we pointed out in the case of taxes on professional groups and the Global Complementary Income Tax. This implies that even if the final progressivity of the system is corrected, in order to reduce evasion it will probably still be necessary to have a set of specific direct taxes levied on income flows from labour and capital rents, with special rates for special sectors (for example, a tax on business profits). Thus taxes of diverse coverage and targets would continue to coexist within the same general tax system.

On similar grounds, it is necessary, especially in underdeveloped countries, to correctly assess for tax purposes not only natural persons but also legal persons. By the same token it would be convenient to use different tax bases besides income. These can be consumption, savings and property. This multiplicity of bases allows for the best form of control of the various sources of tax erosion and evasion. Clearly these diverse channels of tax assessment must be structured in such a way as to be consistent among themselves (i.e. treatment of exemptions and deductions, rate structure, etc.) so that, in spite of diversity, some advance is made toward the overall, single scheme postulated initially.

Moreover, as we pointed out previously, extreme care must be taken in choosing those taxes which possess the highest degree of progressivity and equity. There are two main restrictions that can be properly identified with the functioning of the economic structure. First, the nominal or legal incidence of a tax frequently does not coincide with the real economic incidence of the tax.

A second relevant aspect about the Chilean economy is that, due to an inflationary tradition marked by more or less abrupt and at times unexpected acceleration and deceleration of inflation trends, instances of high capital gains are available to some sectors or social groups. Such increases in real wealth are obviously not the result of direct productive effort, but frequently from merely speculative activities or by random movements in the relative prices and price level in the economy.

Clearly, speculative behaviour modifies income distribution. Most often the change is regressive – since normally the high-income sectors have better mechanisms of information and self-defence – against inflation. This suggests the advisability of establishing a special levy on capital gains, in order to correct undesirable and unplanned alterations in income distribution. This special tax is made necessary by the imperfections of the existing direct-tax schemes, which do not include automatic and rapid mechanisms to assess increases in real and incorporate them to the tax base. Here again we see a dilemma between a "second-best" tax system and the ideal.

Further, we must consider the political restriction. If there is anything that limits the effectiveness of a tax system in the developing world, it is the restriction imposed by the power groups. Any attempt to raise the progressivity of personal income tax or to better assess business sectors, income or wealth has inevitably come up against implicit or explicit opposition.

This limitation is related to the distribution of power in society. And distribution of power is normally correlated with the distribution of property.[44] The "richest" in society have better avenues of access to information and direct influence in government decision-making.

Finally, the implementation of a property tax system is one of the requirements to advance in eliminating the obstacles standing in the way of suitable tax progressivity and fair distribution of incomes. Whether they are direct, assessing wealth itself, or indirect with progressive levies on imputed income from property, such a tax system doubtlessly constitutes a useful fiscal tool to achieve a higher level of social welfare.[45] Such action aimed at property taxation, implies affecting the existing distribution of power which is normally considered overly concentrated.

We should also mention the implications of the tax system for resource utilisation. Of special importance are the policies related to tax incentives, as explained in previous chapters of this study. It seems advisable, based on the historical experience of such incentives in countries such as Chile, to concentrate these mechanisms in the future at the factorial level rather than sectorially or regionally. Because of the problems that exist in the employment area, tax exemptions and fiscal incentives should be modified in order to stimulate greater utilisation of labour and the use of technologies conducive to more rapid growth of employment.

[44] The distribution of property in Chile is heavily concentrated. In 1969 the high-income sector, which accumulated 40 per cent of total family income, possessed at the same time about 70 per cent of privately held assessed wealth.

[45] Moreover, this policy would eliminate one of the sources of "escape" from direct income tax used by wealthy sectors.

In any case, it must be recognised that the role played by the tax system in general is conditioned by the context in which it is implemented. Thus it is indispensable to know what is happening in the other areas of the public budget – for example, the level, structure and destination of public expenditures. One must also examine the price, salary and income policies applied by the countries over time.

This provides a logical ground to begin to analyse the nature and incidence of the rest of public programmes. Later in the book we will examine another public instrument destined to extract resources from high-income groups. It was of significance in Chile. We refer to the direct redistribution of property, by means of Land Reform Programmes or expropriation of industrial enterprises.

TABLE A-1

Incidence of direct taxation, 1969

(All figures in millions of escudos unless otherwise stated)

Income bracket (1)	Distribution of family incomes (%) (2)	Number of families (thousands) (3)	Distribution of families (%) (4)	1.1* Tax on professionals (5)	1.2. Second-category tax on employees (6)	1.3. Second-category tax on blue collars (7)	1.4. Tax on corporate directors' income (8)	1.5. Other Global Income Tax (9)	1.6. Other direct personal taxes (10)
0 – 1	7.6	531.1	29.8	–	–	–	–	–	0.1
1 – 2	20.1	564.1	31.6	–	34.7	82.6	–	56.7	1.3
2 – 3	18.9	314.3	17.6	–	58.8	50.9	–	85.6	2.1
3 – 4	11.2	131.7	7.4	–	42.3	18.9	–	61.5	1.5
4 – 5	8.7	79.5	4.5	–	35.7	9.3	–	58.3	1.3
5 – 6	7.1	52.5	2.9	2.8	33.5	3.7	–	62.5	1.2
6 – 8	8.0	47.7	2.7	6.0	40.9	2.1	–	72.2	1.5
8 – 10	5.9	27.0	1.5	5.2	28.5	0.0	–	52.2	1.0
10 +	12.5	35.6	2.0	58.0	57.4	0.0	10.6	300.4	2.1
Total	100.0	1,783.5	100.0	72.0	331.8	167.5	10.6	749.4	12.1

*These numbers correspond to the order of tax items in Table 4.

TABLE A-1 (cont.)

	2.1.7. On corporate profits			2.1.8. On profits of unincorporated enterprises					
Income bracket (s.v.a.)	on employers (11a)	on consumers (11b)	½ employer ½ consumer (11c)	on capital (12a)	on consumers (12b)	¾ employer ¼ consumer (12c)	¾ capital ¼ consumer (12d)	2.1.3. On rentier income (13)	2.2. Capital gains tax (14)
0 – 1	–	61.3	30.6	3.7	36.8	9.6	12.0	1.7	0.0
1 – 2	–	116.9	58.4	19.8	70.4	19.5	32.5	3.5	0.1
2 – 3	15.8	92.7	54.3	31.1	55.8	23.4	37.2	3.0	0.5
3 – 4	12.8	48.6	30.8	23.7	29.2	15.1	25.1	2.1	0.4
4 – 5	30.1	34.1	32.1	28.7	20.5	23.1	26.6	2.5	0.9
5 – 6	44.8	28.1	36.4	23.8	16.9	31.1	22.1	2.5	1.3
6 – 8	45.7	28.0	36.9	33.7	16.9	31.7	29.5	3.1	1.3
8 – 10	36.7	21.2	28.9	31.1	12.8	25.2	26.5	1.9	1.1
10 +	278.8	33.8	156.3	84.1	20.4	101.0	68.2	6.3	4.6
Total	464.7	464.7	464.7	279.7	279.7	279.7	279.7	26.6	10.2

TABLE A-1 (cont.)

Income bracket (s.v.a.)	3.1. Patrimony of net wealth tax (15)	3.2.1. Real-estate tax on agricultural property: person's portion (16)	3.2.1. employers (17)	3.2.2. Real-estate taxes on non-agricultural property: person's portion (18)	employers (19a)	consumers (19b)	½ consumer ½ employer (19c)	3.2.2. Other property: person's portion (20)	on employers (20a)
0–1	–	–	–	–	–	14.2	7.1	–	–
1–2	–	2.5	–	37.4	–	27.2	13.6	1.8	–
2–3	–	4.9	0.05	39.7	3.6	21.5	12.5	2.0	0.2
3–4	–	3.7	0.04	26.4	3.0	11.3	7.1	1.4	0.2
4–5	–	7.0	0.09	33.7	7.0	7.9	7.4	1.8	0.5
5–6	–	9.5	0.14	33.9	10.4	6.5	8.5	1.9	0.7
6–8	12.8	10.1	0.14	41.5	10.6	6.5	8.6	2.3	0.7
8–10	8.9	7.7	0.11	25.5	8.5	4.9	6.7	1.4	0.6
10+	33.8	32.4	0.84	90.6	64.8	7.9	36.4	5.2	4.3
Total	55.5	77.8	1.41	328.7	107.9	107.9	107.9	17.8	7.2

TABLE A-1 (cont.)

Income bracket (s.v.a.)	Other property taxes: on consumers (20b)	Other property taxes: ½ consumer ½ employer (20c)	3.3. Vehicle licences (21)	3.4. Inheritance and gift tax (22)	Total tax burdens (benchmark) (23)	Incidence of direct taxation = (23/2) (24)
0–1	1.0	0.5	–	0.7	52.7	1.5%
1–2	1.8	0.9	–	1.4	327.4	3.5
2–3	1.5	0.8	6.9	1.8	361.1	4.1
3–4	0.8	0.5	4.9	1.3	227.9	4.4
4–5	0.5	0.5	7.5	1.8	226.5	5.6
5–6	0.4	0.6	9.5	2.2	232.2	7.0
6–8	0.4	0.6	10.4	2.4	282.3	7.6
8–10	0.3	0.4	7.6	1.7	205.3	7.5
10+	0.5	2.4	30.2	6.4	902.1	15.5
Total	7.2	7.2	77.0	19.7	2,817.5	6.1%

TABLE A-2

Incidence of indirect taxation, 1969
(All figures are in millions of escudos)

Income bracket (s.v.a.)	General Sales Tax rate 4.1* (1)	Luxuries 4.2 (2)	Leisure sector 4.3 (3)	Auto-mobiles 4.4 (4)	Neces-sities 4.5 (5)	Non-alcoholic beverages 4.6 (6)	Semi-durables 4.7 (7)	Wines and liquors 4.8 (8)	Heavy taxed items 4.9 (9)	Alcohol 5.1 (10)
0–1	312.8	6.4	11.2	0.1	14.2	5.4	29.9	10.1	4.3	9.4
1–2	573.1	15.1	22.0	1.1	18.2	18.9	47.1	28.1	13.9	24.0
2–3	537.3	14.4	19.2	2.3	12.6	17.5	37.7	20.0	9.6	14.8
3–4	253.1	8.9	8.5	2.1	5.2	8.8	17.5	10.5	17.6	8.0
4–5	174.3	6.3	6.6	1.9	3.2	6.4	11.3	8.1	16.2	6.3
5–6	157.6	4.2	4.7	2.4	2.4	5.1	9.2	5.8	14.5	4.4
6–8	136.1	5.1	6.8	4.0	2.1	5.3	8.7	6.6	17.2	5.2
8–10	100.3	2.5	4.1	3.9	1.3	5.0	6.7	5.9	10.5	4.4
10+	143.3	5.3	7.6	10.7	1.4	6.1	8.8	8.4	26.4	6.9
Total	2,387.9	68.2	90.7	28.5	60.6	78.5	176.9	103.5	103.2	83.4

*These numbers correspond to the order of tax items in Table 4.

TABLE A-2 (cont.)

Income bracket	Tobacco 5.2 (11)	Gas and electricity 6.1 (12)	Liquid gas 6.2 (13)	Petrol (gasoline) 6.3 (14)	Kerosene 6.4 (15)	Oil and lubricants 6.5 (16)	General services 7.1 (17)	Banking 7.2 (18)	Insurance 7.3 (19)	Transport and other 7.4 (20)
0–1	62.6	12.3	2.4	13.7	3.8	4.6	44.8	–	0.2	1.0
1–2	113.2	20.8	6.6	39.2	4.7	13.2	93.0	–	5.3	2.6
2–3	92.3	16.3	7.2	42.0	2.2	14.2	77.5	–	9.1	2.5
3–4	46.2	10.1	3.5	27.8	0.9	9.3	46.1	–	5.3	1.6
4–5	35.9	8.0	3.4	22.7	0.3	7.7	25.1	–	2.5	1.2
5–6	23.5	5.3	1.8	22.0	0.3	7.4	28.1	–	0.8	1.1
6–8	23.5	5.5	1.7	30.1	0.2	10.2	34.4	–	4.8	1.3
8–10	18.2	3.9	1.1	25.8	0.1	8.6	28.9	6.6	3.8	1.0
10+	28.4	7.2	1.5	64.7	0.1	21.8	41.1	14.3	20.3	2.4
Total	443.8	89.4	29.2	288.0	12.6	97.0	419.0	20.9	52.1	14.7

TABLE A-2 (cont.)

Income bracket	Hospital, laundry 7.5 (21)	Entertainment 7.6 (22)	Stamp tax 9 (23)	Tax on interest charged by banks on commercial loans 7.7 (24)	*Total indirect taxes* (excludes tax on interest) (25)	*Total indirect taxes* (includes tax on interest) (26)	Incidence on family incomes (%) (27)
0–1	2.8	1.8	27.7	19.5	51.85	601.0	17.0
1–2	6.6	5.8	111.6	37.2	1,184.1	1,221.3	13.1
2–3	6.1	5.8	131.0	29.5	1,091.6	1,121.1	12.7
3–4	4.5	3.8	81.8	15.5	581.1	596.6	11.4
4–5	2.6	2.8	67.2	10.8	420.0	430.8	10.6
5–6	2.7	2.3	54.8	9.0	360.4	369.4	11.2
6–8	3.1	1.9	64.5	8.9	378.3	387.2	10.4
8–10	2.3	2.0	48.5	54.0	295.4	349.4	12.7
10+	4.7	2.5	106.0	111.3	539.9	651.2	11.2
Total	35.4	28.7	693.1	295.7	5,432.3	5,728.0	12.3

CHAPTER 3

Who Benefits from Government Expenditures?

THE DETERMINANTS OF GOVERNMENT EXPENDITURES

The Government Budget is an important instrument to bring about a more equal distribution of income. The income of the wealthiest can at least potentially be reduced through taxation whereas the living standards of the poor may be improved by directing government expenditures preferentially to those groups.

Before discussing what effects government expenditure may have over the various income groups in developing countries in general and more specifically what effects it had in the Chilean case, we must briefly discuss the underlying factors which determine the level of government expenditures and the relative importance of this variable in the country that concerns us in this study.

The study of the interrelationship between government expenditures and other socio-economic variables is greatly complicated by the fact that unlike firms or individuals, government decisions are the result of a complex collective process, where different institutions, interest groups or the community in general intervene. Thus it is not easy to find a simple behavioural hypothesis which can satisfactorily explain or predict how much and where the government spends its resources.

Since Wagner's law was stated, the literature is rich in attempts to relate public expenditure to other economic variables. Wagner's formulation that the share of government expenditures in GNP should expand as economic growth proceeds has been tested in various econometric studies relating government expenditures and income. Musgrave finds a positive trend towards a higher share of public expenditures over GNP when analysing time series data for the US, UK and Germany in the period 1890–1960.[1] He interprets the trend as reflecting the higher provision of social services that come about as a result of the social and cultural tendencies toward greater equality that develop in most countries as income expands.

The previous relationship breaks down, however, when cross-section data are studied. Musgrave's estimates, based on a cross-section sample of forty-four countries in the period 1953–58, show that the share of government expenditures is significantly correlated with income only at low levels of development (countries with income *per capita* below 600 dollars). During the early stages of the growth process, governments must provide the necessary infrastructure (roads, irrigation, transport) that will allow other investment to be productive. This is particularly relevant given the importance of externalities in those early stages of growth. As development proceeds other factors acquire a much larger significance. No longer the level of income is the best explanatory factor, but the whole character of the development process becomes very important. By this it is usually meant the system of economic organisation prevailing, the degree of urbanisation, the importance of the industrial sector, the distribution of income, the rate of growth and the age composition of the population, the quantity and quality of private services available and their cost, the degree of monetisation of the economy and others.[2]

These various factors influence in a different manner the several components of public expenditures. Thus the empirical studies have necessarily evolved towards a more disaggregated analysis, trying to test diverse hypotheses that explain the behaviour of each of the main components of total expenditures.[3] Musgrave, for example, disaggregates government expenditures in a capital formation component, public

[1]See R. Musgrave, *Fiscal Systems*, Yale, 1969.

[2]See F. Pryor, *Public Expenditures in Communist and Capitalists Nations,* Allen & Unwin, 1968; and J. Lotz, "Pattern of government expenditures in developing countries", *The Manchester School of Economic and Social Studies,* June 1970.

[3]This is the direction taken by the studies of R. Thorn, "The evolution of public finances during economic development", *The Manchester School,* January 1967; S. Lall, "A note of government expenditures in developing countries", *The Economic Journal,* June 1969; J. Lotz and H. Morss, "Measuring tax effort in developing countries", *IMF Staff Papers,* November 1967; Pryor, *op. cit.;* Musgrave (1969), *op. cit.*; Lotz (1970), *op. cit.*

consumption and transfer payments. No clear overall pattern emerges. Thus, it is not possible to predict whether as a net result the share of total expenditures in GNP will rise or decrease as income grows.

On a recent cross-section study by Lotz that includes thirty-seven developing countries, expenditures have been divided into four groups: social welfare expenditures (mainly social security); education and health; defence; and economic services, the latter including things like lending for development purposes, infrastructure, communications, agriculture, industry and community services.[4]

Of the four components of the public expenditures, Lotz's results show that social welfare expenditures seem to be closely correlated to the degree of development.

The second component, education and health, is found to be significantly correlated with *per capita* income, but somewhat surprisingly also with the degree of openness in the economy.[5]

The economic services component of public expenditures, which includes direct government investment and indirect developmental programmes that provides incentives for the private sector, does not behave in an entirely systematic way with respect to the traditional economic variables. Lotz does find an inverse significant correlation between degree of development (using literacy rates as a proxy) and expenditures on economic services, a result that he explains as meaning that "countries at a low stage of intensive development typically allocate a larger proportion of the national income to economic services, because governments at a low stage of development have a bigger need for expenditures on infrastructure, communications and irrigation, than do countries at a more advanced stage of development".[6]

This result is not surprising, and is consistent with Musgrave's,[7] but does not provide an explanation for the behaviour of the economic

[4] Lotz (1970), *op. cit.*

[5] Although Lotz develops a theory of an international "demonstration effect" to explain this, it is much more likely that the degree of openness, being highly correlated with tax revenues available, becomes a good proxy for the revenue-constraint factor. In other words, education and health expenditures would be at least partially determined from the demand side by *per capita* income levels and from the supply side by public financial resources available through the tax system. See Hinrichs, *A General Theory of Tax Structure Change during Economic Development,* Law School Harvard, 1966.

[6] Lotz (1970), *op. cit.*

[7] Musgrave (1969), *op. cit.*

services component at more advanced levels of development. Lotz's findings suggest some correlation of this variable with the revenue constraint factor (measured indirectly by using total government expenditures as a proxy), but the correlation is weak. One reason that the correlation is weak is that variables like the system of economic organisation are left aside in the analysis. If we are dealing with a socialist economy, economic services expenditures will tend to be high. In a capitalist *laissez-faire* type of economy they will be much lower. The extent of government action in the economic sphere is very critically dependent on these non-economic, institutional factors.

Finally, the fourth component is defence. It does not seem to be correlated to any variable in Lotz's study, as indeed in none of the several other previous analyses of government expenditures. This component introduces a completely exogenous variable into the picture, thus one that is very difficult to predict and which is a random element within aggregate public expenditures studies.

The previous discussion illustrates very clearly the unsatisfactory state of the art in the field of theories of public expenditure determinants. Unlike the taxation side, where simple statistical correlations do shed light on some of the main variables affecting tax revenues, government expenditures do not follow such a simple trend. From these studies we can conclude that only a few of the components of public spending (mainly social services) show some stable trend with respect to variables like the degree of development. Others such as economic services are more likely a function of the character of the economy (developed or developing, rich or poor in natural resources, dependent on primary products exports or industrialised); and of the system of economic organisation (socialist, capitalist or mixed economy). These are the factors that we must consider when doing intercountry comparisons of public expenditures, a task we shall undertake next in order to put the Chilean case in the right perspective.

CHILEAN GOVERNMENT EXPENDITURES IN PERSPECTIVE

The Chilean economy is clearly a developing economy at an intermediate stage of development. It shares with most other Latin

American countries the reliance on one primary product as the main source of foreign exchange, the existence of a traditional agricultural sector with relatively abundant land undergoing structural transformation, and the development of a modern capital-intensive industrial sector co-existing with backward traditional activities both in the rural and urban areas.

On the other hand, the system of economic organisation which has undergone dramatic changes in the last 10 years, could be characterised as being that of of a mixed economy with a large state sector, as we shall see next, larger than in most Latin American countries.

The State participation in the Chilean economy can be put in perspective if we compare the share of government expenditures on GNP for several Latin American countries as we do in Table 14. We can see that the State participation in GNP as measured by the public spending–GNP ratio was higher in Chile than in any other country in the late 1960s.

TABLE 14

Public expenditures in GNP for Latin America (in percentages)*

	Years	G/GNP
Argentina	1968–69	27.0
Brazil	1967–68	27.1
Mexico	1967–68	16.6
Colombia	1967–68	14.7
Venezuela	1967–68	22.4
Peru	1966–67	20.4
Chile	1967–68	36.1
Uruguay	1966–67	27.9
Costa Rica	1967–68	19.3
El Salvador	1967–68	14.4
Guatemala	1966–67	12.1
Honduras	1966–67	15.1
Nicaragua	1968–69	16.0
Panama	1967–68	19.8
Dominican Republic	1967–68	20.0
Ecuador	1966–67	22.9
Paraguay	1968–69	17.1
Bolivia	1968–69	22.5

Source: UN ECLA, *Estudio económico de América Latina 1970,* p. 56.

*Total public expenditure includes the General Government plus public investment.

Expenditures of the General Government were 36 per cent of GNP for Chile,[8] but only 27 per cent for Brazil and Argentina, 23 per cent for Ecuador and 28 per cent for Uruguay. These significantly different ratios cannot be explained by differences in *per capita* income, if the abundant empirical findings on this matter are to be believed.[9]

If income *per capita* is not very helpful in explaining the differences, where do they arise from? As the theoretical discussion in the previous section suggests, a disaggregated analysis of the behaviour of the main components of government expenditures might be useful in this respect. A study for the 1960s, comparing various public expenditure components for thirty-seven developing countries including those listed in Table 1, shows Chile to be amongst those spending one of the highest shares of public resources in social services (social security), an average "normal share in public health and education programmes, and a low proportion in defence.[10] Expenditures on economic services appear to be "normal" with respect to the average trend, but since the figures include only the General Government (as defined by UN National Accounts) but not public enterprises and decentralised public agencies, the results are not very meaningful in terms of actual state participation in economic development activities. In spite of that it is quite clear that, even when only the General Government is included, public expenditures in Chile as compared to other Latin American economies seem to be on the high side.

What happens when we compare the level and structure of public expenditures in Chile with that of countries with similar systems of economic organisation, that is mixed economies with large public sectors as some of Western Europe's economies would be? Hansen provides us with an interesting comparative study of public expenditures in seven OECD countries.[11] Using the same definitions as he does we compare his figures with those for Chile in 1965.

We can see from Table 15 that Chile's total government expenditures as a share of GNP are the lowest in the sample with the exception of the US. Although lower than most countries in the sample, the order of magnitude is not too different from the other countries varying two or

[8] As we shall see below the coverage of our analysis is broader than this one. See Table 17.
[9] Musgrave (1969), *op. cit.*; Pryor (1968), *op. cit.*; Lotz (1970), *op. cit.*
[10] See Lotz (1970), *op. cit.* Chile's figures are for 1965.
[11] B. Hansen and W. Snyder (1969), *op. cit.*

TABLE 15

Government expenditures in selected countries as a percentage of GNP, 1965

	Current expenditures[a]	Public investment[b]	Total government expenditures
Belgium	29.1	2.5	34.2
France	34.6	5.3	42.8
Federal Republic of Germany	30.8		35.3
Italy	31.9	3.9	38.3
Sweden	32.9	5.7	42.7
UK	30.3	5.2	37.8
US	25.0	0.5	28.6
Chile	23.4	9.9	33.3

[a] General Government Current Expenditures according to UN National Accounts Classification.

[b] Includes investment of the General Government plus *public enterprises investment.* For Chile it includes Public Sector *direct investment plus developmental loans* given by the Public Sector.

three points around 35 per cent. The Chilean ratio is particularly similar to that of Belgium and the Federal Republic of Germany.[12]

When we disaggregate the figures in terms of current and capital expenditures, we find that Chile's current expenditures (again for General Government only) are also lower as a percentage of GNP than those all countries considered, and close to the US figures. On the other hand, when capital expenditures are compared, including investment by the General Government plus public enterprises investment and decentralised public agencies investment, Chile shows the highest ratio in the sample, 9.9 per cent of GNP as compared to 5.3 per cent for France, 5.2 per cent for the UK, etc. This comparison brings our attention to a very important characteristic of Chile's economic development in the last decade, mainly that of a very extensive participation of the State in investment activities; either directly through the expansion of productive capacity in public enterprises, or indirectly by the increasing importance of a multitude of decentralised government agencies whose task has been

[12] These results are similar to those indicated for taxation in the previous chapter. See Table 1, Chapter 2.

to support and subsidise private investment programmes in most branches of economic activity.

A conclusion of the analysis so far would then be that Chile's above-average share of public expenditures over GNP as compared to other Latin American countries would lie in the inordinately higher expenditures on social security and on the extensive participation of the State in economic activities. This participation is still well below that of a socialist economy as we can see in Table 16, where we give comparative figures for Poland, the UK and Chile (for different years).

TABLE 16

Public spending structure by sectors

	Poland (1960)	UK (1961)	Chile[(a)] (1965)
Current expenditures	21.3	31.1	27.2
Education	4.8	4.5	4.0
Public health	3.5	3.4	3.8
Social security	5.7	6.4	9.5
Defence	3.6	6.7	2.3
Other current	3.7	10.1	7.6
Capital	27.5	3.4	9.9
Total public sector	48.8	34.5	37.1

[(a)] Public Sector Current Expenditures and Direct Public Investment plus Development Loans.

Source: Musgrave (1966) and Chile, *Balances Consolidados Sector Público 1964–1970.*

It is interesting to examine, in Table 16, the sectoral composition of public expenditures for the three countries considered. Current expenditures in education are around 4 per cent of GNP for all three countries, just as those in public health do not vary significantly from an average of 3.5 per cent of GNP. The main difference is in capital expenditures where Poland's public investment is 27.5 per cent of GNP, in Chile 9.9 per cent and in the UK 3.4 per cent. The pattern that emerges from Table 16 is one in which the proportion of resources devoted by the government to the "social sectors" in Chile is equivalent to that of a socialist country and also to that of a welfare-state type of economy such as the UK, with the exception of social-security expenditures that are higher in Chile than in the other cases considered.

With respect to expenditures in direct economic activities the Chilean case is a very interesting one. The State participation has been above that of mixed Western European types of economies. The government has had in the past a decisive participation in the allocation of resources in the economy. Whether this participation helped improve the distribution of income will be one of our concerns in the rest of this chapter.

INCIDENCE OF GOVERNMENT EXPENDITURES: SOME METHODOLOGICAL ISSUES

In the previous section we learned about the importance of government expenditures in the Chilean economy, its evolution through time and the relative significance of its various components, mainly expenditures on economic services, on the social sectors and in administration and defence. Before embarking on the analysis of the effects of government expenditures over the various socio-economic groups, we shall presently discuss some general issues posed by the methodology used in this type of "incidence" study.

Government expenditures' incidence studies are of a more recent origin than tax incidence studies. The first one on expenditures was done by Barna in 1945.[13] Since then various other studies have been carried out.[14] All of them attempt to measure the effects of public expenditures over the general welfare of the population by using income as a catch-all variable representing changes in welfare.

These studies take into account only the direct effects of expenditure with no consideration of the changes in the level of economic activity or employment and the alterations in the relative prices of productive factors that might occur as an indirect result of the economic activity of the government.[15] On the other hand, the studies generally measure the

[13] T. Barna, *Redistribution of Incomes Through the Fiscal System,* Oxford, 1945.

[14] For a survey of studies on developing countries see Bird and de Wulf (1973), *op. cit.* and de Wulf (1974), *op. cit.*

[15] de Wulf (1974), *op. cit.*

incidence of public expenditures when all other variables, like taxes, remain constant.

Two different sets of problems arise when measuring the direct effects of public expenditures. One refers to the problem of identifying the beneficiaries of the policy, the other to the actual form of measurement of the benefit in quantitative terms.

Most studies identify beneficiaries in terms of their relative position in the income-distribution scale. A few others consider criteria like urban-rural,[16] like region or sector of activity, or like technological strata (modern, traditional).[17]

The identification of who benefits depends, of course, on the shifting hypothesis considered in the study. It is true that for a large share of public expenditures very little shifting of benefits occurs. This is true of expenditures in social services and general administration. It is basically in the expenditures that go directly to the economic activities, like, for example, credit to the private sector, where forward shifting of benefits to consumers or background shifting to the productive factors might take place. Most studies have dealt with economies where the bulk of public expenditures have gone to social services, administration and defence, which explains why the problem of shifting of benefits from one group to another has been largely ignored.

A critical assumption in these studies is how general expenditures in administration like central government, the judiciary and defence are assumed to affect socio-economic groups. There are two main alternative assumptions used: one, that these types of expenditures equally benefit all of the population.[18] The other, that they benefit more those already better off, that is that they reinforce the existing distribution of income in the economy.[19] Given that these expenditures are a large proportion of the total, the results can vary significantly according to which assumption is chosen.

[16] Snodgrass, "The fiscal system as an income redistribution in West Malaysia", Economic Development Report No. 224, Harvard University, 1972.

[17] PREALC, *Situación y perspectivas del Empleo en Ecuador,* Santiago, 1976.

[18] Gillespie (1967), "Effect of public expenditures on the distribution of income", in R. A. Musgrave, *Essays in Fiscal Federalism,* Brookings Institution, 1967.

[19] M. Urrutia y C. E. Sandoval, "Política fiscal y distribución del ingreso en Colombia", in A. Foxley, *Distribución del ingreso,* Fondo de Cultura Económica, México, 1974.

Identifying beneficiaries of public expenditures is just one side of the problem. The other consists in measuring the value of the benefits obtained. The usual assumption here is that benefits are equal to the cost of producing public goods and services. The weakness of the approach has been extensively discussed in the literature and we shall repeat it here.[20] Most criticisms refer to the following elements: on the demand side, how does the public evaluate the benefits received from government expenditure? Services might on one extreme be considered of low quality and generally useless; or they might be thought of as essential to satisfy basic needs, as, for example, child-nutrition programmes for the very poor. On the supply side, by equalising benefits to costs we might be inflating the value of the benefits by the degree of inefficiency of the public agency that provides the services although the reverse might also be true: massively produced and distributed public goods and services might benefit from economies of scale and decreasing costs.

Whatever the shortcomings in the approach, no comprehensive alternative has been designed, and all studies up until now have largely used the criterion of evaluating the benefit derived from government expenditures at production costs.[21]

Moreover, the studies do not usually distinguish between components of public expenditures that have a different economic effect on the groups affected by them. One such distinction might be between asset-creating expenditures and consumption-oriented expenditures. The first need not be capital outlays only. Several types of current expenditures, as in education and health, do have an impact in asset creation though improvements in the quality of human resources.

Another possible distinction might be with respect to the time horizon in which the programme produces its effect. It might be a once-and-for-all effect (income transfers) or a more permanent one (new investment). When both are added, one must be aware of the very different way in which the welfare position of the recipient is affected by one or the other.

Not all effects of public expenditures are explicit. Particularly this is the case with those that are oriented to the directly productive sectors. These often consist of credit policies, technical assistance programmes,

[20] Musgrave and Musgrave (1974).
[21] See de Wulf (1974).

etc. If the price at which these services are provided (like the interest rate on loans) is below the social opportunity cost, then an implicit subsidy is being given in favour of those who have access to the cheap credit or technical assistance programme. A similar thing may occur when the prices of goods produced by nationalised enterprises are undervalued. Almost no attempt has been made in the traditional incidence studies to tackle this problem and thus it has been largely ignored.

Finally, we have already mentioned that indirect effects of public expenditures, although important in principle, have not yet been incorporated in incidence studies. An adequate treatment of the problem requires developing a general equilibrium model, where all interrelationships between the public sector and the rest of the economy are made explicit, particularly the distributive and employment aspects. This type of model has not been designed yet in an operational sense, thus the treatment of the problem remains inadequate and the approach to indirect incidence effects partial and incomplete.

Given the methodological limitations of these studies it has been recommended that they should not concentrate exclusively on the formal exercise of measuring incidence against an ex-ante distribution scale, but that more disaggregated sectoral policy-oriented studies might prove to be more relevant and useful for policy purposes.[22]

The approach we followed shares several of the shortcomings of other studies, particularly in that it values the benefits of most public programmes in terms of their costs. But some departures were attempted from the traditional method. A "target group" in terms of redistribution policy was identified, consisting of the poorer 30 per cent of the population, which roughly constitutes the poverty groups in Chile, according to various definitions.[23] Our study of public expenditures, without ignoring the effects throughout the income scale, focuses more sharply on the poverty groups.[24]

[22] Bird and de Wulf (1973), *op. cit.*; de Wulf (1974), *op. cit.*

[23] Instituto de Economía, Universita Católica de Chile, ODEPLAN, *Mapa de la extrema pobreza en Chile,* 1975.

[24] In doing this, we are evaluating public expenditure policy not in terms of its stated objective in 1969, but in terms of what now seems a high-priority objective in development programmes. In this sense we are not being fair in the evaluation of a policy whose goal was not poverty erradication only, but many other things simultaneously.

At the same time and with the idea of identifying groups more relevant for a sociological analysis of fiscal policy, we disaggregated the results in terms of the social strata (low, middle and high).[25]

Another departure from traditional studies is that when the State participation in the economic sphere is analysed, the income classification is used as a secondary element *vis-à-vis* the technological stratification, observed in the various economic sectors. This is assumed to be the main element explaining the heterogeneity in income arising from technologically segmented productive sectors.

The study of spending in social services is enriched by distinguishing between asset-creating expenditures and consumption-oriented programmes. The first should play a key role as a redistributive mechanism, as has been pointed out recently in several publications,[26] given that the lack of so-called ''complementary assets'' seems to be one of the critical bottlenecks that prevent poverty groups (a large proportion of which are small producers or independent workers) from increasing productivity and eventually incomes.

Another element which is present in our study is the explicit treatment of subsidies as an instrument used to redistribute in favour of poverty groups. The effects of subsidies policies on these groups was examined in most instances.

Finally, an attempt has been made to disaggregate the data and study incidence effects not only for each of the main public institutions within a particular sector of activity, but also for the various programmes that each institution implements in the year of our study.[27] Obviously we cannot report on each of these here. We shall try in the next sections to extract from the excessively detailed partial studies those elements which seem of more general validity not only for the country that concerns us here but for other developing countries as well.

INCIDENCE OF GOVERNMENT EXPENDITURES: A GENERAL ANALYSIS

The study of incidence of government expenditures in Chile was done for 1969. The selection of this particular year was the result of several

[25] See Chapter 5.

[26] Chenery *et al.*, *Redistribution with Growth,* Oxford University Press, 1974.

[27] One hundred and forty different programmes were examined in detail as part of the basic research for this book.

considerations. The first and most important one was the availability of data. Consolidated National Budget expenditures disaggregated at the level of programmes of public institutions were available for that year.[28] Size income distribution and household expenditures figures were also available from surveys done in 1968 and 1969 as well as other sector-specific surveys (for example in the health sector).[29]

The study covers the most extensive definition of government: General Government plus autonomous public institutions. This corresponds to the concept of public sector. The study proceeds by separating real from financial expenditure by the government. The first, net of self-generated income,[30] is allocated among income groups or economic strata, according to the type of expenditure. The second, which basically represents loans given by public institutions, is dealt with by calculating the amount of subsidy they imply and later assigning the subsidy among income groups or economic strata.

Real government expenditures are valued at their cost, in order to measure benefits. A separation is made between those that imply an increase, either at present or in future periods, of assets available to the groups being considered, from expenditures that merely increase consumption of families.

The benefits of a particular expenditure programme are measured differently when they refer to economic services provided by the government in the productive sphere than when they consist of programmes in the social sectors (education, health, housing). In the productive sectors, expenditures are first assigned to the technological strata they are directed to (handicrafts, small industry, medium and large industries; or minifundia versus medium and large agricultural holdings, etc.). Once assigned by stratum, income-distribution figures for each stratum are used to estimate the effects on family income of the several expenditure programmes preferentially oriented to each stratum.

In the case of social services, expenditures are allocated according to the income distribution of those directly using or receiving the services provided by the government.

[28] Ministerio de Hacienda, *Balance Consolidado del Sector Público,* Santiago, 1973.

[29] Instituto Nacional de Estadísticas (1969), Instituto Nacional de Estadísticas (1974), Ministerio de Salud (1970). For more details see Chapter 2.

[30] The largest item in ''self-generated income'' is the government revenue from traded goods produced by public sector institutions.

The subsidies estimated in this study are those implicit in loans given by public sector institutions with developmental or social purposes.[31] The sources of subsidies in developmental loans are several: low or negative real interest rates, overevaluation of the local currency, affecting credits financed through external resources (foreign capital); and debt repayment below negotiated levels. These subsidies are measured with reference to the theoretical income stream that should be returned to the government, if the social opportunity cost of capital were to be covered (estimated at 10 per cent a year). The present value of the difference between the theoretical income stream and the effective loan repayments constitutes the present value of the subsidy. It depends not only on nominal interest rates, but on indexation schemes that take account of inflation, and on the period and size of the loan.

The coverage of credit subsidies is not complete in this study. Credits given by the State Bank are not considered, given that they are not included in the Consolidated National Budget. Thus the conclusions that we may reach, might be biased and have to be taken with caution.

After these preliminary methodological considerations, we can now summarise some of the results.

The order in which we shall analyse the results will be the following. We shall first examine where has the government concentrated its effort in terms of relevant target groups for a redistributive strategy. Have government programmes focused preferentially on poverty groups, or have the resources been used to support the relatively modern, higher income, sectors in the economy? This is the issue we shall deal with in this section. The next chapter will describe the main sectoral expenditure programmes in detail and will integrate sectoral results into a size-distribution-of-income picture, where the traditional incidence exercise will show us how much of each type of expenditure actually benefited the various income groups. An important point here will consist in examining how much of the resources mobilised in poverty-oriented programmes were of direct benefit to the poor, and what proportion could be considered a "leakage" to other non-target socio-economic groups.

The determination of where government efforts have been concentrated in terms of public expenditures and with a view on the

[31] One example of the latter would be public loans to build or buy houses.

distribution of income problem requires a definition of the target groups one would consider as of high priority in the redistribution strategy. This does not mean that the government actually and explicitly considered the very same groups as targets of the policy. In fact the government has always dealt with a multiple-target objective function. But an ex-post evaluation of redistributive policies necessarily requires a certain, albeit arbitrary, definition of the target groups. Only then is it possible to have a yardstick against which to evaluate the redistributive impact of the policies. The exercise is legitimate as an ex-post evaluation, done from the point of view of optimal redistributive policy.

Preliminary studies measuring relative levels of welfare in Chile using indicators such as education, type and quality of housing, sanitary conditions, etc., point out that a proportion in the order of 30 per cent of the population could be considered as living in absolute poverty conditions.[32] This proportion is roughly equivalent to that of families whose income is less than or equal to the minimum salary. We somewhat arbitrarily defined this group of families as a target group, in the sense that for a redistributive strategy to be successful, public resources should be preferentially directed to that group.

Expenditure programmes benefiting poverty groups shall be classified under two headings; what we call ''progressive programmes'' and ''poverty programmes'' as such.

''Progressive programmes'' are defined as those in which the poor obtain a proportion of the total benefits arising from the programme, which is larger than their initial share in total family income, which is 7.6 per cent.

''Poverty programmes'' are defined as those where benefits are largely concentrated in poverty groups, in such a manner that not only does their income share increase but also the absolute benefit per family is larger for the poor than for the average household. In other words, a programme is classified under this heading when the proportion of benefits falling on poverty groups is larger than the latter's proportion in the total population, which is 29.8 per cent.

Public resources involved in so-called progressive programmes improve the relative income position of the poor, although the absolute expenditure per family might still be lower for poor *vis-à-vis* rich families.

[32] Instituto de Economía (1975).

Public expenditures in so-called poverty programmes imply, on the other hand, that the resources not only improve the poor relatively to others but also that the government spends more per poor family than it does for the average household.

Another distinction that we made when classifying poverty-oriented programmes is that of asset-creating programmes and mainly consumption-oriented expenditures. The first are those that increase the productive capacity and income potential of poverty groups (physical capital, education and health expenditure). The second are those that mainly increase present welfare levels of the target groups (welfare payments, food subsidies) with no clear direct effect on their future earning capacity.

To be sure, some types of expenditures are of a dual nature; they simultaneously increase present welfare levels and the income-earning capacity in the future. It is the case of expenditures in health, education and to some extent housing. They are classified under one or the other heading according to which effect seems to be the most important. Thus, for example, expenditures in education are classified as asset-creating whereas housing expenditures are considered as mainly consumption oriented.[33]

Summing up, the classification of government programmes that will follow in the next pages is the result obtained after the incidence analysis was made for each and every one of 140 expenditure programmes. The incidence analysis measures how the incomes of each group in the economy are affected by each type of public expenditure.

The detailed results of the traditional incidence exercise will not be reported until Chapter 4. The criteria used to distribute benefits among income groups and the shifting assumptions are indicated in Table 24 (see Chapter 4). There the main expenditure programmes are identified, and a description of the contents of the programmes, of assumptions made concerning beneficiaries, and statistical series used, are presented.

We shall postpone a discussion of what is behind the assumptions until the chapter on sectoral incidence.

[33]The line is drawn looking at direct benefits to the poverty group. This explains why transport expenditures and other capital outlays are classified as "consumption oriented". A different situation emerges if the evaluation were done from the point of view of all groups in society.

The data used originates in the Consolidated Public Budget figures for 1969, but are not necessarily equal to it. One reason is that we have separated real from purely financial expenditure. The first are assigned directly according to the way they benefited the different income brackets. The second, consisting of loans, are not assigned entirely but only in the fraction which constitues a subsidy. In other words, we have tried to get closer to an economic concept of what constitutes the benefit from a loan. We have not (at this stage) added up real expenditures and subsidies. They are presented separately, given that they measure different things: the first measures a current flow and the second the present value of future income gains due to the subsidies.

Having clarified the nature of our calculations, we can proceed to report on the main aggregate results in Table 17. Table 17 summarises the conclusions of the incidence exercise by classifying expenditures and subsidies' programmes according to whether they turned out to be "progressive programmes" or they benefited other non-target groups.[34] Table 18 gives the composition of expenditures plus subsidies per sector according to whether they are "progressive", "poverty programmes", or other. Table 19 indicates the proportion of resources devoted to asset creation *vis-à-vis* those that have mainly a consumption effect over poverty groups.

The results show that of total expenditures allocated through the public sector, two-thirds were involved in programmes increasing the relative income share of poverty groups. As we have already warned, this does not mean that the benefits to the poor are equal to 67 per cent of public expenditures. In fact, our classification does not take into account the "leakages" from "progressive programmes" toward other groups.[35] It should be clear that many of the programmes incorporated under this heading did not have as a purpose to exclusively support the poor at the expense of the rest of the population. That is the case of education and public health expenditures. It is also true of credit policies for small industry or small- and medium-sized mining concerns. Within these

[34] The latter can be calculated by subtracting the resources involved in "progressive programmes" from the total.

[35] Note that given the "optimality-criteria" we used for this classification, the term "leakage" includes here a series of benefits which may have satisfied other goals of public programmes (provision of public goods, development, etc.).

TABLE 17

Effects of government programmes over poverty groups. (million escudos) 1969

	Total		Progressive programmes[a]				Poverty programmes[b]			
			Asset creating		Mainly consumption oriented		Asset creating		Mainly consumption oriented	
	Exp.	Subs.	Exp.	Subs.	Exp.	Subs.	Exp.	Subs.	Exp.	Subs.
Economic Services										
(1) Land reform	223	199	223	199						
(2) Support to small farmers	91	70	91	70			91	70		
(3) Agricultural development	114	28	96							
(4) Conservation of natural resources	140		114							
(5) Irrigation	104									
(6) Distribution of agricultural products	91				91					
(7) Other agricultural expenditure	46		46							
(8) Industrial develop.	9	28								
(9) Support to small industry	25	6	25	6						
(10) Sugar mill	161									
(11) Other industrial expend.	31									
(12) Mining develop.	37	20	37	20						
(13) Other expend. in mining	60									
(14) Transport: air, sea	508				144					
(15) Transport: railroads, urban	639				639					

(16) Highways	652									
(17) Other transport expend.	385									
(18) Communications	301				216					
(19) Energy	212				212					
(20) Other infrastructure expend.	26									
(21) Other expend. for develop. promotion	292									
Sub-total	4,146	351	632	295	1,302	–	91	70	–	–
Social Services										
(22) Public health	1,751		1,568				1,555			
(23) Social welfare	89				89				33	
(24) Housing	510	976			446	908				94
(25) Education	2,842		2,066				195			
(26) Social security	5,376				4,227				820	
Sub-total	10,568	976	3,634	–	4,762	908	1,841		853	94
Administration and Defence										
(27) General admin.	658				658					
(28) Defence, policy, foreign rel., comunal govt. and justice	2,468				2,182					
(29) Public debt	2,182				2,182					
Sub-total	5,307				2,840					
Total	20,021	1,327	4,266	295	8,904	908	1,932	70	853	94

(a) Programmes where more than 7.6 per cent of the expenses benefit families who earn the minimum salary or less.
(b) Programmes where more than 29.8 per cent of the expenses benefit families who earn the minimum salary or less.

Notes to Table 17

(1) CORA, ICIRA
(2) INDAP
(3) CORFO AGRICOLA, ODEPA, IIA, SOCOAGRO
(4) SAG, INFORE, INFOPE
(5) DIR. RIEGO
(6) ECA
(7) SUBS. MIN. AGRICULTURA, MIN. TIERRAS
(8) CORFO INDUSTRIA
(9) SERCOTEC
(10) IANSA
(11) DIRINCO, DIR. TURISMO, SUBS. MIN. ECONOMIA, CORMAC, INDUST.
(12) ENAMI
(13) SERVICIO MINAS DEL ESTADO, CORFO MINERIA, SUBS. MIN. MINERIA, CORMAG MINERIA
(14) EMPREMAR, EMPREPORT, DIR, OBRAS PORTUARIAS, LAN, DIR. AEROPUERTOS, I. AERONAUT.
(15) FFCC DEL E., ETC.
(16) DIR. VIALIDAD
(17) DIR. GRAL. OBRAS PUBLICAS
(18) CORPEOS, ENTEL
(19) ENDESA, ENAP
(20) CORFO ENERGIA, COCHEN, INST. HIDRAULICA, SERVICIOS ELECT.
(21) CORFO, DRAW-BACK
(22) SNS, SERMENA, SCHEH, AGUA POTABLE STGO., DIR. DEPORTES DEL E., SUBS. MIN. SALUD
(23) CREDITO PRENDARIO, SENDE, MIN. DEL TRABAJO, CONSEJO DE MENORES
(24) CORVI, CORHABIT, CAJA CENTRAL, A y P, COU, D.O.S., CORMU, DIR. PAVIMENTACION, MIN. VIV.
(25) MIN. EDUCACION, INAEB, INACAP, IER
(26) EMPART, CANAEMPU, SSS, otras cajas
(27) MIN. INTERIOR, MIN. HACIENDA
(28) MIN. RELACIONES, MIN. DEFENSA, MUNICIPALIDADES, JUSTICIA, POLICIA
(29) DEUDA PUBLICA

TABLE 18
Distribution of public expenditures
(percentages)

	"Progressive programmes"	Other	Poverty programmes	Other
Total	67.3	32.7	13.8	86.2
Economic services	49.6	50.4	3.6	96.4
Agriculture	75.9	24.1	7.6	96.4
Industry	11.9	88.1	–	100.0
Mining	48.7	51.3	–	100.0
Infrastructure	44.5	55.5	–	100.0
Social services	80.6	19.4	24.2	75.8
Public health	89.5	10.5	88.8	11.2
Social welfare	100.0	–	37.1	62.9
Housing	91.1	8.9	6.3	93.7
Education	72.7	27.3	6.9	93.1
Social security	78.6	21.4	15.3	84.7
General expenditures	53.5	46.5	–	100.0

Source: Table 18. (Expenditures and subsidies are added in Table 19.)

TABLE 19
Distribution of expenditures that increase income share of the poor
("progressive programmes")

	Asset-creating	Mainly consumption
Total	31.7	68.3
Economic services	41.6	58.4
Agriculture	91.3	9.7
Industry	100.0	–
Mining	100.0	–
Infrastructure	–	100.0
Social services	35.3	64.7
Public health	100.0	–
Social welfare	–	100.0
Housing	–	100.0
Education	100.0	–
Social security	–	100.0

Source: Table 17. (Expenditures and subsidies are added.)

strata, there are very poor independent producers and rather modern small-scale enterprises, as we shall later see when examining sectoral results. The policy benefits more than proportionately the poor independent producer, but it also benefits the other small- and medium-sized producers belonging to the modern sector.

Leakages also appear in the implementation stage of the expenditures policy, that is, programmes designed to support the poor are applied in such a way that non-target groups have also access to its benefits. This is often the case with agricultural development programmes which emphasise support of the small producer through cheap credit, subsidised imports and technical assistance, but in the end those who have better access are the medium-sized modern producers. This is due to the greater organisation and political power of medium-sized farmers *vis-à-vis* small producers; to the administrative difficulties of reaching a very large number of small independent producers; and to inefficient public control of where resources are actually going to.

Another approach to the problem is to measure the proportion of public spending programmes largely concentrated on poverty groups, that is those where more than 29.8 per cent of total benefits accrue to these groups, implying that the benefits per household are larger for the poor than for other groups. We find that 14 per cent of total resources could be actually classified as being spent in "poverty programmes" as such (see Table 18). Under this definition fall the following programmes: support to small farmers, public health, social welfare, a small part of public housing programmes (site and services and self-contruction programmes), programmes to up-grade skills of blue-collar workers, and some social-security programmes (blue-collar workers' family and retirement allowances, family allowances for pensioners).

Figures also show (see Table 18) that expenditure programmes in the social sectors were oriented to the poor in a larger proportion than public spending in directly economic activities. In fact 80 per cent of public expenditures in social sectors had a "progressive" character, as compared to only 49 per cent in the economic activities (economic services). Table 17 shows that over 70 per cent of expenditures on public health, public education and government-sponsored housing programmes preferentially oriented to the poor.

As far as the productive sectors are concerned, our results show that public resources in "progressive" programmes were about half of the total. But only 3.6 per cent of resources devoted to economic programmes could be classified as forming part of "poverty programmes" as such. Expenditures in the industrial sector were of a particularly regressive nature. Eighty-eight per cent of total resources were used in programmes whose main beneficiaries were the modern medium- and large-scale enterprises. On the other hand, public programmes in the agricultural sector revealed a marked redistributive character, not only because of the expenditures in land reform, but also because of very important schemes of support to small farmers.

Programmes in the mining sector and in infrastructure, although with some effect on poverty groups, tended to be less selective in their approach. We will be able to explain the different orientation of the programmes when dealing with the sectoral analysis in the next chapter.

If we look now in Table 19 exclusively at those programmes that increase the income share of the poor, we find that about one-third of public resources used had an asset-creating effect, *vis-à-vis* those that had a purely consumption effect. The former includes expenditures in Land Reform, developmental expenditures oriented to small producers (rural and urban), primary education and vocational training within the social services sectors. Of those having mainly a consumption effect, expenditures in social welfare, social security and public transport were particularly important. Were these relative shares between asset-creating and consumption-oriented pro-poor programmes close to the optimal mix? That basically depends on two factors, whose relative importance we have not been able to evaluate yet. Consumption-oriented public expenditures are particularly necessary when basic subsistence consumption levels are not reached by poverty groups. This justifies and gives higher priority to publicly sponsored consumption supporting schemes, like food subsidies, etc. If basic subsistence needs are met (however inadequately), asset-creation schemes have an obvious priority, since they are the more efficient instrument to allow poverty groups to increase their earning capacity in the future.

On the other hand, the mix is directly related to the nature of poverty, If it is a temporary situation, or a condition of retired and handicapped people, consumption-oriented programmes will be better. On the contrary when poverty affects working people and is a permanent condition, more permanent solutions are required so asset-creation programmes should play an important role.

The figures in Table 19 by themselves do not allow us to judge whether the proportion allocated to both types of programmes was the most adequate to the nature of the poverty problem in Chile, although they are important, at least in the sense of illustrating that a relatively significant amount of resources in poverty programmes probably had a long-term effect in increasing productivity and the income-earning potential of the poor. These results are consistent with the hypothesis that government expenditures in Chile have played a very significant role as a redistributive instrument. The public spending effort, particularly in the provision of social services available to the poor (education, health, housing) in government support of small producers and in financing land tenure changes in the agricultural sector, implied the mobilisation of vast amounts of resources through the National Budget and through a large number of public institutions and decentralised agencies that were in charge of implementing the redistributive programmes. In order to better understand the specific contents of these programmes and illustrate how the redistributive effects were actually measured, we must proceed to a more disaggregated analysis of public expenditures. This is done in Chapter 4.

CHAPTER 4

Government Expenditures: Sectoral Programmes and Overall Incidence

The previous chapter dealt with a general analysis of government expenditures in Chile, focusing on their relative importance as compared with other countries and on their main characteristics, particularly from the point of view of their effect on poverty groups.

We shall now proceed to a more disaggregated analysis, measuring the incidence of individual programmes over income groups. One hundred and forty different expenditure programmes were analysed. In order to facilitate a comprehensive treatment, they have been classified here under two headings: public expenditure programmes in the economic sectors and spending programmes in the social sectors.

Some sectors have been selected, where a more detailed description of methodology and contents of the programmes will be made. These are agriculture, industry and transportation in the general category of programmes focusing on economic sectors. Health, education and housing receive special attention in the treatment of the so-called social sectors.

In the last part of the chapter, we put together the results for all 140 programmes and perform the incidence exercise, to end up with a discussion of the policy issues that emerge from the quantitative analysis of beneficiaries of the programmes.

EXPENDITURE PROGRAMMES IN THE ECONOMIC SECTORS

Nearly 21 per cent of total government expenditures corresponded to public activities in the directly productive sectors. They consisted of public investment, loans to the private sector, general economic support of small producers and land reform. The programmes were particularly important in agriculture, and industry and transportation.

When we examine government expenditure programmes in directly productive activities in Chile in 1969, we get a cross-section view of four types of programmes: direct government investment and financial support schemes for modern large-scale public or private firms; investment and production activities not clearly oriented to any particular group (mainly transportation, energy and communications); cheap credit and technical assistance for the less productive small-scale enterprises; and comprehensive economic and institutional support to the new groups emerging as a result of asset redistribution schemes, mainly land reform.

The four types of economic intervention we have just described probably had a different impact over the various income groups. What that effect was is what interests us here.

We must begin by briefly discussing a basic element that creates a differential effect of the policies over the various socio-economic groups. This is the segmentation of the structure of production into several heterogeneous productive strata, ranging from the more backward activities of the self-employed in the traditional or informal sector, to the semi-modern small-scale production units, to the technologically advanced large-scale capital-intensive productive units. If we consider the technological characteristics of Chilean agriculture, mining and industry, we find diverse types of production activities within each sector. The differences, essentially in scale of production, relative capital-labour intensity, and productivity levels, result in wide income disparities.

The largest number of individuals work in the more backward activities, yet the scale of production is the smallest. The more modern units are few but larger and highly productive.

How were public resources distributed among the various technological strata identified in the following tables and how did the characteristics of each stratum affect the distribution of benefits among families? Let us examine some of the expenditure programmes which seem more meaningful from this point of view in the agricultural, industrial and transportation sectors.

AGRICULTURAL SECTOR

The institutions which best represent public policies in the agricultural sector in the period under analysis were the Corporation for Development (CORFO), the Institute of Agricultural Development (INDAP) and the Land Reform Corporation (CORA). In 1969 CORFO supported the agricultural sector basically through loans given to medium- and large-sized farmers. The beneficiaries of the credits were few (1,400 producers out of 260,000). They were charged real interest rates of around 7 per cent, for loans given for a period as long as 5 years. The loans were used to buy machinery and introduce new crops.

INDAP, on the other hand, oriented its activity exclusively to support low-income minifundia producers. It gave training, technical assistance, promoted the organisation of production co-operatives and provides the co-operatives with cheap credit. The purpose of the loans was varied: finance working capital needs, purchase machinery and finance changes in types and methods of cultivation. The total volume of credits given was similar to that provided by CORFO for large producers, but the effect extended to a larger number of families. The conditions of the loans were extremely favourable: no readjustment for inflation, nominal interest rates between 9 and 12 per cent (with inflation around 30 per cent per year) and periods of up to 5 years for paying back.

The Land Reform Corporation (CORA) was the executive agency engaged in the expropriation of farms and in the organisation and technical and financial support of the new "Reformed Sector" productive units.[1] CORA expenditures were directed to land acquisition (10 per cent of total expenditures), to investments in infrastructure in the newly expropriated land (20 per cent) and to providing financial support in the form of loans for the Reformed Sector producers (48 per cent). Credit was given to pay salaries, working capital, purchase of inputs and investment. The volume of loans was double what CORFO was giving to the large private-sector farmers and the conditions were as follows: loans given to finance current expenses and working capital were not readjustable for inflation and nominal interest rates were not higher than 12 per cent. This amounted to 70 per cent of the loans. The rest, given to

[1] Chapter 7 deals with Land Reform.

finance new investment, was indexed to inflation but the interest rate was only 4 per cent.

So here we have three institutions, one supporting the medium- and large-sized productive stratum, the other the low-income small producers, and the third transferring assets away from latifundia owners and in favour of those salaried agricultural workers who constituted the labour force in the expropriated farms.

One important effect of credit policies in the agricultural sector was that large subsidies were transferred to those producers who had access to any of the public loans available.

In order to have an idea of the size and distribution of the subsidy between strata, we have calculated the present value of the difference between the flow of payments that should be payed back during the period of the loan if the opportunity cost of capital were charged (10 per cent real interest rate) and the effective payments.[2]

We can observe in Table 20 the relative size of the subsidies implied by the various types of loans. They range from 63 per cent of the value of the loan in the Land Reform sector to 20 per cent in the private sector of large producers. These are very large subsidies. We shall later discuss some policy issues that are raised by looking at these figures.

Let us, for the moment, note the following. The most influential factors in the rate of subsidy are the absence of provision for indexation

TABLE 20

Credit policies in the agricultural sector

Strata	Loans	Interest rate	Indexing with inflation	Effective recuperation	Percentage subsidies/ loans
Land		12[(a)]	No		
Reform	315	4[(b)]	Yes	48.0	63.0
Small farmers	110	9–12	No	75.0	51.0
Agricultural	147	7	Yes		20.0

[(a)] Loans for working capital (70 per cent of total loans given).
[(b)] Loans for capital investment (30 per cent of total loans given).

[2] Effective payments are lower than the "opportunity cost" measurement because interest rates charged are lower than 10 per cent in real term; and because not all loans are paid back. Effective recuperation of loans was 48 per cent of expected recuperation in the Land Reform Sector and 75 per cent in the small-farmers' sector.

with respect to inflation and the low effective recuperation rate. The former is more important for small producers and was deliberately used to discriminate in their favour. The second is a non-programmed subsidy (like the rate of tax evasion). It is high for small farmers, perhaps reflecting an inability-to-pay problem at the very low levels of income of minifundia producers. It is also very high for Land Reform enterprises. This probably reflects the lack of budgetary and financial control in the Land Reform area and as a consequence of that, that the enterprises were able to operate with no budget constraints and subject to no penalty for not fulfilling self-financing targets. This type of problem, which we also observe when nationalised industrial enterprises are examined,[3] is a recurrent one which deserves some more discussion elsewhere.

Several other public programmes, apart from the three just mentioned, have been examined as part of this study. Some of them, like irrigation, were not particularly directed to one productive stratum. Consequently they tended to benefit all kinds of producers, large and small, although probably in proportion to their relative share of agricultural land; others, like the food-price subsidy schemes, benefited consumers rather than producers; finally some public expenditures in agriculture like those used in the conservation of natural resources were probably of benefit to the whole of the population. When these types of hypotheses are formalised for each of the public expeditures programmes in agriculture, it is possible to estimate the repercussions of these programmes over the distribution of income among families, and particularly over poverty groups.

A summary of the assumptions used to distribute benefits by income brackets is given in Table 21 and it might be useful to look at it for a moment and discuss briefly some of the methodological problems posed by the use of the particular assumptions chosen.

Shifting assumptions are always more or less arbitrary and ours are not exceptions. They assume a certain type of behaviour of economic agents which constitutes a simplification of reality. If we take just one example, we have assumed that the benefits of CORFO's developmental loans were distributed among agricultural producers in proportion to their relative income share. This means that we are implicitly assuming that

[3] See Chapter 7.

there is no shifting of the benefits towards farm labour, nor forward shifting to consumers. Obviously, the no-shifting assumption implies certain hypothesis about how the agricultural labour and goods markets function. The implicit hypothesis is that the demand curve faced by producers is perfectly elastic. This means that the prices of agricultural products need not be affected by the fact that the cost of capital is subsidised. The only effect of the latter would be to allow agricultural producers to make an income gain which is not transferred to nor shared with consumers.

Once we introduce an assumption like this, we must make sure that it is a reasonable one from the point of view of our knowledge of how markets really operate. In this case the hypothesis is sustained by the fact that a very small number of producers received the subsidised loans and that very probably none of them held a monopoly position in the market, given the type of land tenure prevailing at the time.

But when we say that no shifting occurred, we also hypothesise that no backward shifting to the factors took place. The net gain, due to the lower cost of capital, was not transferred to workers in the form of higher wages or more employment. For the former to be true, the labour-supply curve must be perfectly elastic. But in that case there would be a positive employment effect. We have hypothesised that given the low number of producers benefiting from the subsidised loans, the employment effect would be negligible.[4]

Obviously the introduction of each of these assumptions influences and may often bias the results in a certain direction. One must be aware, then, of the nature and relative magnitude of these biases because they certainly condition the types of results one gets from the incidence exercise.

Another possible source of bias in the incidence estimates is caused not so much by arbitrary shifting assumptions as by data constraints. For instance, CORFO credits were not available to small farmers, yet since no income distribution data excluding small producers were available, the aggregate income distribution profile of all agricultural producers including small farmers was used to distribute the subsidies. In the case of

[4]A similar conclusion is achieved if the substitution among different crops, induced by the subsidies, is considered.

Land Reform, in which the beneficiaries of the policies were the workers incorporated to Land Reform areas, the data used were the income distribution of all agricultural wage earners, because no figures were available for the Land Reform group of workers alone.[5]

Finally, a particular bias may be compounded when several assumptions are made simultaneously in order to determine who benefits from a certain type of expenditure. Let us take the case of irrigation. There, we have assumed that irrigation programmes benefit private producers *vis-à-vis* the Land Reform sector, according to the proportion of total land held under one or other tenure system.

We later on assume that within the private producers sector, benefits are distributed in proportion to income, and within the Reformed Sector in proportion to agricultural workers income in general. Then when both sets of assumptions are combined in one result, the biases involved in each one of them are compounded.

This rather long warning note about possible arbitrariness and biases in assumptions, already a customary feature of incidence studies, serves us well to introduce Table 22. There we summarise the distribution of benefits by income groups, that result when all expenditure programmes in agriculture are considered. Although a sensitivity analysis of the effects of using several alternative assumptions is generally recommended, our results here report on only one set of assumptions, those indicated in Table 21.

The aggregate results show a high progressivity in the benefits of public-expenditure programmes in the agricultural sector. Poverty groups (those comprised in the 0–1 income bracket) received two and a half times a larger share of benefits from the programmes than they do of total households' income. The next bracket (1–2) also benefits more than proportionately from public expenditures, while all other groups receive a smaller proportion of benefits than their income share. This high progressivity in benefits from agricultural expenditures is in sharp contrast with results for the industrial sector as we shall see next.

[5]Although average incomes and income growth rates were calculated from survey data, it was not possible to have the dispersion of wages within the Land Reform sector. See Chapter 7.

TABLE 22

Incidence of benefits in agricultural sector, 1969 (million escudos)

Income bracket (min. salary)	Land Reform	Support to small farmers	Agricultural develop-ment	Conserva-tion natural resources	Irrigation	Food distrib-ution	Other	Total benefits	Distribution of total benefits (%)	Families income distrib. (%)
0–1	84.7	48.0	24.4	29.7	4.2	18.4	9.6	219.0	19.8	7.6
1–2	175.7	32.7	31.6	42.4	11.3	28.1	14.0	335.8	30.4	20.1
2–3	88.4	20.4	17.1	24.6	9.7	18.8	7.6	186.6	16.9	18.9
3–4	40.9	12.2	10.6	12.7	6.0	8.3	3.9	94.6	8.6	11.2
4–5	16.0	9.8	4.6	7.8	8.3	5.2	2.2	53.9	4.9	8.7
5–6	8.0	6.9	6.0	5.1	10.6	3.5	1.7	41.8	3.8	7.1
6–8	1.7	11.4	7.1	5.6	11.0	3.0	1.7	41.5	3.8	8.0
8–10	3.8	6.9	6.0	4.5	8.5	2.0	1.3	33.0	3.0	5.9
10+	2.1	12.7	34.6	7.6	34.4	3.3	3.6	98.3	8.8	12.5
Total	421.3	161.0	142.0	140.0	104.0	90.6	45.3	1104.2	100.0	100.0

INDUSTRIAL SECTOR

We shall briefly describe now two of the more significant government activities in the industrial sector in 1969. The first one consisted of development loans given to medium- and large-scale private industrial enterprises. The second was a credit and technical assistance programme by the Service of Technical Cooperation (SERCOTEC) directed to small industry and handicrafts.

CORFO credit policies in the industrial sector did not greatly differ from those in agriculture. Loans were oriented to medium-sized enterprises. The amount and conditions of credits are given in Table 23, where they are compared with those supplied by SERCOTEC to small industry. The conditions do not differ very much. Both imply real interest rates between 3 per cent and 7.5 per cent and payment periods of up to 8 years. The volume of credit given to small industry and handicrafts considered together (representing 42 per cent of the labour force in industry) is only 20 per cent of the total. Thus, although the subsidies as a proportion of the value of the loans are similar for the three strata, fluctuating between 17 and 20 per cent of the loans, the absolute amount is much larger for the medium-scale industry.

TABLE 23

Credit policies in the industrial sector

Strata	Volume of credit (million escudos, 1969)	Interest rate	Indexing	Percentage subsidies/ loans
Large- and medium-sized industry	139	7.5	Yes	20.6
Small industry	25	3–7.5	Yes	17.0
Handicrafts	10	3–7.5	Yes	17.0

The public programmes to benefit small industry did not exclusively consist of loans, though. An equally important programme was that of preparing projects, training personnel and giving general technical assistance to small firms. These programmes implied public expenditures about the same size as all loans for small industry and handicrafts taken together. The impact of this policy falls on the same productive stratum and we shall consider both effects together, when calculating how the benefits of these policies distribute among income brackets.

As we can see, expenditure programmes in the industrial sector do not differ too much from those in agriculture, except for two factors: the relative intensity of programmes supporting the less productive small-scale producers is much lower in industry; and no asset redistribution scheme was underway in the industrial sector during the year we are presently analysing. As we shall see, both factors will be decisive in explaining the different distributive outcome of expenditure policies in industry *vis-à-vis* agriculture.

In distributing the benefits of industrial credit and expenditure policies among families, the same procedure was followed as with respect to the agricultural sector. The incidence assumptions are indicated in Table 21. The distribution of benefits of CORFO loans is supposed to fall entirely on employers, that of SERCOTEC credits on small-scale and independent producers (using the distribution of income of the latter as the yardstick).

When the implications of these assumptions are estimated, plus those for other public programmes in industry, a distributive picture emerges, which is depicted in Table 24. Benefits in the industrial sector follow a

TABLE 24

Incidence of benefits in industrial sector, 1969
(millions escudos and per cent)

Income brackets (minimum salaries)	Industrial development	Small industry	Sugar beet	Other industrial expenditures	Total benefits	Distribution of total benefits	Distribution of family income
0 – 1	1.2	2.5	12.2	2.3	18.2	7.0	7.6
1 – 2	7.5	5.5	32.4	6.2	51.6	19.8	20.1
2 – 3	7.1	5.2	30.4	5.9	48.6	18.7	18.9
3 – 4	3.7	2.8	18.1	3.5	28.1	10.8	11.2
4 – 5	3.4	2.7	14.0	2.7	22.8	8.7	8.7
5 – 6	2.0	2.4	11.4	2.2	18.0	6.9	7.1
6 – 8	3.6	2.9	12.9	2.5	21.9	8.4	8.0
8 – 10	1.1	1.8	9.5	1.8	14.2	5.5	5.9
10 +	7.8	5.2	20.1	3.9	37.0	14.2	12.5
Total	37.4	31.0	161.0	31.0	260.4	100.0	100.0

slightly regressive pattern. Only programmes oriented to the small industry and handicrafts are progressive. But these are of limited scope and coverage. This means that the overall pattern is one of benefits concentrated in the modern, large- and medium-scale productive units. Thus, government action in the sector contributes to a concentration rather than a redistribution of income. On the other hand, it does little to improve the situation of the independent producers and workers in informal sector activities in urban areas, groups that constitute the core of the urban poor.

TRANSPORT SECTOR

Public activity in the transport area normally absorbs a considerable amount of resources. In the year our estimates refer to, they exceeded 10 per cent of the total expenses and subsidies provided by the State. The tasks undertaken by the public sector in this field can be divided into the building of roads, ports and airports on the one hand, and the direct provision of certain services (railways, air transport, sea transport and urban passenger transport) on the other. For reasons of space we shall here analyse one programme of each type, i.e. road-building and railway transportation. These are the two which absorb most resources; each one consumes about one-third of the total expenditure in the sector. However, the estimates contained in Table 28 include all the expenses.

With regard to transportation, market-behaviour analysis and the use of assumptions derived therefrom concerning shifting of benefits they are more difficult to undertake than in the cases of Agriculture and Industry. The main difference rises from the universal character of transport subsidy, as any user obtains the benefit – either passenger or cargo – whereas in cases previously examined a certain specific section of the population reaped the benefit. Consequently, it is probable that in transportation the benefits be shared by the many economic agents taking part in this activity. When dealing with movement of cargo, the producers will probably be favoured, as their costs go down; the consumers, if they receive the product at a lower price; and the transporters, whose operation and maintenance costs will be less. The difficulty lies in knowing the size of the benefits for each of them.

Concerning passenger transportation, no doubt the passengers themselves enjoy the total subsidy except when they travel in collective vehicles, in which case they probably share it with the service companies.

Let us see how this view applies to the works of road and railroad. The road expenses are channelled through six different programmes. The most demanding one is maintenance and repair of the road network. We have supposed here that the benefits of this programme are distributed in proportion to the use made by the passengers and cargo vehicles of the network. In the latter instance, we also suppose that the benefits are shared equitably by transporter consumers and producers.[6] Other individual programmes are those which bring about an increase in traffic capacity and thus expedite traffic circulation (broadening of roads, multi-level crossings, etc.) and those which improve the quality of highways (especially the paving of dirt or gravel roads).[7]

Programmes were also evaluated for the building of new roads, roads of penetration giving farmers the means of reaching new markets, international connections and urban roads. Again the distributive consequences differ. The first benefit the farmers; the second favour all the population of the country; and the urban works benefit families living in towns and cities.

With regard to railway transportation, this was the object of large transfers in 1969. The relative importance of subsidy to passengers and to cargo can be determined as a function of the difference between rates charged and cost estimates as calculated by the State railway company.[8]

After incorporating in incidence computation the above assumptions and the estimates for the rest of public transport programmes, we obtain the general distributive outline of the sector (Table 29). This comes out to

[6] If we had had available an estimate of the elasticity of demand and supply, it would have been possible not to fall into the arbitrariness of distributing benefits in equal shares.

[7] These two programmes may seem alike; however, their distributive consequences are quite different. While the first fundamentally benefits passenger vehicles, the second helps to reduce the costs of transporting cargo and people and to increase the period of time in the year when roads are passable. Congestion mainly affects passenger vehicles, whereas cargo vehicles do not make high speed and therefore do not benefit so easily by works intended to expedite circulation.

[8] In order to assign these resources among families, we use distribution of passengers according to income levels and relative distribution of income among all the inhabitants of the country, as proxy to the beneficiaries of cargo transportation.

be regressive. In other words, as a result of public outlays in transportation, families with incomes over five "minimum income" improve their participation in revenue, while the other ones suffer detriment. The programmes which do most towards income concentration are those connected with airways and road transportation.

SOME POLICY ISSUES FROM INCIDENCE RESULTS IN THE ECONOMIC SECTOR

The previous results suggest some policy issues that might be useful to discuss at this point. The first refers to the general nature of public action in the productive sectors. In the industrial and transportation sector the government undertakes simultaneously programmes that support all productive strata (big producers and small producers) and various types of enterprises (public enterprise and private activities). The government does a little bit for everybody. This necessarily results in the predominance of "traditional" resource allocation, meaning a reinforcement of the traditional pattern of production, concentrated in the large- and medium-sized modern industries, given that these groups hold a larger share of power in the economic system. The distributive implication is, as we have seen in the previous section, that of generating an over-all regressive pattern in the distribution of benefits among income groups.

Policies in the agricultural sector, on the other hand, did have a clearer direction and consequently more selectivity in terms of target groups. The relative importance of resources allocated to each of the programmes, clearly reveals two explicit or implicit targets in agricultural policies: that of rural workers incorporated into land reform areas and that of minifundia producers. Given that a large proportion of families belonging to these strata were also low-income families, the selection of target groups was consistent with income redistribution, and the over-all impact was progressive. The *a priori* selection of target groups was essential in changing the emphasis in agricultural development programmes and in allowing decision-makers to effectively discriminate when resources were being allocated, thus reducing "leakages" to non-target groups to a minimum.

Leakages were particularly important in credit policies. A large share of subsidised credit went to producers with a capacity to pay the opportunity cost of capital. In fact 80 per cent of total subsidised credit in industry was obtained by large modern enterprises. In agriculture, 20 per cent of credit went to non-target groups. These leakages probably had various negative effects. First, they effectively reduced the access to credit by low-income groups. Secondly, they had a regressive effect on income

TABLE 25

Incidence of benefits in transportation sector, 1969
(millions of escudos and per cent)

Income brackets (minimum salaries)	Air transport	Sea transport	Urban transport	Roads building	Railways	Others	Total	Distribution of total benefits (%)	Distribution of family income (%)
0–1	19.1	15.6	5.9	33.9	46.1	26.2	150.0	7.0	7.6
1–2	55.7	33.3	14.8	94.5	117.3	68.5	380.3	17.6	20.1
2–3	51.2	28.1	10.6	91.2	111.6	63.9	356.2	16.6	18.9
3–4	28.9	15.6	5.8	58.0	81.8	41.6	232.2	10.8	11.2
4–5	22.7	11.4	4.8	50.8	50.5	30.4	170.3	7.9	8.7
5–6	52.3	9.3	2.8	50.8	36.1	33.1	184.7	8.6	7.1
6–8	44.3	9.9	2.8	67.7	45.9	37.4	208.0	9.7	8.0
8–10	21.8	7.4	1.7	54.1	32.5	25.8	143.4	6.7	5.9
10+	33.6	13.8	2.4	150.5	65.3	58.2	324.1	15.1	12.5
Total	329.6	144.4	51.6	651.4	587.1	385.1	2,149.2	100.0	100.0

distribution. Thirdly, they probably induced the introduction of capital-intensive technologies in the new government-subsidised investments.

The access to subsidised credit was severely limited, except for a very reduced number of producers. Total number of loans given to small industries in 1969 was in the order of 550 and there were 25,000 small producers, which means that less than 2 per cent of the total were actually covered by the government programme. Loans given through CORFO to medium- and large-sized farmers were not distributed more evenly. Loans reached only 0.6 per cent of total productive units. Thus the concentration of credit did not only affect one stratum (small producers) *vis-à-vis* large producers, but the previous figures also suggest that their distribution within each stratum was not even. It is not clear then that income distribution *within* the poorer small-scale producers improved as a result of credit policies. It depends on who, among small producers, had in fact access to the subsidised loans: those relatively well-off or the poorer marginal producers.

The limited access to cheap credit signifies that some rationing mechanism was probably established, regulating just who should benefit from the subsidy. Obviously aggregate figures do not reveal what this rationing system was, but surely it did exist and was *de-facto* selective. The selectivity criteria, if not explicitly stated, probably was a function of size, power and influence. None of these criteria are quite consistent with a poverty eradication-oriented expenditure programme, unless those who have the power and influence are precisely the poor.

Another important point suggested by our results is that the inability to pay back loans given by the government might be a severe limitation to extend the poverty programmes in order to cover a larger share of the low-income, small, or independent producers. Our results, for example, showed that only 75 per cent of funds loaned to small agricultural producers was ever paid back. The case of small miners, not reported in our previous results, is even more dramatic; only 40 per cent of funds were actually paid back to the government agency administering the programme that supports the activities of medium- and low-scale copper producers. If one considers that the income of a minifundia producer is typically half the minimum salary, and that 50 per cent of small miners have an income below the minimum salary, it is easy to understand the difficult option faced in this area: either the programmes are expanded to sustain higher incomes, risking an even lower effective recuperation of loans due to inability to pay, or they are "cut down to size", on the basis of giving access only to those who can pay.

The alternative of some producers paying back the loans and others not is clearly inequitable and inefficient. It is inequitable in the sense that once the principle is accepted that only some pay, the government is no longer able to control the allocation of subsidies among small producers. Those producers who do not pay back or who pay a lower share of the original loan receive a higher subsidy. They might be those whose incomes are lower, but also they might not. A non-programmed subsidy is established, with non-programmable results in terms of redistributive effects.

The second alternative, consisting of cutting the programme down to size on an ability-to-pay-real-costs principle, effectively ensures that most of the subsidies will go to medium-income non-target groups, reinforcing the concentrated-income pattern existing before the government intervention.

As a consequence, the ability-to-pay problem is related to the problem of leakages: the higher the requisites for loan repayments, the larger the proportion of loans going to non-target groups, because these are precisely the groups capable of repaying the full amount of the original loan.

The issue we have raised so far suggests some policy corrections that might prove efficient for the income-redistribution strategy as a whole. One is that the policies should be made more selective, thus reducing the leakages, by doing away with subsidies for non-target groups. In other words, those who have ability to pay should pay the full amount of the loans or services provided by the State.

What would the alternatives be for small and independent producers that belong to the poverty groups? A first problem here is whether all small-scale producers should receive the same kind of support and the answer is probably negative. As we saw when characterising the productive sectors, several types of producers exist within the small-scale production activities. We found a residual group that we classified as the "Informal Urban Sector"; another stratum formed by handicrafts and still another one consisting of small industry as such. Productivity levels between the former and the latter differed by more than 100 per cent. We also found three different productive and technological strata within the small mining sector, covering from the independent part-time miner who gets a lease to work a very small mine to the small-scale but modern mining enterprise. The productivity levels between one and the other might differ on a ratio of 1 to 10. A similar statement can be made with respect to agriculture.

The heterogeneous nature of productive activities in the traditional sectors of the economy, where the poor are concentrated, forces policy-makers to consider different kinds of remedies to problems that are essentially different from an economic point of view. One sector of small-scale producers is a potentially efficient one. Productivity levels have been held off probably because of insufficient access to basic complementary inputs like working capital, technical assistance, new technologies. Restricted access might have been an explicit government policy, or more likely the result of automatic self-exclusion on the part of small producers, due to inability to pay. Whatever the reason behind the unequal access to complementary inputs, it is clear that it can be remedied by removing the obstacles preventing them from obtaining these inputs at a reasonable price. The policy would make sense because, once the barriers to higher productivity are done away with, the small-scale production activities should become dynamic, and highly labour-absorptive ones.[9] Besides guaranteeing access, subsidies might be justified for this stratum whenever the low initial productivity prevents them from having a surplus large enough to pay back loans, technical services, etc., that the government provides. However, as productivity grows and a large surplus is generated, the amount of the subsidies should be gradually decreased.

It is quite obvious that for this type of policy to be successful, the government must at all times know what it is giving to whom in terms of subsidies. If these are hidden behind low nominal interest rates, partial inflation-indexing schemes and varying coefficients of "effective loan recuperations", the task becomes almost impossible. A better alternative might well be to charge the full cost of the loans (or the cost of the public services provided, be it technical assistance, marketing or whatever) and match this with a direct transfer to small producers, earmarked to the paying back of that fraction of the value of the loan or services that exceeds a certain proportion of their income.

The problem is quite different with respect to the stratum of marginal producers. These are basically under-utilised, unskilled self-employed workers and independent producers. Productivity is extremely low and unlikely to rise even with access to cheap credit or other intermediate inputs. In fact, these activities are bound to disappear as economic development proceeds, so if they are sustained by the government, it is only because of their significance in terms of employment (between 10 and 20 per cent of employment in the industrial and agricultural sectors according to Tables 21 and 22). Economic policies towards these activities should focus on retraining of the labour force involved, so as to allow

[9] The experience of Japan is quite interesting in this respect.

them to move into more productive activities. The best policy here does not consist of providing subsidized credit, but perhaps just giving access to technical training programmes for which the beneficiary pays a fraction of his income, the rest being paid by the government.

EXPENDITURE PROGRAMMES IN THE SOCIAL SECTORS

Public expenditures in the social sectors account for 54 per cent of total expenditures, as was seen in Table 17 in Chapter 4. When examining comparative data for developing countries in the first part of this chapter, it was observed that Chile was ranked in the above average category as far as social-security expenditures (as a share of GNP) were concerned and in the "normal" or average category with respect to expenditures in other social sectors such as health and education. We have dealt with social security in another chapter, so we shall concentrate here on the latter.

Programmes in the health sector

Health needs in a developing country like Chile are enormous. Of those services available, almost 70 per cent of out-patient visits and 90 per cent of in-patient services are provided by the public health system.

Does the public health system contribute to reduce inequalities in the provision of health services? This is what we shall deal with in this section.

The system of public health is divided up into several institutions in Chile. The main ones are the National Health Service (SNS), that absorbs 80 per cent of total public resources devoted to health, and the National Medical Service for Employees (SERMENA). The first one is supposed to give preferential attention to blue-collar workers and the non-insured groups (like the self-employed), although it does not in principle exclude other groups. The services are largely provided free of charge. SERMENA, on the other hand, covers the white-collar workers and provides services which are financed jointly by the State (between 70 per cent to 50 per cent of the cost) and the users (paying between 30 per cent and 50 per cent of the cost). Besides these two institutions, there are others devoted to hospital construction (SCEH) and to providing health services to specific groups.

In order to determine the beneficiaries of public health programmes, we used the results of a survey taken on a national level by the Ministry of Public Health in 1968.[10] The sample consisted of 9,287 households. The data allowed us to determine which income groups had access to services provided by the National Health Service (SNS) during that year. We have assumed that the situation did not change in 1969. The services covered by the survey are out-patient visits (medical and dental) and in-patient (treatment in hospitals). For other services not covered in the survey we have used various assumptions that will be described below.

Besides in- and out-patient services, the SNS undertook a food and epidemy-control programme, a child-nutrition programme consisting of free distribution of milk for low-income school children, sanitary improvements in slum areas and homes for orphans and the aged.

The beneficiaries of these programmes were determined as follows: for in-patient and out-patient services we used the health survey data which give us directly the information of who had access to these services; we then assumed that the food and epidemy control benefitted all the population equally; that the nutrition programme benefits children of blue-collar workers' families; and that sanitary improvement and homes for the aged and orphans benefit poverty groups only.

When these assumptions are applied to the expenditure data, we obtain the results shown in Table 26. All National Health Service programmes are clearly redistributive. The benefits are more progressively distributed than income, the poverty groups obtaining 37 per cent of the benefits (*vis-à-vis* a 7.6 per cent of total income). The share is even larger than the proportion of families below the poverty level (29.8 per cent), which implies that the benefit per family in absolute terms is larger for low-income than for higher income households. This is the opposite of what seems to be the pattern as reported by studies in other countries.

The results for other institutions (besides the National Health Service) are shown in Table 26. Hospital construction programmes are also progressive, a reflection of our assumption that public hospitals and clinics are used in the same proportion as in-patient and out-patient

[10]The results are described in Ministerio de Salud, ''Recursos Humanos de Salud en Chile'', Santiago, 1970.

TABLE 26

Distribution of benefits—Public Health sector
(By income brackets)

	National Health Service	Employees health service	Hospital construc-tion	Total sector	Benefits per family	Benefits as % of average income
0–1	37.0	3.4	36.2	33.4	1099	16.5
1–2	36.0	25.5	31.0	35.0	1086	6.6
2–3	14.3	27.0	15.7	15.7	876	3.1
3–5	7.7	23.1	9.7	9.5	786	1.7
5+	4.5	21.1	7.4	6.5	695	0.7
Total of average	100.0	100.0	100.0	100.0	981	3.8
Percentage share of total expenditure	79.7	9.9	5.8	100.0		

services per income bracket. The Employees Health Service programmes benefit the white-collar workers which means that in terms of income distribution it benefits middle-income groups more than the poor as can be seen in Table 26.

The distribution of benefits for the Public Health Sector as a whole, depicted in Table 26 has a strong progressive pattern, both in relative and absolute terms. Benefits are equivalent to 16 per cent of a poor family's income, but only to 0.7 per cent of a well-to-do family's income. The first type of family would receive the equivalent to 1.099 escudos as benefits during the year, where the latter's would not be higher than 695 escudos.[11]

Of course, the previous results are not at all surprising. In fact, if one compares the incomes of the families who had access to public health services *vis-à-vis* those of the families who used the private health facilities, we will find a very clear stratification according to incomes: low-income families using the public health facilities, high-income families using private health services.

The progressive character of public expenditures in health does not imply that basic health needs are satisfied for the whole of the

[11]We must remember that benefits are being valued at the cost of providing the service.

population. In fact, one of the targets that the Public Health System in Chile has stated for many years is that of providing services for all the population. The scarcity of resources has made this impossible. What in fact happens, then, is that health services are somehow "rationed". Low-income groups receive some service from the public sector, although below what could be considered as an acceptable minimum by experts' recognition. Since the poor do not have any alternative available, and the public health system cannot cope with satisfying basic health needs for everybody, the service they get is insufficient and of generally low quality.

Given resource scarcity, it is apparent then that the nature of health programmes should be revised. If there are no resources to provide services for everybody, then public action should concentrate selectively on those groups whose basic needs are not satisfied. In order to illustrate the implications of such a shift in the policy, we have taken the minimum number of out-patient medical and dental consultations required per year, per person, according to the Pan American Health Organisation, used it as a measurement of basic health needs and calculated the deficits that arise, per income bracket, when the minimum standard is compared with actual services provided through the private sector. We have *a priori* defined as a policy target the satisfaction of basic needs for everybody. Given that, as income grows, families are able to use more of private services, we calculate the net deficit (after private services have been accounted for) to be met by the Public Sector.[12] This is, of course, larger for poverty groups and decreases with income. For example, the net deficit to be covered by the State for out-patient consultations is roughly equal to two visits per year for poverty groups, one visit per year for those in the 3–5 income bracket and zero for families in groups above that as can be seen in Table 27.

Evaluating the deficits at the actual costs of the services in 1969, we calculate the resources required to provide them through the Public Health System, and the relative distribution required of these resources among income groups for the policy objective to be fulfilled. These results are indicated in Table 27. They show that a selective policy of meeting basic health needs for those who do not have the alternative of

[12] The use of private health services by income brackets is obtained from *Ministerio de Salud* (1970).

TABLE 27

Required allocation of public health expenditures to satisfy minimum health needs (By income brackets)

	Out-patients, medical, visits *per capita*	Out-patient, dental, visits *per capita*	Required expenditures		Actual expenditures, distribution, %
			Mill. escudos	%	
0–1	1.9	1.0	194	47	33
1–2	1.7	0.8	145	35	35
2–3	1.4	0.4	54	13	16
3–5	0.9	0.1	21	5	10
5+	–	–	–	–	6

paying for private services would imply allocating 47 per cent of the expenditures in the 0–1 income bracket *vis-à-vis* the 33 per cent this income group actually received in 1969.

The amount of resources required by this new, more selective policy would not be too different from total health expenditures in 1969. Our calculations show that 13 million out-patient medical visits would be required instead of the 12 million effective in 1969, but the access to them would be more selective.

In terms of sectoral allocation, this policy would certainly imply devoting more public resources to rural health programmes, since 60 per cent of the population below the poverty line lives in rural areas. In terms of occupational category, independent workers who are not affiliated to social-security schemes and who constitute half of the rural and urban poor are another obvious target group for a more selective policy.

The central point in the previous discussion is one of almost general validity for social sectors' expenditure policies in developing countries. It is a fact of general occurrence that social policies are defined in terms such that they should benefit all the population. What in practice occurs is that, due to the scarcity of public resources, the public services effectively provided for are insufficient, so that it becomes a privilege to have access to them. Very often it is the organised, politically powerful middle-income groups that most benefit from them, leaving sectors of the low-income population outside of the system. The alternative, of not attempting to provide subsidised services to all but only to those with inability to pay, might well be a more efficient and equitable one.

PUBLIC HOUSING

Public housing programmes have been an important part of government expenditures in Chile. Nearly 4 per cent of GNP has been devoted by the government to finance various housing schemes. Of the 510,000 housing units built in Chile between 1960 and 1972, 306,000 were directly built by government agencies, and about half of the rest were built by the private sector but financed through public funds. During 1969 nearly 40,000 new housing units were initiated plus 15,000 site and services solutions.

The main agencies in charge of housing programmes are the following: the Housing Corporation (CORVI) which builds houses and apartment buildings under a "Popular Savings Plan (PSP) for those families registered in the Plan and for Social Security institutions. The Housing Services Corporation (CORHABIT) administers the Popular Savings Plan, collecting payments from the families participating in the Plan and assigning the houses once they are built by CORVI. It also finances and gives technical support to self-construction programmes. These two institutions do most of the low-budget housing projects.

The government also gives financial support to the Savings and Loans System (SINAP), in fact subsidising the houses financed by savings and loan associations. The houses built under this system are larger (140 square metres *vis-à-vis* a maximum of 70 square metres for CORVI houses) and certainly more expensive than the units built by CORVI.

Another institution, the Urban Renewal Corporation (CORNU), is devoted to urban improvement, a part of which consists in building apartment buildings in urban renewal zones. The type of housing is similar to that of the Savings and Loan System.

As in the case of health services, there is a large unsatisfied demand for low-budget housing in Chile. Of a total of 78,294 applications in the Popular Savings Programme[13] only 15,278 were fulfilled in 1969. Nearly 60 per cent of the applications were for the cheapest site and services programme, but only half of those who applied for this type of solution were able to meet the savings requirements of the programme.

[13] This was the cheapest housing programme in 1969.

What the previous figures strongly suggest is that demand exceeded by far the capability of the public sector to provide housing solutions to poverty groups: only 20 per cent of the total applications were met. The figures for the Site and Services programme also indicate that an important proportion of the population did not have the "capacity to pay" even for the minimal site and services solution. This means that this group was severely limited to satisfy their minimum housing needs. This is a problem which we shall come back to later on because it is a very critical one and of importance for social services in general.

The conditions under which financing was provided by the State for the various schemes are given in Table 28 as well as the average income of beneficiaries in each programme and the subsidies implied by the loans.

The subsidies were calculated with reference to a social rate of interest assumed to be 10 per cent in real terms. The subsidy is explained by several factors: low nominal interest rates (beteen ½ and 2 per cent for most programmes), partial readjustment of debt outstanding with respect to inflation and undervaluation of the building cost by the State construction agency.[14] The subsidies are calculated, as elsewhere in this chapter, in terms of the present value of income gains obtained throughout the period of debt repayment.

Table 28 clearly shows a strong correlation between size of loan and income. Loans for the higher-income groups are almost 20 times the value of the loans given to poverty groups, generally slum dwellers. A second point is that monthly mortgage payments as a share of income are lower for expensive housing schemes (middle and high-income groups) than they are for many of the low-budget houses and flats. The difference is particularly striking when social-security financed housing for employees is compared with the Popular Savings Plan's small houses. The first required that on the average the employee pays 16 per cent of his monthly income as mortgage payment. For the buyer of the latter the percentage goes up to 25 per cent.

Subsidies as a share of the value of the loan are extremely high, 70 per cent on the average, except for the Savings and Loans System where it is closer to 20 per cent. The lowest subsidy as a percentage of the value of

[14]General administrative costs are not considered, nor the increase in costs due to inflation.

TABLE 28

Characteristics of housing loans

	Maximum loan	Annual interest* rates, %	Required savings over size of loan, %	Monthly mortgage, payments over income	Subsidy as % of loan	Average yearly income beneficiaries escudos
PSP site and services, partial	8,300	½	9.5	11.8	70.4	5,280
PSP site and services, total	7,900	½	18.2	9.8	72.1	5,980
PSP self-construction	19,000	1	18.1	20.4	70.8	6,760
PSP small home	25,300	2	18.0	25.0	68.3	7,950
PSP small flat	37,700	2	15.0	18.4	76.5	10,470
Social security, white-collar plan	142,000	2	None	15.9	77.4	13,830
Social security, blue-collar plan	60,000	2	None	17.4	72.7	9,350
Savings and loans	140,000	10	20.0	19.8	19.4	37,660

*Excludes indexation schemes. Loans were partially readjusted for inflation.

the loan is obtained by those with a higher income. This is because the readjustment scheme for the inflationary factor is close to 100 per cent in the Savings and Loans System, and much lower in the others.

The way these subsidies are distributed by income brackets is shown in Table 29. The distribution was done by analysing mostly unpublished figures obtained from the loans' applications under the different programmes. The Housing Service Corporation programmes, which include the PSP, are shown to have the most progressive effect. The Savings and Loans subsidies' distribution is, on the other hand, highly regressive with benefits concentrating in middle- and high-income groups.

From the results reported in Table 29, we can see that the overall effect of the public housing programmes favours the poverty groups, also those in low-income, non-poverty brackets (the 1–2 and 2–3 brackets) in a proportion higher than these groups' share of families' income. In relative terms, the benefits to poor families amount to 5 per cent of their income, whereas in the other extreme in the income scale benefits amount to 0.9 per cent of average family income. But the benefits (or expenditures) per family in absolute terms increase as income grows, they are in fact four times larger for families in the top of the scale, as compared to those in the bottom. This result differs from that found in the health sector.

It is interesting to compare the distribution of benefits in the first column of Table 29, with the distribution of families by income brackets of the slum dwellers, according to the Houshold Expenditure Survey data (see last column in Table 29). If we use the latter as a rough indicator of how resources should be distributed in order to solve the problem of those whose minimum housing needs are not satisfied (target group for the housing policies), we should conclude that in spite of the relative progressivity in the distribution of public housing expenditures, there is an ample margin to redistribute more, reducing the leakages going to middle- and high-income groups. This can be achieved not eliminating these programmes, but reducing the amount of hidden subsidies behind them.

If the previous considerations were implemented, the system would then evolve towards one where basically the low-budget, minimal housing units would be subsidised. As in health and other sectors, subsidies would be selective, explicit and programmed. Efforts on the supply side to

TABLE 29

Incidence of benefits in housing, 1969
(Millions of escudos)

	Housing Corporation (CORVI)	Housing Service Corporation (CORHABIT)	Savings & Loans System (SINAP)	Urban Renewal Corporation (CORMU)	Sanitary constructions (DOS)	Other	Total	Distribution of benefits (%)	Distribution of income (%)	Distribution of families (%)	Slum dwellers income distribution (%)
0–1	55.1	50.6	–	9.5	25.7	38.7	179.6	12.1	7.6	29.8	36.4
1–2	231.5	102.2	3.4	21.7	38.6	79.4	476.8	32.1	20.1	31.6	49.0
2–3	147.4	26.5	25.9	25.3	24.6	52.5	302.2	20.3	18.9	17.6	11.2
3–4	114.2	5.6	22.4	17.9	10.9	32.2	203.3	13.7	11.2	7.4	2.8
4–5	49.0	1.7	18.9	12.6	6.9	18.6	107.7	7.2	8.7	4.5	0.5
5–6	22.4	1.2	12.8	8.1	4.5	11.8	60.8	4.1	7.1	2.9	–
6–8	31.2	0.3	14.6	9.2	4.1	13.8	73.2	4.9	8.0	2.7	–
8–10	2.7	0.1	11.2	6.0	2.3	7.0	29.3	2.0	5.9	4.5	–
10+	2.6	–	22.7	11.5	3.3	13.1	53.2	3.6	12.5	2.0	–
Total	656.0	188.3	132.0	121.7	120.9	267.4	1,486.1	100.0	100.0	100.0	100.0

reduce the cost of the standard housing unit would, of course, help in decreasing the subsidy given to low-income families, thus allowing to extend the programmes to more families, with the same resources.

The access to the minimal housing solution should not be limited because of low income. Poor families would pay a fixed maximum proportion of their income for housing, and the rest would be financed by the State.[15]

Educational programmes

In Chile the public sector provides education directly to 77 per cent of the students and grants a subsidy to private schools which absorb the rest of the students. In this way, practically, the students in the country – 2.5 million in 1969 – are favoured in some measure by the State's disbursement in this area.

The Chilean system comprises four levels of teaching: pre-basic; basic education, which is compulsory for all children of school ages and which lasts 8 years; medium education, of 4 years' duration, dedicated to study of humanities or technical professional subjects; and university (higher) education, following careers which demand 3 to 7 years of study.

The expenditures at each teaching level were divided by the respective number of students, assigning the benefits by strata according to the number of families who have members studying in each level of the educational system. We also considered the resources assigned to the National Institute for Training (INACAP), which provides training to people already working. We included also expenses assigned for feeding the school children – which benefit 60 per cent of the children in basic education – and for helping students of scanty means; this work is done by the National Committee for School Aid and Scholarships.[16] Lastly – as in the Health sector – expenses for the School Building Society were considered, besides administrative disbursements and those for general planning of the schools system: the former were assigned to students of basic and medium levels, in accordance with the proportion

[15] See a more detailed proposition in J. P. Arellano, "Elementos para una política de vivienda social", *Estudios de CIEPLAN,* No. 5, Santiago, December 1976.

[16] The assignment of these benefits was made on the basis of mostly published data, taken from the requests for loans for the diverse programmes.

TABLE 30

Incidence of benefits in public education, 1969
(Millions of escudos)

Income brackets (minimum salary)	Primary education (1)	Secondary education (2)	Professional education (3)	Univer-sities (4)	Training for workers (INACAP IER) (5)	School aid and scholarships (JNAEB) (6)	Others (7)	Distribution of total expenditures: Millions escudos (8)	% (9)	Families income distribu-tion (%) (10)
0–1	201.8	29.6	28.7	48.1	15.3	45.2	49.6	418.3	14.7	7.6
1–2	397.4	89.6	72.8	215.6	32.3	44.3	109.2	961.2	33.8	20.1
2–3	244.2	94.0	58.0	124.9	13.8	24.3	75.2	634.4	22.3	18.9
3–4	107.6	43.1	21.1	107.0	4.7	10.5	35.9	329.9	11.6	11.2
4–5	36.2	16.9	12.3	56.6	1.7	3.6	14.0	141.3	5.0	8.7
5–6	12.4	6.2	4.5	31.0	0.3	1.3	5.4	61.1	2.1	7.1
6–8	13.5	11.1	8.6	49.6	0.3	1.4	7.9	92.4	3.2	8.0
8–10	6.2	4.0	3.7	14.8	0.1	0.6	2.9	32.3	1.1	5.9
10+	15.5	13.6	5.8	128.0	–	1.5	12.7	177.1	6.2	12.5
Total	1,034.8	308.1	215.5	775.6	68.5	132.7	312.8	2,848.0	100.0	100.0

of buildings destined to each educational level, while general expenses were distributed in the same way as the total public expenditure for education.

In Table 30 we show the results of our incidence exercise. We see how the poorer families receive as subsidy less than one-fifth of what the higher-income level people get as an average. This difference arises from the almost entirely free university education, access to which is easier for students from homes with higher or medium incomes. If the State were to stop financing higher education, these differences would be substantially reduced. Our estimates show that in this case the benefit obtained by the latter represent no less than 29 per cent of their income which we must compare with 6 per cent in the case of the more wealthy homes. This result is explained by the highly redistributive incidence of basic education: about 85 per cent of the expenditure on this level goes to the three lower strata, which make up about 78 per cent of the families in the nation.

Adding up the social sectors

Our study of the social sectors has been restricted so far to health, housing and education. Although the information available would allow us to do a similar kind of analysis for social security, and social welfare expenditures, we shall not do so in order to avoid excessive length. We summarise results for the social sectors in Table 31.

As expected, expenditures in the social sectors are highly progressive when compared to the income shares of the various income groups. However, the effect is not progressive enough as to imply a larger benefit per family in absolute terms for the poor families *vis-à-vis* the high income groups, 29.8 per cent of families below the poverty line receive 18.1 per cent of total benefits, whereas at the other extreme 2 per cent of families get 4.6 per cent of benefits. The relative position of the poor is improved but still more resources are being spent per family in the non-target groups.

We are now in a position to pass on to the last section in this chapter where we shall put together the various sectoral results to illustrate on the overall incidence of government expenditures programmes.

TABLE 31

Incidence of benefits in the social sector
(Millions of escudos and %)

	Public Health	Social Welfare	Housing	Education	Social Security	Total	Distribution of benefits	Distribution of income	Distribution of families
0–1	583.8	25.2	179.6	504.6	798.9	2,089.2	18.1	7.6	29.8
1–2	612.7	36.5	476.8	756.5	1,391.3	3,278.2	28.4	20.1	31.6
2–3	275.2	13.0	302.2	530.8	1,089.7	2,204.7	19.1	18.9	17.6
3–4	103.2	6.3	203.3	267.8	604.9	1,188.9	10.3	11.2	7.4
4–5	62.8	4.3	107.7	186.6	431.1	796.5	6.9	8.7	4.5
5–6	35.9	1.1	60.8	122.0	299.8	519.4	4.5	7.1	2.9
6–8	33.7	1.0	73.2	168.2	328.2	600.2	5.2	8.0	2.7
8–10	18.6	0.5	29.3	114.6	172.7	334.7	2.9	5.9	1.5
10+	24.9	0.7	53.2	190.8	258.9	531.0	4.6	12.5	2.0
Total	1,750.7	88.6	1,486.1	2,841.9	5,375.5	11,542.8	100.0	100.0	100.0

TOTAL INCIDENCE OF GOVERNMENT EXPENDITURES

We can now proceed to integrate all the sectoral results in order to have an overall picture of public expenditures incidence.

Before we do that, we must make explicit the treatment given to General Expenditures of the government. These include two main components: the first one consists of purely administrative expenditures that the General Government must do in order to be able to perform its function in the social and economic sectors. Debt repayment also falls under this category. The benefits arising from these types of expenditures are assumed to be distributed as the sum of benefits resulting from all other programmes.

A second item in General Expenditures is constituted by expenditures in defence, police, foreign relations and justice. These are specific functions of the government, and can be considered as pure "public goods" in the sense that they are intended to benefit all of the population in the same proportion. Often this is not the case, either because of insufficient public resources available or due to unequal access to the services. That is why it is sometimes assumed that the benefits from these types of public spending are distributed according to the relative income shares of each group.[17] This we do in Version 1 (Table 32).

Another hypothesis concerning these expenditures is that they in fact equally benefit all of the population. This we assume in Version 2 of total incidence results (Table 32).

If we look at Table 32 we shall find that the distribution of total benefits turns out to be progressive (that is pro-poor) all along the income scale. The lowest income groups ("poverty groups" according to our definition) obtain 15.1 per cent of benefits which is higher than the 7.6 per cent that was their income share. The effect is progressive for the first three income brackets. They gain more than proportionately from public expenditures. They also get more as a proportion of their income. The gains for the poor are a bit lower than their income (equivalent to 91 per cent of their income) whereas in the other extreme of the scale, the gain is only equivalent to 28 per cent of income.

[17] Urrutia y Sandoval (1973), *op. cit.*

TABLE 32

Total incidence of government expenditures

Income brackets	Expenditures (millions escudos)				Percentage distribution of			Benefits per family (escudos)		Incidence of benefits over family income	
	General		Total public sector		National income	Total public expenditures					
	Version 1 (1)	Version 2 (2)	Version 1 (3)	Version 2 (4)	(5)	Version 1 (6)	Version 2 (7)	Version 1 (8)	Version 2 (9)	Version 1 (10)	Version 2 (11)
0–1	616.6	1,249.4	3,217.9	3,851	7.6	15.1	18.1	6,059	7,520	91.0	108.9
1–2	1,225.7	1,555.4	5,482.9	5,813	20.1	25.7	27.3	9,719	10,304	58.6	62.2
2–3	991.7	956.9	3.950.5	3,916	18.9	18.6	18.4	12,569	12,459	44.9	44.5
3–4	569.0	460.9	2,201.7	2,094	11.1	10.3	9.8	16,721	15,900	42.3	40.2
4–5	419.1	298.4	1,533.6	1,413	8.7	7.2	6.6	19,287	17,769	37.9	34.9
5–6	328.5	207.8	1,153.6	1,033	7.1	5.4	4.8	21,975	19,675	34.9	31.3
6–8	370.6	219.9	1,306.8	1,156	8.0	6.1	5.4	27,391	24,232	35.1	31.1
8–10	256.4	130.7	827.0	701	5.9	3.9	3.3	30,609	25,957	30.1	25.5
10+	530.0	228.2	1,639.3	1,337	12.5	7.7	6.3	46,089	37,604	28.2	23.0
Total or average	5,307.6	5,307.6	21,313.3	21,313	100.0	100.0	100.0	11,950	11,950	45.8	45.8

Note: In Version 1, general expenditures are distributed according to families' income. In Version 2, according to population (equally for all families).

Although the relative gains are larger for the lower-income groups, benefits measured in absolute terms increase with income. A rich family obtains as an average (under the assumptions in Version 1 results) 7.6 times the amount of benefits a poor family does. This result is consistent with that obtained in other studies.[18] One reason for it is that public programmes are not *a priori* conceived in terms of benefiting just one group. Thus their benefits spread through the various groups more or less evenly. Those who are less in number tend to get a larger amount than the others. On the other hand, programmes specifically directed at high-income groups (i.e. loans to large industrial enterprises), even if relatively small in terms of the total amount of public resources devoted to it as compared to other programmes (i.e. primary education), may imply a large gain per family due to the reduced number of families that have access to such programmes.

Our results are heavily dependent on the shifting assumptions used. Our Version 2 results show a larger relative gain for the poor (their share of benefits goes up to 18.1 per cent) and the difference in absolute benefits per family *vis-à-vis* the highest income bracket decreases from 7.5 times to 5 times. Thus, the results prove the high sensitivity to the assumptions chosen to assign general administration expenditures. In spite of that, the basic conclusions of the exercise remain the same: the effect of public expenditures is such that it tends to benefit more than proportionately the poor *vis-à-vis* other groups.

[18] See de Wulf (1974), *op. cit.*

CHAPTER 5

What does Social Security do to Incomes?

1. INTRODUCTION

Social security has two different objectives. One is to guarantee income support for the aged, the disabled and dependent survivors. The other is to mitigate the decline in living standards when the earnings of the head of household are interrupted because of retirement, disability or death, and even to supplement incomes if they are considered insufficient to attain a standard of living that is adequate by society's standards. In sum, social security is a system with an earnings-replacement objective (at all levels of income) as well as a welfare objective of proving aid to the poor in society. Both of these purposes have a redistributive content, they affect – directly or indirectly – the final distribution of personal incomes.

Given the quantitative importance that the benefit programmes of social security have assumed in modern days – some 25 per cent of total public expenditures in the Chilean case – and the costs and effects of their financing, it is of great interest to understand the existing inter-relationships between the social-security system and income distribution, especially if social security represents an important set of public instruments available for effecting such distribution.

The aim of this chapter is to explore such effects and to produce a statistical estimate of the post-social-security state of income distribution for Chilean families.

First, the Chilean social-security system is described in terms of its coverage, cost and structure of benefits. Second, the incidence effects of financing the system through payroll taxes is analysed, assessing in particular the question of who bears the final burden of social-security taxes.

Then we determine the incidence of social-security expenditures and draw a picture of the net redistributive effects of both benefits and contributions. Finally, our policy conclusions propose to identify the critical elements of the system, as well as present various alternatives for a reform of social security to enable it to perform an enhanced income-redistribution role, and to positively affect the welfare levels of an ample category of poverty groups.

In spite of this we will simply refer to social security throughout this chapter and we will not be considering here all its functions. Specifically, medical care and housing finance that are important parts of social security have been analysed in Chapters 3 and 4, so, they will be omitted here.

2. THE COVERAGE, COST AND BENEFIT STRUCTURE OF THE CHILEAN SOCIAL-SECURITY SYSTEM

The Chilean system is fairly sophisticated, with a vast proliferation of plans and institutions for the concession of benefits. There are more than 150 types of plans, with more than 35 institutions for social insurance, ruled by some 2,000 legal texts. To understand how such a proliferation came about, we must say something about the historical development of the system.

Although originally conceived as schemes working on the actuarial basis, the system evolved into the *"common fund"* scheme, where the connection between actual contributions by individuals, and retirement benefits as well as other types of allowances, was practically lost. There were two main reasons for this.

(a) the increasing imposition by the State of "welfare-type allowances" to be paid by each institution out of its own funds, and out of limited fiscal aid for earmarked purposes (health, family allowances, etc.);

(b) the inefficiency and limitations imposed by the capital market, aggravated by ill-conceived legislation (for example, the impossibility of using readjustment or indexing clauses), did not allow the social-security capitalisation system to maintain the real value of its assets in the process of escalating inflation in the economy.

The combination of redistributive elements introduced through state regulation or legislation and the efficiency problems in the administration of the funds led to the degradation of the basic programmes.

Legislation as old as the year 1924 created the "Caja del Seguro Obrero" (later to be called Servicio de Seguro Social) which was to cover all *blue-collar* workers' needs for health services, sickness subsidies, disability and retirement pensions. The origin of this programme coincided with a period of marked social legislation passed in favour of workers, and with an increasing democratisation process in the political arena. The period was characterised by rapid mobilisation of the working-class movement, and the pressures exerted in the form of social demands. This blue-collar-worker service started as a "common-fund" system, to which the State, the employers and blue-collar workers themselves had to contribute. The legislation quite conscientiously established an investment mechanism to assure adequate capitalisation of the fund.

The birth of the white-collar workers' system is of somewhat different character. By Decreto-Ley No. 857 of December 1925, the "Caja de Empleados Particulares" was created as a simple institution of forced private savings, whose objective was the financing of a retirement scheme and an indemnity for years worked. If an employee ceased to work, he was entitled to get back his capitalised funds.

Similarly, the public sector employees' social-security programme dates from as early as 1858, the year in which the Caja de Ahorros de los Empleados Públicos was founded, a savings institution run entirely on individual *voluntary* contributions. After the voluntary system of savings failed in 1889, contributions were established on an obligatory basis. The turning-point for social legislation in Chile was the year 1925, when the "Caja Nacional de Empleados Públicos y Periodistas" was established, with a "definitive" text being drafted by 1930. The institution has undergone numerous legal modifications up to the present.

Gradually, but with accelerating speed, more and more programmes and benefits were added to the responsibility of the social-security institutions in a financing scheme that diverged from the initial identification of contributions and benefits. The "common-fund" approach prevailed in practice, and was reinforced by the establishment of benefits such as family allowances, housing loans in aid, broadening of health services and a partial scheme of unemployment subsidies in some plans. The redistributive character of the system was in this way established more firmly.

Historically, then, we observe an evolution in which the system gains in redistributive effect, but loses from the point of view of the maintenance of the real value of funds and benefits.[1]

Nevertheless, the preceding elements led to a tendency by relatively well-to-do pressure groups (bank employees, large-scale state enterprise workers, high ranks in civilian groups, etc.) to withdraw from the general institutions and create private plans among their own kind with greater advantages from the point of view of their own benefits. Hence, high-income-level employees tended to group among themselves in institutions of reduced membership, producing a potential erosion on the financial system of the general plans. This tendency explains – in part – the vast and excessive proliferation of plans.

In terms of the number of affiliated persons, there are three major institutions – the Servicio de Seguro Social, the Caja de Empleados Particulares (EMPARI) and the Caja Nacional de Empleados Públicos y Periodistas (CANAEMPU) – which account for around 90 per cent of all affiliated persons in the economy (contributors).[2] (We have focused attention on the benefits provided basically by these three, in the analysis of distributive incidence patterns.)

On a nationwide basis, social security has also extended rapidly, so that in recent years more than two-thirds of the population have been covered by one programme or another.

It is important to disaggregate the information in terms of the structure of coverage by occupational categories in order to have a clear picture of the distribution of protected and unprotected sectors of the population. As we explained in the first section of this chapter, the structure of non-affiliated groups represents the limits to the redistributive potential that the system may attain.

Table 33 constructed on the basis of the only reliable source of information on this matter shows that some 786,800 workers were lacking any protection, and that they were concentrated in two categories which

[1]Of course, it does not follow that the first produces the second effect, even though there is a coincidence in this case.

[2]See Table 33.

TABLE 33

Labour force distributed by occupational category: affilitation by social-security programme, 1967
(in percentages of total labour force)

Occupational category	Social security programme: Blue-collar workers	White-collar workers	Public servants and journalists	(Military, policemen, bank employees, etc.) Other programmes	Non-covered	No information	Total
Employers	0.1	0.2	–	–	1.2	–	1.5
Self-employed, independent	5.8	0.7	0.2	0.4	13.5	0.9	21.5
White-collar workers	0.8	10.0	7.0	3.6	1.9	0.5	23.8
Blue-collar workers	36.5	0.1	0.3	1.5	7.7	0.9	47.0
Non-remunerated relatives	0.6	–	–	–	3.7	1.2	5.6
Unemployed that had not worked before	–	–	–	–	0.4	0.4	0.8
Labour force	43.9	10.9	7.5	5.5	28.4	3.9	100.0

Source: Instituto Nacional de Estadísticas, Muestra Nacional de Hogares, Marzo-Junio 1967. (Encuesta suplementaria sobre algunos aspectos de asistencia médico y hospitalaria de la mano de obra.)

Percentages are calculated on the basis of an estimated total labour force of 2,773,900.

normally belong to the bottom part of the income distribution: self-employed workers, which account for nearly half of the unprotected labour force, and blue-collar workers, which represent 27 per cent of all unprotected workers.

In the first category, a vast majority belongs to the rural sector and are groups constituted mainly by minifundia producers and temporary rural workers. These sectors are normally considered as being below poverty standards.

Another important group among non-affiliates[3] is formed by "non-remunerated relatives". This category normally prevails in the informal urban sector, and in handicrafts and small industrial establishments.

The unprotected minifundia peasants (smallholders) in agriculture, the rural migrants, workers operating in the informal sector, in handicraft and small industry in the cities, will be important when we trace the incidence model of contributions and benefits from the Chilean social-security system. Although these sectors of the population are left out of social-security benefit programmes, they do contribute to the financing of such programmes, either through direct or indirect mechanisms, as we listed previously.

The magnitude of resources handled by the Chilean social-security system is important. In terms of gross national product, social-security receipts represented around 12 per cent, and social-security expenditures amounted to 10–11 per cent of Chilean GNP.[4] These standards are high if compared with the shares of GNP represented by social security in other Latin American countries of a similar level of development.[5] Thus we may expect that the impact of the system in terms of national aggregates (consumption, savings, incomes, etc.) is of significant dimension.

The structure of benefits of the Chilean social-security system is fairly diversified and complete, ranging from the provision of various kinds of

[3]A large percentage of employers seem also to be non-affiliated, although this has changed in recent years with the establishment of social-security programmes for the retail business and trucking sectors.

[4]Higher percentages result if aggregation is done directly by adding each institution's figures without consolidation of interinstitutions transfers, and if social-security transfers to the health and housing sectors are added to the expenditures' side.

[5]For homogenous intercountry comparisons in this respect see ILO, *The Cost of Social Security, 1967–71,* Geneva, 1976.

pension programmes for the insured worker and his relatives to family allowances and various supplementary transfers. There are differences between the Cajas or institutions, with blue-collar workers showing a lower density in the functions covered by their programme, as opposed to the situation of white-collar workers in the private and public sectors. This is illustrated in Table 34.

Of the total value of benefits distributed in 1969 by the social-security system, almost one-third was paid in the form of family allowances; pensions and other retirement benefits accounted for 58 per cent; loans and other transfers represented 7 per cent; and unemployment compensation accounted for no more than 2 per cent of the funds distributed.

The last figure is consistent with one of the major flaws of the system in terms of coverage, since the programme of subsidies to the unemployed is more nominal than effective in the Chilean case. It is interesting to observe also that more than 90 per cent of the benefits allocated were accounted for by pensions and family allowances.

Finally, in spite of the deficiencies, the Chilean social-security system appears to rank comparatively high in terms of the combined standards of maturity, coverage and the various indicators of equality in the financing and benefit structure. A comparative study for Argentina, Chile, Mexico, Peru and Uruguay ranks the Chilean system in second place, after Uruguay.[6]

The earlier appearance of legislation in the Chilean case, the higher percentage of the total population covered and the more homogeneous distribution in the number of benefits which are conferred by the various programmes are all factors tending to compensate for some of its comparative inequalities.

3. INCIDENCE OF THE PAYROLL TAX

Social-security contributions represent a large share of the financing of the Chilean system. In the year 1969, almost 60 per cent of social-security revenues came from contributions. Of this total, approximately one-third

[6] Carmelo Mesa-Lago, *Social Security in Latin America: Pressure Groups, Stratification and Inequality,* Center for Latin American Studies, University of Pittsburgh, 1975.

TABLE 34

Benefit structure of Chilean social-security system

	Pensions													
	To the insured				To the relatives of the deceased						Others			
Institutions	Old age	Disability	Working years	Unemployment	Widow	Invalid widower	Sons	Mother	Father	Brothers	Life insurance	Death allowance	Supplements	Withdrawal of contributions
Blue-collar														
Servicio Seguro Social	x	x			x	x	x					x		
Capremar-Triomar	x	x			x	x	x	x				x		
Cajas Hípicas (PP. y JJ.)		x	x	x	x	x	x	x	x		x	x		x
Cajas OO. Municipales	x	x	x		x		x	x	x			x		
White-collar														
Caja EE. Particulares	x	x	x		x	x	x	x	x			x	x	x
Organismos Auxiliares	x	x	x		x	x	x	x	x			x	x	x
Capremar-EE. y Ofic.	x	x	x		x	x	x	x	x	x	x	x	x	x
–Agent. Aduana	x	x	x		x	x	x	x	x			x	x	x
Canaempu-Periodistas	x	x	x	x	x		x	x	x		x	x	x	x
Caja Bancaria y Bco. Chile	x	x	x	x	x	x	x	x	x		x	x	x	x
Caja de Agua Potable	x	x	x	x	x		x	x			x	x	x	x
Caja de Amortización	x	x	x	x	x	x	x	x	x		x	x	x	x
Cajas Hípicas (EE.)														
Public servants														
Caja de EE. Públicos	x	x	x	x	x		x	x		x	x	x	x	x
Caja de la Defensa	x	x	x	x	x		x	x	x	x		x		
Caja de Carabineros	x	x	x	x	x		x	x	x			x	x	
Caja de Emp. de FF.CC.	x	x	x	x	x		x	x	x			x	x	x
Caja Banco del Estado	x	x	x	x	x	x	x	x	x	x	x	x	x	x
Caja Banco Central	x	x	x	x	x	x	x	x	x		x	x	x	x
Caja EE. Munic. Repub.	x	x	x	x	x	x	x	x	x		x	x	x	x
Caja EE. Munic. Stgo.	x	x	x	x	x	x	x	x	x	x		x	x	x
Caja EE. Munic. Valpo.	x	x	x	x	x		x					x	x	x

was obtained from employee contributions, whereas two-thirds came from employer contributions or payroll tax. In terms of the public budget, the payroll tax represented more than all of the tax revenues generated by copper, and about 60 per cent of all direct taxation. It is evident that a financing instrument of such magnitude produces some of the most significant redistributive effects produced by the social-security system.

When judging the incidence of social-security contributions four basic questions seem in order: (a) are they to be considered as payments for benefits obtained on a *quid pro quo* basis, or are they to be treated simply as taxes? (b) Are contributions universal or selective in their coverage? (c) Is the legal contributory scheme proportional, progressive or regressive in terms of the income base on which it is levied? (d) How does market structure render effective incidence divergent from legal incidence? In the following analysis of the Chilean case, we shall see that the answers to these questions will prove crucial for determining the actual incidence of contributions.

Further, average yearly contribution rates are relatively high in terms of the wage bill, and the modal rate represents over 50 per cent of taxable wages and salaries. From a legal point of view the total "tax" rate is the result of a combination of contributory rates whose receipts are earmarked for the financing of different types of benefits.

It is interesting to point out the differences between employee and employer contributions.

First, legal contributory rates by employers are almost four times as high as the rate by employees, so that it is the classic "payroll tax" which finances the bulk of contributions.

Secondly, tax-rate components for worker contributions are mainly directed to social-security funds which tend to be more associated with individual-type benefits such as the retirement and pension allowances (see Table 35). On the other hand, employer contributions are largely devoted to finance collective-type benefits such as family allowances and the like.

Thirdly, in the case of blue-collar workers, the legal contributory rate by workers has tended to be relatively more stable over time than the employer rate. The employer rate has been multiplied by eight throughout the period 1952–70, whereas the worker rate had risen five times.

All these differences, added to other evidence, led us to perform a distinct incidence analysis of contributions by employees and contributions by employers in spite of the fact that, in theory, there is no basis for a sharp distinction between the incidence of the employee portion of contributions and that of the payroll tax.

TABLE 35

Social-security contributions: legal contributory rates and their destination[(a)]

White-collar (Caja empleados particulares)			Blue-collar (Servicio seguro social)		
Destination	By the worker	Tax rate % By the employer	Destination	By the worker	Tax rate % By the employer
I. Retirement fund	5.0	5.0			
II. Pension fund	3.0	3.0	Pension fund	5.5	12.0
III. Indemnisation		8.33	Indemnisation		2.0
IV. Family allowances	2.0	21.50	Family allowances	2.0	22.0
V. Health	1.0	2.5	Health		
VI. Other	2.75	3.65	Other	1.25	3.15
Total rate	13.75	43.98	Total rate	8.75	39.15

[(a)] All of these contribution rates relate to the situation for active workers; contributions by pensioners are of much lower rates and represent discounts over gross allowances.

Source: Seguridad social, *Estadísticas 1968,* Superintendencia de seguridad social, Chile.

We assumed that the burden from employee contributions remained on workers themselves, either because this minor portion of contributions was visualised by labour simply as another direct tax on earned income or because at least in part this share of the contributions could be considered by workers as equivalent to the current benefits they receive from social security plus the discounted money value of the rights acquired for future benefits from the system (pensions and retirements).[7] The assumption of not shifting *employee* contributions is thus incorporated into the incidence results presented in the next section.

In general, however, we think that the bulk of contributions are seen as a non-compensated burden by the young active labour force, a view which is consistent with the nature of the common fund (*reparto*) scheme on which the Chilean social-security system is based. Such a scheme is characterised – as explained in the first section of this paper – by a disassociation between contributions and benefits, from the point of view of the labour force.

[7] For an analysis which assumes that this evaluation by workers could also extend to part of the employer contributory rates see PREALC, *Acción de los ministerios de trabajo en la política del empleo del grupo andino,* Santiago, 1975, PREALC/87.

This we think is one of the basic aspects of Chilean payroll tax incidence: the fact that contributions are levied on one group of the population (the young active and employed labour force) which does not directly visualise and associate these with the benefits that social security distributes to a different group of the population (the old inactive labour force, the unemployed, the disabled, the inactive dependants). This way of financing social security introduces a wedge between the maximum amount that firms are willing to pay for the services of workers (the demand for labour) and the minimum values at which the same amount of labour could be obtained (labour supply).

The incidence effects of such a wedge or distortion introduced in the labour market have special characteristics in the Chilean case, which makes it diverge from the traditional analysis on payroll taxes.

The typical labour market in Chile is characterised by three main elements; it is a market with persistent disequilibria, subject to important institutional factors (such as minimum wage and other protective labour legislation) as well as subject to the interplay of trade-union behaviour. These elements, plus the fact that a considerable and pervasive degree of imperfections exist in the goods markets (mostly related to oligopoly power and pricing behaviour by firms) imply that payroll tax shifting analysis is not straightforward.

In particular, we have worked on the following general hypothesis with respect to the effective incidence of the payroll tax:

(i) a considerable part of employer contributions is shifted forward to consumers through the force of institutional labour protective factors (minimum wages, trade union practices, etc.) and the pricing behaviour of Chilean firms (monopoly practices and cost mark-up);
(ii) part of the payroll tax is shifted back on workers themselves, mainly in the context of inflation and wage readjustment negotiations;
(iii) in specific sectors of the economy and for special labour groups, both the employer and the employee are able to escape the tax by shifting the burden to the State itself, through one or another form of legal and illegal evasion.

The first hypothesis corresponds to a widespread belief on the part of

Chilean social-security experts to the effect that it is consumers in general who bear most of the cost of social-security contributions.[8]

This view is founded – in part – on the effects that an institutionalised wage barrier produces in the labour market, so that employer contributions cannot be financed through a reduced take-home pay.

Also, its other economic foundation lies in the widespread practice of pricing on the basis of "average cost plus a mark-up", practice which is most frequent in Chilean enterprise decisions, as we explained in Chapter 2.

With such a behaviour by firms, social-security contributions (which form part of average costs of production) end up being transmitted forward to consumers. This transmission is assured by the general context of oligopoly and lack of competition in Chilean goods markets, and by the macro context of persistent inflationary trends.

In an inflationary milieu in which prices are changing continually, there is an *a priori* basis to expect a higher degree of tax shifting than in an alternative milieu.

The second general hypothesis is related to the study of incidence in a dynamic setting. Here, explicit consideration is given to labour unions and their behaviour in wage negotiations.

The issue is that social-security contributions, by stepping up the effective cost of labour, represent an inhibiting element on the bargaining power of trade unions and workers in their demands for wage improvement. In wage negotiations and in collective bargaining, social-security contributions will be taken into account by management, since employers normally do not think about the cost of labour in terms of wage rates only but consider all other labour-related costs. Hence, the relative strength of unions is lowered in negotiations because of the existence of this particular way of financing the social-security system.

A case study for Chilean industry by Peter Gregory showed the sensitivity of employers with respect to social-security contributions: " . . . interviews with factory managers revealed that they were pursuing this substitution (capital for labour) within the limits permitted by the availability of scarce foreign exchange (used in bringing in capital goods

[8]See, for example, the opinions of authorities on the subject such as Carlos Briones, Luis Orlandini, Juan Gutiérrez and Juan P. Soto as expressed in the influential study *Antecedentes Bàsicos y análisis del estado actual de la seguridad social en Chile,* Seguridad Social No. 98.

which are largely imported). Most of them declared they were motivated to a large extent by a desire to reduce their payroll tax. . . ."[9]

The menace of this substitution against labour is probably present in wage negotiations, thereby placing in jeopardy the potential achievement power of unions.

Thus employer contributions will be partially shifted back to workers, in the context of the year-by-year process of negotiating wage readjustments to keep up with inflation.

The actual degree of backward shifting depends on a series of elements, among which are the degree of social-security coverage existing in any one labour market, the conditions of entry and exit in such a market, the demand conditions, the kind of manpower, etc.

If we focus on one type of labour, say skilled labour, we may see that there are various pressure groups in the Chilean case which are able to escape incidence and force it on the State.[10] This is done in the form of agreements between labour and enterprise, so that only a minimum part of work compensation is established in the form of a wage or salary. Agreements of this type are frequent in the case of labour groups such as professionals, who normally receive a significant share of their earnings in the form of honoraria, which become non-taxable for social-security purposes.

These become ways of forcing incidence on the State, since the social-security system finds itself with equal or higher welfare obligations demanded by the old and newly insured population, but with less real resources to face these demands.[11] The State in turn "defends" itself by transmitting the burden to private households in the forms of increased taxation, increased inflation, reductions in the average level of some of the socal-security programmes, and lower-quality services. These are significant forms of incidence which escape traditional measurement.

[9]See Peter Gregory, *Industrial Wages in Chile,* New York State School of Industrial Labour Relations, Cornell University, New York, 1967.

[10]See Section 2 for a description of how these groups led to a proliferation of social-security programmes in Chile.

[11]Evidence for twenty-three plans, for example, showed that for the period 1956–64, social-security expenditures grew at an annual rate of 10.2 per cent, whereas receipts from contributions grew only at an implicit rate of 5.8 per cent per year. See E. Aninat, "Nuevas alternativas para el sistema chileno de seguridad social", Documento No. 6, CEPLAN, 1971.

The preceding analysis provides the ground for allocating the burden from the payroll tax to consumers in general and to workers. This is the basis of the calculations shown in Table 37. It would be important to see how this aggregate picture applies in the case of particular sectors of the labour force. In this sense a more complete analysis would have consisted in disaggregating the incidence effects according to the various differentiated labour markets in the economy. Unfortunately the data did not permit such a disaggregation. In any case a general effect which is important to consider is that the payroll tax contributes to higher levels of unemployment than would be the case with an alternative source of social-security financing. This is because of its interference with the capital/labour choice in production.

For the economy as a whole, there are estimates which show that – if some of the hypotheses we have worked with are true – the impact of the payroll tax on the aggregate rate of unemployment is very significant.

Three studies which elaborate on expected variations in employment brought about by substituting alternative tax-finance schemes for the existing payroll tax in Chile conclude that the positive employment effects would range from a minimum of 8 per cent to a maximum of 25 per cent.[12] In the case of the industrial sector as a whole, such a rise in employment would be close to 10 per cent of man-years in the industrial labour force. For agriculture we could expect an increase of 2.5 per cent in terms of the number of men actually employed in the sector.

These positive changes in employment to be derived from the policy described are quite significant, if contrasted with the low labour-absorption coefficients that the Chilean economy has shown over time. Also, they would have positive effects on workers in the non-covered and informal sectors (the self-employed, independent producers, etc.) due to the "tightness" which such a policy change would introduce in the demand/supply conditions confronted. Thus we may conclude that the existing payroll tax is generating considerable regressive effects.[13]

[12] These estimates refer to man-years. See E. Aninat, "La eliminación del sistema de cotizaciones previsionales: estimaciones de su impacto sobre el empleo", *Estudios de Planificación,* CEPLAN, No. 9, 1971; PREALC, "Acción de los ministerios de trabajo en la política del empleo del grupo andino", Cap. II, Santiago, PREALC/87, 1975; N. Villagrán, "Proposición de un nuevo sistema de financiamiento de los fondos previsionales y sus implicancias sobre el nivel de empleo en el sector agrícola", Tesis de postgrado departamento de economia agraria, Universidad Católica, Santiago, Chile, 1975.

[13] Balance consolidado del sector público, 1969.

Being true that in all labour markets we observe a common phenomenon of forward and backward shifting of payroll taxes, it is important to note that the exact degree of these shiftings varies from group to group, and that the intervening direct and indirect variables are normally of a differentiated character. This must be surely kept in mind when evaluating the over-all redistributive results, so as to qualify our aggregate incidence estimates.

4. REDISTRIBUTIVE EFFECTS OF THE CHILEAN SOCIAL-SECURITY SYSTEM

In this section we proceed to allocate the burdens and benefits arising from the social-security system (in 1969) to the various classes of family incomes. The incidence exercise is based on a disaggregation of the information presented in the consolidated budget for the public sector into the relevant groups of contributors and beneficiaries. Although emphasis has been placed on the experience of three main groups, blue-collar workers in the Servicio de Seguro Social, white-collar workers in the Caja de Empleados Particulares, and public servants in the Caja Nacional de Empleados Públicos y Periodistas, the data for all other programmes has been also incorporated in our results, in consolidated form.

Intensive use has been made of the distribution series of family incomes by occupational categories from the National Survey on Family Incomes (1968) and the incomes data and expenditures information obtained from the Survey on Households Budgets (1969). The income distribution series of both surveys were made compatible, and the income base for each bracket was adjusted so as to correspond with total (adjusted) household incomes from national accounts.

Again, we measure the distribution of burdens and benefits along an income scale expressed in terms of "annual minimum income" units, and we distinguish nine income classes on the basis of such units.

The distribution of burdens is based on the working hypothesis described in the preceding section; the allocation of benefits is in direct relation with the nature of each kind of benefit and the income situation of the corresponding beneficiary.

We start by presenting the allocation of burdens arising from employee contributions, the payroll tax and other receipts.

4.1. The incidence of social-security receipts

The structure of financing of the Chilean social-security system will prove important in terms of its redistributive incidence. The ranking in the relative importance of financing sources is as follows:

(i) employer contributions (37 per cent of the total);
(ii) fiscal support and earmarked tax receipts (30 per cent of the total);
(iii) employee contributions (23 per cent of the total);
(iv) receipts from the sale of goods and services and other (6 per cent of the total);
(v) income from capital (4 per cent of the total).

Therefore, the biggest determinants of redistributive incidence at this level will be social-security contributions and special earmarked taxes (about 90 per cent of all receipts).

We have allocated each of the amounts contributed by active blue-collar, white-collar and independent workers, as well as by pensioners from the blue-collar and white-collar ranks.[14] Here we proceeded on the basis that no shifting of these contributions occurred so that the burdens rested on workers. We allocated employer contributions in the private sector, assuming that a major portion of the payroll tax was shifted forward to consumers and that the rest fall back on workers, through the mechanisms outlined in the preceding section.

The distribution of employer contributions in the public sector was done following the incidence profile of total taxation in Chile (direct and indirect), according to the results reached in our chapter on the incidence of taxation (see Chapter 2).

Earmarked tax receipts comprise a series of special levies established as surcharges on various kinds of indirect taxes, special tax rates on direct taxes and fees which resemble user-charge costs on various services (municipal services, race-tracks, etc.). The list of such levies is long and detailed, with the characteristic that individual items in it represent small amounts. Although they are related to the social-security system in the sense that tax receipts are devoted to the financing of its various programmes, the distribution of the income burdens they impose must be in line with total tax incidence.

[14] We allocated employer contributions in the private sector assuming that four-fifths of them were shifted to consumers, and one-fifth of them were shifted as a burden on workers. In any case see note no. 6 on Table 36 for sensitivity analysis.

Direct current income received by the social-security institutions in the form of charges for the various services rendered was deducted from the expenditures side, reducing the net benefits received by social-security beneficiaries.

Other receipts and transfers were consolidated at the aggregate level, since no double counting should be allowed when one looks at the social-security system as a whole from the point of view of its net effects on the incomes of families.

The relatively minor receipts due to rents from investment and asset sales were not included in the incidence exercise, given the difficulties of estimating the incidence of income from capital rather than of current income.

Table 36 presents a summarised description of the distribution series used for the allocation of burdens in accordance with our previous considerations. These series are the basis for the fiscal incidence results of Table 37.

Incidence results, that is, figures showing burdens as a proportion of family incomes in each bracket, follow a regressive pattern as column 15 in Table 37 indicates. The average burden from contributions and earmarked taxes is about 11 per cent of total family incomes, with a range going from 13.8 per cent in the first bracket (poorest families) to 8.3 per cent in the highest income bracket (richest families). The three upper-income classes contributed amounts which, as a proportion of their incomes, are less than the average effective contributory rate.

The distribution of burdens shows that it is basically the middle-income class (brackets III to VI) that makes the highest absolute contribution to the financing of the system. This class, which covers around one-third of total population and accumulates about 45 per cent of total family incomes, finances by itself almost half of the total costs of the system. This is consistent with the nature of the main programme of the Chilean social-security system, since they are largely middle-class oriented in their affiliates, coverage and programme structure.

Indirectly, though, the system seems to affect significantly the income situation of poor families. This is mainly because of the tax-shifting to consumers and the regressiveness of such incidence, since more than half of the burden reported in the lower echelons is explained by the forward shifting of the payroll tax (compare for the first two brackets, columns 7 and 13).

TABLE 36

Incidence of social-security receipts

Legal incidence	Effective incidence	Distribution series used
Item		
I. Social-security contributions		
1. *Worker contributions*		
Active population		
1.1. Contributions by blue-collar workers	Blue-collar workers(1)	Distribution of income of families headed by blue-collar worker (survey on family incomes)(1)
1.2. Contributions by public servants	Public servants(2)	Distribution of income of employees in government services (survey on household expenditures)(3)
1.3. Contributions by (private) white-collar workers	White-collar workers(3)	Distribution of income of employees working in the private sector (survey on household expenditures)(3)
1.4. Contributions by independent workers	Self-employed workers(4)	Distribution of income of self-employed workers (survey on family incomes)(4)
Inactive population		
1.5. Blue-collar pensioners	Blue-collar pensioners(5)	Distribution of pension incomes (survey on household expenditures)(5)
1.6. White-collar pensioners	White-collar pensioners	Distribution of pension incomes (survey on household expenditures)(5)
2. *Employer contributions*		
2.1. Employer contributions in the private sector	Consumers in general and workers in general(6)	Four-fifths of the total according to the distribution of total household expenditures (survey on household expenditures) One-fifth of the total according to the distribution of incomes of families headed by blue-collar and white-collar workers respectively (survey on family incomes)(6)
2.2. Employer contributions by public sector	Taxpayers in general	Distribution of direct and indirect taxes (from "Fiscal Instruments and Redistribution: The Incidence of Taxation", *op. cit.*)(7)
3. *Earmarked tax receipts*	Taxpayers in general(8)	Distribution of direct and indirect taxes (from "Fiscal Instruments and Redistribution: The Incidence of Taxation", *op. cit.*)(8)

(continued)

Notes to Table 36

(1) By Law 16840 of May 1968 the old ceiling on the amount of earnings which could be taxed for social-security purposes in the industrial sector was abolished (the limit was the equivalent of forty-two minimum wages of industry and commerce, or around 2.6 s.v.a.). Therefore in 1969, the only taxable ceiling in the Servicio de Seguro Social was the one for agriculture workers (equivalent to 1.5 times the average daily salary in industry, or around 0.7 s.v.a.) but this was of little quantitative importance since only 13.8 per cent of all contributions to the Servicio Seguro Social, came from agriculture. In any case, and if we combined both ceilings, we would obtain a maximum ceiling of 2.4 s.v.a., and we can see in column 1 of Table 43 that 83 per cent of the burden from contributions by blue-collar workers lies in the range of 0–3 s.v.a. (the first three income classes).

(2) The regressive effect of the existing ceiling on taxable earnings in the case of public employees, equivalent to 8 s.v.a., has been incorporated in the incidence calculations.

(3) The existing ceiling on wages subject to the social-security tax on the case of white-collar workers affiliated to the Caja Empleados Particulares, equivalent to 6 s.v.a., has been incorporated in the incidence calculations.

(4) Independent workers of commerce and other sectors who lacked a social-security programme were offered by law the possibility of affiliating to the Servicio de Seguro Social, and only to that institution.

(5) Contributions by pensioners were distributed in line with the distribution of "pension income" for families headed by pensioners, according to estimates processed on the basis of the information in the Survey on Family Expenditures. Data did not, however, permit further disaggregation into the particular income distribution series of pensioners of blue-collar and white-collar origin.

(6) Sensitivity analysis of allowing for some portion of the payroll-tax burden to remain on the employers' shoulders showed that the incidence profile tended to follow a relatively more proportional trend (i.e. similar shares of income sacrificed at the different income brackets) than the regressive pattern shown by our findings. This, however, mainly affects the middle- to high-income brackets and is not very significant given the probable minor share of the total burden that would in practice remain at the firm's level.

(7) We assume that fiscal contributions must be financed, in the end, out of general funds in the public budget (mostly taxation).

(8) It is possible (but not definitively clear) that it is indirect tax levies which supply an important part of these receipts. Thus the distribution would lie more closely to that for the incidence of indirect taxes, rather than general taxation.

The regressiveness of the contributory scheme is coherent with the functioning of the financing system. The structure of contribution rates, the relative evasions by programme, and the ceilings imposed on earnings subject to contributions are all explanatory factors.

A clear example of this fact is what happens with the earnings subject to contributions. In the Caja de Empleados Particulares, white-collar workers are only subject to social-security contributions for earnings up

TABLE 37

Social-security receipts: incidence results
(millions of escudos 1969; all programmes)

	Social-security contributions						Payroll tax								
	Active			Pensioners			Private sector								
Family income brackets	Blue-collar (1)	Public servants (2)	White-collar (3)	Independent workers (affiliated) (4)	Blue-collar origin (5)	White-collar origin (6)	Burden on consumers (7)	Burden on blue-collar workers (8)	Burden on white-collar workers (9)	Public sector (10)	Earmarked tax receipts (11)	Total burdens (1–11) (12)	Relative distribution of burdens (%) (13)	Relative distribution of family incomes (%) (14)	Incidence on family income (%) (15)
I	43.6	1.1	3.9	5.7	9.6	45.0	263.3	31.9	1.9	9.2	72.0	487.2	9.4	7.6	13.8
II	132.7	28.9	54.5	8.5	16.0	75.3	500.6	97.2	28.1	22.1	172.6	1,136.5	21.9	20.1	12.2
III	81.0	65.0	121.3	7.7	12.7	59.9	396.9	59.4	47.6	21.6	164.1	1,036.6	20.0	18.9	11.8
IV	29.9	48.2	99.3	5.4	7.5	35.6	209.4	21.9	34.4	11.7	91.0	594.3	11.5	11.2	11.4
V	15.0	43.5	106.6	3.9	5.1	24.3	145.6	10.9	28.9	9.4	73.0	466.2	9.0	8.7	11.5
VI	5.9	38.6	101.3	2.2	3.5	16.3	121.6	4.3	27.1	8.5	66.0	395.3	7.6	7.1	12.0
VII	3.4	50.1	23.9	2.6	3.9	18.4	119.7	2.5	33.0	9.5	73.9	340.9	6.6	8.0	9.2
VIII	–	30.6	18.0	2.5	1.8	8.3	91.7	–	23.0	7.9	61.6	245.4	4.7	5.9	8.9
IX	–	37.5	37.6	2.9	2.8	13.3	145.6	–	46.5	22.2	173.5	481.9	9.3	12.5	8.3
Total	311.5	343.5	566.4	41.4	62.9	296.4	1,994.4	228.1	270.5	121.5	947.7	5,184.3	100.0	100.0	11.1

to the equivalent of six annual minimum incomes (6 s.v.a.), and in the case of public servants affiliated to the Caja Nacional de Empleados Públicos y Periodistas, the limit climbs only up to the equivalent of eight annual minimum incomes (8 s.v.a.). Therefore, two of the more well-to-do groups of workers in the economy benefit from ceilings which represent a distortion to the apparent proportionality in legal contributory rates.

Finally, it is interesting to point out the fact that social-security contributions have a more regressive incidence pattern than that shown for general taxation. Table 38 illustrates this.

TABLE 38

Redistributive effects of social security and taxation in Chile (percentages)

Income brackets (s.v.a.)	Relative distribution of direct and indirect tax burdens (2)	Relative distribution of social-security receipts (burdens) (3)	Relative distribution of pre-tax family income (1)
I	7.6	9.4	7.6
II	18.1	21.9	20.1
III	17.3	20.0	18.9
IV	9.6	11.5	11.2
V	7.7	9.0	8.7
VI	7.0	7.6	7.1
VII	7.8	6.6	8.0
VIII	6.5	4.7	5.9
IX	18.2	9.3	12.5
Total	100.0	100.0	100.0

Hence, social-security contributions represent an inadequate mechanism for generating public funds if judged solely from the redistributive point of view.[15] This will become an important policy issue when evaluating the alternatives for reform.

4.2. The incidence of social-security expenditures

The two principal items in the expenditure programmes of Chilean social security are pensions and family allowances. These represented

[15] See Conclusions for a discussion of this matter.

90 per cent of the total value of benefits distributed. It is interesting to see how two elements of such a different character, the "welfare-oriented" family allowances and the "insurance-oriented" pensions, form the core of the mixed social-security system in Chile.

Table 39 reveals the benefits received by blue-collar and white-collar workers and public servants, under each of the programmes. This information summarises, in aggregate form, the data for each programme.

Blue-collar pensioners, which represent 60 per cent of all pensioners in the country, received 30 per cent of all pension benefits distributed by the system, whereas white-collar pensioners from the private and public sectors of the eonomy representing 40 per cent of the total number, received 70 per cent of the total value of pension benefits. This fact is a

TABLE 39

The structure of social-security benefits
(1969, in percentages)

I. *Family allowances*			32.5
1. Actives		29.0	
– Blue-collar workers	(10.2)		
– Public servants	(3.3)		
– White-collar workers	(15.5)		
2. Pensioners		3.5	
– Blue-collar	(1.1)		
– Employees	(2.4)		
II. *Pensions and other social insurance benefits*			58.3
– Blue-collar		17.3	
– Employees		41.0	
III. *Loans and other benefits*			7.2
– Blue-collar		1.8	
– Public servants		0.9	
– White-collar		4.5	
IV. *Unemployment allowances*			2.0
– Blue-collar		0.5	
– Public servants		1.0	
– White-collar		0.5	
Total social security benefits			100.0

Source: Balance Consolidado del Sector Público de Chile, 1969–1970, Ministerio de Hacienda, Dirección de Presupuestos.

good illustration of the limited scope of Chilean social security, in terms of the redistributive role it can play on the expenditures side.

The preceding statement must in any case be qualified in – at least – two ways. First, if comparisons are made not with respect to the numerical importance of labour groups but with respect to their original income basis, the system may still produce important redistributive effects. This is due to the meagre income shares going to the mass of workers located at the bottom of the pre-social-security distribution of incomes.

A second qualification relevant to the Chilean case is that considerable redistributive effects may be occurring inside a particular programme, within each labour group. There are programmes such as family allowances which clearly favour lower-income groups in relation to the rich minorities in the cajas. This "intra distribution" of benefits may also significantly alter the distribution of incomes. In fact it is this second kind of effect which largely explains the net progressive character that incidence results show for the expenditures side of social security.

The incidence exercise is more straightforward here than for contributions. Considerable effort went into the detection of the most significant benefit programmes in each of the social-security systems and the identification of their direct beneficiaries. Then, the best income distribution series available for each group of beneficiaries was utilised for allocating benefits along our family income classes. Table 40 contains a listing of the distribution series used for each programme.

Incidence results are reported on Table 41. The distribution of benefits as a proportion of incomes shows a progressive pattern with social-security programmes representing 22.6 per cent of the incomes of the poor (first income class), a rate that is continuously lowered as we advance through the income scale until it reaches only 4.5 per cent of the incomes of the rich bracket (IX).

The relative distribution of benefits (see column 5.3, Table 41) shows that Chilean social security is largely a programme for the middle class (households in the III–IV range). This group receives the highest absolute share of total benefits, some 45 per cent of the system's allowances, while at the same time bearing a very high proportion of the system's financing. Thus, social security in Chile is a programme largely *financed by* and for the benefit of the middle classes.

TABLE 40

Social-security programmes and their beneficiaries

Programme or benefit	Distribution series used for beneficiaries of the programme
I. *Active population*	
1. Blue-collar	
1.1. Family allowances	Distribution of the number of blue-collar households throughout the income scale (survey on family incomes)
1.2. Indemnisation and unemployment allowance	Distribution of incomes of blue-collar families (survey on family incomes)
1.3. Other blue-collar benefits	In line with distributions 1.1 and 1.2 combined
2. White-collar (private sector)	
2.1. Family allowances	Distribution of the number of white-collar households in the private sector (survey on household expenditures)
2.2. Unemployment allowances	Distribution of allowances according to the Caja de Empleados Particulares statistics (adjusted to the distribution of white-collar households in the private sector), (survey on household expenditure)
2.3. Loans	Distribution of incomes of white-collar households in the private sector (survey on household expenditures)
2.4. Other white-collar benefits	In line with distributions 2.1, 2.2 and 2.3 combined
3. Public servants	
3.1. Family allowances	Distribution of the number of white-collar households in the public sector (survey on household expenditures)
3.2. Unemployment allowance	Distribution of incomes of white-collar households in the public sector (survey on household expenditures)
3.3. Other benefits	In line with distributions 3.1 and 3.2 combined
II. *Inactive population*	
4.1. Family allowances to pensioners	Distribution of households with pension incomes (survey on household expenditures)
4.2. Pensions	Distribution of pension incomes (survey on household expenditures)
4.3. Retirement	Distribution of pension incomes (survey on household expenditures)
4.4. Desahucio (severance pay)	Distribution of households with pension incomes (survey on household expenditures)
4.5. Loans	Distribution of households with pension incomes (survey on household expenditures)
III. *Operating expenditures and administrative costs*	
5.1. Various expenditures	In line with the results of all previous distributions

TABLE 41

Social-security expenditures: incidence results

	I. Benefits to the active population									
	Blue-collar			White-collar				Public servants		
Family income (s.v.a.)	Family allow-ances	Indemnisation and unemployment allowance	Other blue-collar benefits	Family allow-ances	Unemploy-ment allowances	Loans	Other white-collar benefits	Family allow-ances	Unemployment allowances	Other benefits
	(1.1)	(1.2)	(1.3)	(2.1)	(2.2)	(2.3)	(2.4)	(3.1)	(3.2)	(3.3)
I	157.8	3.2	28.2	25.2	2.1	0.2	5.2	0.2	0.1	0.2
II	238.3	9.7	43.3	132.5	7.6	3.4	27.4	2.0	3.6	4.2
III	86.7	6.0	16.2	186.1	7.0	7.7	38.5	2.9	8.0	8.1
IV	22.8	2.2	4.4	108.8	4.1	6.3	22.8	1.6	6.0	5.7
V	8.8	1.1	1.7	91.5	3.0	6.7	19.2	1.1	5.4	4.9
VI	2.6	0.4	0.6	70.2	2.1	6.4	15.1	0.8	4.8	4.2
VII	1.6	0.3	0.4	73.3	1.1	8.4	15.7	0.8	6.2	5.2
VIII	0.5	0.1	–	42.6	0.6	6.3	9.5	0.7	7.0	5.8
IX	–	0.1	–	58.4	0.9	13.1	13.9	0.6	8.5	6.9
Total	519.1	23.1	94.8	788.6	28.5	58.5	167.3	10.7	49.6	45.2

TABLE 41 – continued

Family income (s.v.a.)	II. Benefits to the inactive population					Operating expenditure and adminis-trative costs	Total distribution of benefits	Relative distribution of benefits (%)	Relative distribution of family incomes (%)	Incidence on family incomes (%)
	Family allow-ances	Pensions	Retirement allowances	Desahucio (severance pay)	Loans					
	(4.1)	(4.2)	(4.3)	(4.4)	(4.5)	(5.1)	(5.2)	(5.3)	(5.4)	(5.5)
I	55.4	447.7	0.6	6.7	1.3	64.8	798.9	14.9	7.6	22.6
II	50.3	748.2	0.9	6.1	1.2	112.6	1,391.3	25.9	20.1	14.9
III	33.5	595.0	0.8	4.1	0.8	88.3	1,089.7	20.3	18.9	12.4
IV	15.5	353.4	0.4	1.9	0.3	48.7	604.9	11.2	11.2	11.6
V	9.7	241.5	0.3	1.2	0.2	34.8	431.1	8.0	8.7	10.7
VI	5.4	162.0	0.2	0.6	0.1	24.3	299.8	5.6	7.1	9.1
VII	5.2	182.6	0.2	0.6	0.1	26.5	328.2	6.1	8.0	8.8
VIII	2.7	82.5	0.1	0.3	0.1	13.9	172.7	3.2	5.9	6.3
IX	2.5	132.5	0.2	0.3	0.1	20.9	258.9	4.8	12.5	4.5
Total	180.2	2,945.4	3.7	21.8	4.2	434.8	5,375.5	100.0	100.0	100.0

It is interesting to note also that the relative distribution benefits reported in Table 41 lie very close to the relative distribution of benefits constructed on the basis of *personal* income, subject to social-security levies, according to the distribution series for affiliated workers obtained from each of the cajas.[16] The first one shows percentages somewhat concentrated at the upper echelons, which is as it should be given the alternative definition of the income base (family incomes).

In terms of each of the main social-security programmes there are significant differences in the distribution of benefits to the active contributors and their dependants by income classes.[17] If we summarise the allocation of programmes in this way, we observe that three-quarters of the benefits received by the Servicio de Seguro Social will go to the two poorest income classes, almost three-fifths of total benefits in EMPART will be received by households in the middle-income range, and 40 per cent of benefits in CANAEMPU will accrue to upper-income classes (the last three income brackets).[18]

In this sense, a gross classification of the three principal social security programmes in the country indicates that the Servicio de Seguro Social is pro-poor, whereas the Caja de Empleados Particulares as well as the Caja Nacional de Empeados Públicos y Periodistas are predominantly middle-class oriented. These differences, which are consistent with the nature of the labour groups in each programme, provide an idea of the final use of fiscal support to these institutions.

It is useful now to illustrate briefly the distributive character of programmes financed by social-security plans, but whose services are supplied by other institutions in the public sector.[19] This is the case of transfers made to the public health system, comprised of the Servicio Nacional de Salud and the Servicio Médico Nacional de Empleados (SERMENA), in recompense (partial) for the health services provided to

[16] This alternative base for incidence, which has the advantage of greater disaggregation, was utilised in a previous draft of this paper, A. Foxley, E. Aninat and J. P. Arellano: "What does social security do to incomes?", mimeo CEPLAN, first draft.

[17] Given our sources of information for the family income distribution of pensioners, it was not possible to disaggregate this distribution in terms of the pensioners of each of the cajas.

[18] Benefits included in this comparison are family allowances, indemnisations and unemployment allowances, and other minor benefits.

[19] Given that we are following the consolidated budget presentation of the public sector, health and housing expenditures were analysed apart from social security. See Chapters 3 and 4 of this book.

social-security contributors and their dependants. Also included are transfers to the Public Housing Agency, CORVI, which help finance the construction of housing facilities for workers belonging to the system. In 1969, 21 per cent of the receipts of the Servicio Nacional de Salud came from social-security transfers, some 66 per cent of the receipts of SERMENA came from the cajas and the housing agency CORVI received about 69 per cent of its financing from the social-security system.[20]

A comparison of findings on benefit distribution in the health and housing programmes with the distribution pattern of direct social-security benefits is as shown in Table 42.

TABLE 42

Family income (s.v.a.)	Relative distribution of health and housing benefits directed to social-security contributors (%)	Relative distribution of total direct benefits from social security (%)
I	14.0	14.0
II	31.0	25.9
III	21.2	20.3
IV–V	22.0	19.2
VI–IX	11.2	19.7
Total	100.0	100.0

Therefore, if we were to include the health and housing benefits in the distribution of social-security benefits, the effects would be to strengthen its progressive character, since the share of benefits for low middle-income classes would rise from 65 per cent up to 74 per cent of the total, and this shift would be at the cost of higher-income echelons. This is then another specific illustration of how the system achieves a positive redistributive role on the expenditures side.

The social-security system, however, still shows important inequalities in terms of the inter-institutional distribution of *per capita* benefits. If we use this second perspective for comparisons, some interesting insights

[20]The normal share of finance provided by the social-security system to CORVI is much lower than the 1969 figure.

into this problem appear. Let us discuss these features for the case of pension programmes.

Pension programmes in Chilean social security are the kind of benefit which – in relative terms – correspond more closely to individual "earned rights", or capitalisation schemes. The value of pensions obtained is at least intended to be in line with the value of contributions made in the name of each worker.

In practice, however, the actual relation between individual contributions and pension benefits is tenuous, although there are notorious differentials in the value of pensions allocated by the different programmes given the very distinct income basis of their affiliates. This is explained by the nature of the common fund scheme, which supposes that the contributions of a particular worker are directed not only to the financing of his own pension benefits, but also to cover those of fellow contributors in the programme, as well as to provide other general allowances.

Inequalities in the value of pensions among different programmes must not be explained solely in terms of the different income bases of the members belonging to each social-security institution. There are numerous institutional inequalities which have arisen in the development of Chilean social security, and which correspond to various kinds of privileges acquired over time by specific pressure groups, and which society has accepted explicitly through social legislation by allowing these privileges to regulate the operations of particular social-security régimes.[21]

It is illustrative to compare, for example, the character of retirement pensions for various types of programmes or categories of workers. There are discriminations both in the prerequisites established for retirement by each programme as well as in the computational method utilised for calculating the level of actual pensions. Normally, one can say, both elements appear to be working to the relative advantage of the upper-middle and high-income groups.

The most flagrant example of violation of "horizontal equity" principles was that blue-collar workers were required not only to have reached

[21] Carmelo Mesa-Lago, *op. cit.*, has produced a vivid description of the effects generated by pressure groups over the workings of various Latin American social-security programmes, including Chile.

65 (men) or 55 (women) years of age but also to show a minimum of 800 to 500 weeks of insurance or affiliation to the system. White-collar workers, in contrast, needed but one year of contributions to the system in order to be eligible for retirement benefits. In 1965, for example, 7,693 applications for pensions made by blue-collar workers were rejected by the Servicio de Seguro Social on grounds that they lacked one or other type of prerequisite; about 6,500 of those applications would have perfectly met the prerequisites demanded by the Caja de Empleados Particulares for granting the pensions.

On other grounds, there are instances of discrimination even within subgroups of the insured population of a given institution. We can cite the case of the Caja de Empleados Públicos y Periodistas in the public sector. For a great majority of its affiliates, the basis chosen for calculating the amount of a pension was the average in declared earnings subject to social security the worker had for the last 36 months before retirement; for other groups, it was the average of the 12 last monthly earnings (Empresa Portuaria de Chile), and for still others, it was the last paycheck on the basis of which contributions were paid.

The Chilean social-security system is still plagued with many types of discrimination in this area, distortions which generally have the effect of diminishing the redistributive power the system might have.

The result of all these factors lead to the following differentials in terms of the average level of the retirement pension in each programme (1969).

Retired public servants – on average – obtained a pension whose value was 3.9 times that of a retired blue-collar worker's pension.

The average retired blue-collar workers obtained a pension which would typically satisfy some 43 per cent of the individual annual poverty-line standard (if defined, more or less arbitrarily, as the equivalent of one "minimum income"). Since this is unsatisfactory as a sole source of livelihood, it becomes necessary for such a pensioner to try to engage in part-time employment even at an advanced age.

Finally, the aggregate distribution of the value of pensions per household shows a profile of inequality, according to our findings. The value of pensions per household in an upper-income group (bracket VII) is 4½ times the pension value of a typical household in the poorest group. This is another indicator of the inequalities existing between retired people in different states of "need".

5. CONCLUSIONS

Preceding sections have analysed the incidence features arising from the sources of financing and from the expenditure items of social security. The main findings revealed regressiveness on the contributions side, and progressiveness on the benefits side.

In the case of social security it is not very meaningful to aggregate the effects of contributions and benefits by income classes, since taxes are levied on a specific group in the population whereas benefits are received by another group. Nevertheless it might be useful to have an idea of the net income effects produced by the system throughout the different income classes from the point of view of changes in the welfare of *all* existing households.

When comparing social security with the workings of other programmes in the public budget or with the effects of alternative social insurance and transfer arrangements, it is of interest to have a general idea of the net income distribution effects that occur throughout the existing system. Table 43 summarises the incidence results obtained from sections 1 and 2, and provides the resulting "post-social security" income distribution (in relative terms).

A comparison of columns 2 and 3 in the table shows that it is the first two income classes which obtain absolute net gains from the social-security system as a whole, although these do not appear to be very spectacular.[22]

Other income classes see their income shares unaffected (or slightly diminished) because of the effects of social security, as indicated by the "post-social security" income distribution (column 4).[23]

Taken as a whole, there is no doubt that the Chilean social-security system redistributives incomes in the right direction.

We must still consider whether there are policy alternatives which can improve the redistributive role played by social security, and which may make the system more efficient in terms of the allocation of resources in the economy.

[22] Since the total value of expenditures is somewhat larger than the total value of the social-security receipts we have distributed, absolute net gains do in fact extend up to the fourth income bracket.

[23] The relative distribution presented in column 1 is not exactly "pre-social security" since some of the transfers of the system as well as employee contributions are included in its income base (survey on family incomes).

TABLE 43

Redistributive effects of social security: net incidence

Family income (s.v.a.)	% distribution of pre-social-security incomes[(a)] (1)	% distribution of social-security contributions (2)	% distribution of social-security expenditures (3)	% distribution of post social-security incomes[(b)] (4)
I	7.6	9.4	14.9	8.2
II	20.1	21.9	25.9	20.6
III	18.9	20.0	20.3	18.9
IV	11.2	11.5	11.2	11.2
V	8.7	9.0	8.0	8.0
VI	7.1	7.6	5.6	6.9
VII	8.0	6.6	6.1	7.9
VIII	5.9	4.7	3.2	5.7
IX	12.5	9.3	4.8	12.0
Total	100.0	100.0	100.0	100.0

[(a)] Survey on family incomes.
[(b)] Considers the effects of burdens and benefits from social security.

The most salient finding of our study is the regressive effect of social-security contributions and their negative impact on the standard of living of families located in the poorer echelons. The finance mechanism of social security appeared to wipe out 14 per cent of the gross family incomes of poor families.

The payroll tax had negative effects on employment levels in the economy, as an analysis of its interference with the allocation of resources showed. Different classes of labour markets were affected in distinct ways, but in each the level of employment seems to be lower than what it would otherwise be, were it not for the increase in labour costs due to employer contributions for social security. The non-affected sector experienced negative income effects through the indirect implications of the payroll tax mechanism. All of this generated changes in the primary distribution of earnings at the functional and sectoral levels, which damaged the direct redistributive role played by social security.

The preceding elements indicate that one of the most urgently needed reforms rests on the financing side of the system. The clear advisability of replacing the payroll tax by alternative sources of financing signals one of the policy changes to be undertaken if improvement in both equity and efficiency standards is desired.[24]

The issue is more generally valid if we consider the situation in other Latin American countries. In the case of Venezuela, for example, even though employer contributions represent a lower percentage of the wage bill (11–13 per cent) than in Chile, the positive employment effect arising from the substitution of the payroll tax mechanism could reach 2.1 per cent.[25] For other Latin American countries, where the productive structure is similar and where contributions represent higher percentages of wages and salaries, we could expect even more significant employment effects.

We have already described the changes in the level of employment to be expected in the Chilean situation (between +8 and +25 per cent). The studies estimating such changes have proposed four alternative sources for financing the system.

One postulates that receipts from employer contributions could be adequately recouped through increased profit-tax collections resulting from the abolishment of payroll contributions, united with a convenient set of tax-rate surcharges at the level of the comprehensive personal income tax (Global Complementario).[26]

If the 40 per cent payroll tax is eliminated, it is clear that the value of profits and/or wages would be expanded, therefore allowing for the use of increased income and profits taxation.

A second postulates that a general value added tax could conveniently substitute for employer contributions and be neutral with respect to allocation of resources and labour/capital choices at the production level.[27]

A third study specialised for the agricultural sector, proved that increased real-estate taxes could provide for the social-security financing of rural workers. Such financing today is levied on landlords in the form of payroll contributions.

There are certain differences between the new financing alternatives from the incidence point of view, since they affect different groups or

[24] Because of its relatively minor importance and for other reasons considered previously in the text, employee contributions could remain at present levels.

[25] PREALC, "Acción de los Ministerios de Trabajo", *op. cit.*

[26] E. Aninat, *Nuevas Alternativas para el Sistema de Seguridad Social Chileno.*

[27] PREALC, "Acción de los Ministerios de Trabajo", *op. cit.*

sectors in society. Findings of Chapter 2 indicate that the Global Income Tax (Global Complementario) and real-estate tax alternatives would rank first from the redistributive point of view due to their progressive character.[28] Practical experience with the value added tax in Chile has shown that – in the end – it becomes nothing else but a general tax on consumption, and this has a regressive incidence pattern. The partial forward shifting of the profits tax occurring in Chilean market structure indicates that this alternative would also have its problems.

However, first-best policy alternatives usually suffer from lower degrees of freedom from the political point of view, and are harder to implement.[29] Second- or third-best alternatives – such as the value added tax – might be more feasible from a practical point of view. In this sense, then, it is probable that the most realistic kind of reform would consist in a combination of these new sources of finance.

What is clear is that society at large, workers in general, and poverty groups in particular would definitely gain by the replacement of the payroll tax by any of the alternatives mentioned.

On the benefits side, we found a progressive impact. The two cases of family allowances and pension benefits represent the two poles here.

The redistributive character of family allowances implies that these should be reinforced within a social policy framework which emphasises vertical equity. Also, our analysis indicates that the introduction of a common average allowance for all cajas is positive. Similar social-security transfers should play an important role in elevating the standards of living of poor families.

The identification problem for pensions we described,[30] and other characteristics of the administrative side, seem to support an *a priori* hypothesis that a more decentralised system could prove relatively more "efficient" in the case of pension benefits.[31] This would eventually mean higher-quality services for beneficiaries and pension levels which

[28] N. Villagrán, "Proposición de un Nuevo Sistema de Financiamiento de los Fondos Revisionales . . .".

[29] Empirical estimates for the Global Income Tax alternative showed that for some income brackets nominal tax rates would have to climb to unexpectedly high levels. See E. Aninat, *op. cit.*

[30] We refer here to the disassociation between contributions and benefits; see Section 3.

[31] For example, we would expect a reduction in the administrative costs of the programmes, costs which actually range between 5 and 10 per cent of total receipts.

would correspond more closely to the value of individual forced savings realised.

The issue here is not only the actual level reached by the specific benefit and the quality of service rendered, but the very nature or philosophy of the social-security system itself. Thus, there seems to be an option here between the high redistributive power of a centralised direct transfer system and the relative efficiency of a decentralised scheme.

Up to the present, the Chilean political process has implicitly supported a mixed scheme which is somewhat closer to the first type of arrangement. And our study has proved that its redistributive role has been – on average – positive.

In any case, social-security reform need not be comprehensive or complete. There are numerous instances for improving the character and efficiency of the system without altering its nature. Examples of "small" policy changes are: introduction of readjustment clauses and real interest charges on personal loans distributed by the cajas, reorientation of these to groups or sectors showing the highest urgency of need as indicated by income levels; reorientation of state support in order to supplement the levels of minimum income pensions for blue-collar workers; limitation and even abolition of flagrant discriminations in pension programmes; elimination of the ceilings established on earnings subject to contributions (if contributions continue to exist); regulation of the portfolio of assets maintained by social-security institutions; specialisation of the functions performed by each caja or system, and introduction of a higher degree of supervision and control so as to lower the administrative costs of the system.

Finally, there is the question of coverage and of policies to reach in one way or another needy groups which today are left out of social security.

The non-covered population is composed mainly of self-employed groups (48 per cent of the total), by blue-collar workers (26 per cent), by non-remunerated relatives (14 per cent), and others. The logic of the social-security schemes that were structured for wage and salary earners dictates the exclusion from coverage of those sectors of the labour force which works independently. But at the same time, it is none the less true, that the latter groups have a series of urgent unsatisfied needs.

Non-covered blue-collar workers are most likely workers engaged in occasional jobs or in the rural sector where social legislation is least enforced.

The great problem with the non-covered self-employed is that a vast majority are located in low-productivity activities (craftsmanship, vendors, minifundia, etc.). Their income standards are such that around 65 per cent have family incomes under two minimum-income units (2 s.v.a.). The policy conclusion here, then, is that a programme of benefits independent of the contributions side would have to be designed for this group.

The financing problem is due to the fact that for this class of worker it becomes difficult to shift the contributions burden to other economic agents, such as to customers, as was possible for more typical groups. Demand conditions faced by the self-employed are unstable and precarious, so that it would be quite probable that if contributions were established they would end up lowering the net effective benefit that the programme intended to distribute.

Therefore, the best alternative for financing this new programme would be through general taxation.

Also measures such as opening up existing health facilities to provide services to uncovered groups would clearly render the system more powerful in terms of welfare.

To sum up, the preceding policy alternatives show that there is ample room for improving existing social-security systems without changing their nature. We have also illustrated that decisions about social-security taxes and benefits are closely interrelated with other tax and benefit decisions in the public budget. If a clear understanding of the specific welfare objective and income maintenance role of social security constitutes the guide for action on the benefits side, and if it is recognised that the system should be financed by the best method available at a given time, then we should expect social-security programmes to become more equitable and efficient than they are today.

CHAPTER 6

Net Incidence of Government Expenditures, Taxation and Social Security

Previous chapters measured separately the effect of public expenditure, taxation, and the social-security system on families falling within various income brackets. In this chapter we will bring together the partial findings in order to estimate the net effect of the public budget, and to draw some policy conclusions that will make it possible to increase the redistributive impact of fiscal and social-security policies.

Table 44 summarises the partial results of the expenditures, taxation, and social-security incidence studies, and compares them with the original income distribution.

According to the data in Table 44, budget expenditure shows a progressive effect on income distribution, since the position of the poorer groups improves significantly at the expense of families in the higher-income brackets. Families in the lowest bracket obtain a proportion of expenditure benefits significantly higher than their participation in national income (between 15 per cent and 18 per cent as compared with 7.6 per cent).

The brackets constituting what might be termed the middle groups obtain benefits in almost an equal proportion to their income participation, whereas families within the upper brackets derive benefits from public expenditure in a proportion substantially inferior to their relative incomes.

The tax system, on the contrary, shows an allocation of the tax burden almost proportional to the structure of income distribution by brackets with the exception of the highest bracket, whose contribution to

TABLE 44

Incidence of expenditures, taxes and social security

Family income brackets (minimum salary)[a]	Distribution of families	Original income distribution	Incidence of expenditures[b] Alternatives I	II	Incidence of taxes	Incidence of social security Income	Expenditures
0 – 1	29.8	7.6	15.1	18.1	7.6	9.4	14.9
1 – 2	31.6	20.1	25.7	27.3	18.1	21.9	25.9
2 – 3	17.6	18.9	18.6	18.4	17.3	20.0	20.3
3 – 4	7.4	11.2	10.3	9.8	9.6	11.5	11.2
4 – 5	4.5	8.7	7.2	6.6	7.7	9.0	8.0
5 – 6	2.9	7.1	5.4	4.8	7.0	7.0	5.6
6 – 8	2.7	8.0	6.1	5.4	7.8	6.6	6.1
8 – 10	1.5	5.9	3.9	3.3	6.5	4.7	3.2
10 or more	2.0	12.5	7.7	6.3	18.2	9.3	4.8
Total	100.0	100.0	100.0	100.0	100.0	100.0	100.0

[a] Incomes were converted to US dollars using the exchange rate in effect at the time of the survey (1969). The minimum salary was equivalent to US $670 that year.

[b] In alternative I, general expenditures were assigned according to the original distribution of family income; in alternative II this was done according to the distribution of the number of families per bracket.

financing state expenditures appears to be more than proportionate. The findings for this bracket, however, should be interpreted with utmost care. Problems of underestimation of this group's income figures, as yielded by the Family Income Survey, have been discussed in a previous chapter. In the higher brackets, composition of income is more varied, thus offering greater possibilities of undervaluation.[1]

Correction of the income data for the highest bracket against the National Accounts statistics indicate that this group's participation in national income might approach one-fourth of the total family income in the economy.[2] If this latter figure were a better estimate of the real

[1] Components such as interest, dividends, capital gains and profits are more important in the higher-income brackets and make the higher incomes more difficult to check than incomes from labour. To the extent that the former are mis-stated in the survey, incomes appear undervalued. There is assorted evidence that this is actually so in the case of the survey used for this study. See E. Aninat, "Ajuste de los ingresos familiares de la encuesta INE a los datos de ingresos de cuentas nacionales", CEPLAN, 1975.

[2] *Ibid.*

position of the higher-income groups, their tax burden would actually be less than proportional to their income participation.

Nevertheless, if we ignore for the time being the top brackets' income estimates, the incidence of the tax system on the remaining groups is nearly proportional.

With regard to social security, its net effect is positive for the poorer groups, relatively neutral for brackets between US $1,340 and US $4,020 and slightly negative for families whose incomes are above US $4,020.

Table 45 shows income distribution after incorporating the total government effect, that is, the combined effect of public expenditure, taxation, and social security for each income bracket.

Alternative I allocates general government expenditures in line with original income distribution. Under alternative II, these general expenditures are allocated according to the number of families per brackets.

It can readily be seen that with either alternative, state action entailed a significant improvement in income distribution. This is particularly true with regard to the increase in the share accruing to the poorer families within the first two brackets and to the decrease in the share of total income enjoyed by the wealthier families.

In order to facilitate international comparisons, the distributions before and after government programmes have been estimated according

TABLE 45

Income distribution after government effect

Family incomes (min. salary)	Family distribution	Original income distribution	Distribution considering the effect of the government	
			Alternative I	Alternative II
0 – 1	29.8	7.6	10.5	11.8
1 – 2	31.6	20.1	22.6	23.2
2 – 3	17.6	18.9	18.9	18.8
3 – 4	7.4	11.2	11.1	10.9
4 – 5	4.5	8.7	8.2	8.0
5 – 6	2.9	7.1	6.4	6.1
6 – 8	2.7	8.0	7.4	7.1
8 – 10	1.5	5.9	5.1	4.8
10 or more	2.0	12.5	9.8	9.3
Total	100.0	100.0	100.0	100.0

TABLE 46

Income distribution before and after government effect
(Percents of total income)

Deciles	Original family income	After government intervention	
		Alternative I	Alternative II
1°	2.4	2.5	2.7
2°	2.6	3.5	4.3
3°	3.5	5.0	5.5
4°	5.5	6.0	6.5
5°	6.0	7.0	7.0
6°	7.0	8.0	8.0
7°	9.0	9.0	9.0
8°	11.5	12.0	12.0
9°	17.5	16.0	16.0
10°	35.0	31.0	29.0
Total	100.0	100.0	100.0

to a classification by deciles. Table 46 shows the income shares of the different deciles in the population.

The foregoing data should constitute a basic element to evaluate government performance during the period under review. Normally, this performance has been examined only according to results in terms of economic growth. Nevertheless, if it is acknowledged that national objectives are – or should be – those of bringing about simultaneously both economic development and greater equality among the social groups, then the efficiency of government programmes should of necessity be measured in accordance with results achieved in both objectives.

In this study, aggregate findings show without doubt that state action was relatively successful, at least from the point of view of a redistribution objective.

It is worthwhile to analyse the effect on social groups of the government budget.

Effects on social groups

The results of our study can be interpreted as to their effect on certain social groups or strata, instead of on income brackets.

Raczynski has stratified population using an indicator that combines income, educational and occupational situations.[3]

By applying this indicator to the data in the present study, three strata are identified: a bottom group, comprising 60 per cent of the families, whose incomes are below US $1,340; a middle stratum representing 33 per cent of the households, with incomes fluctuating between US $1,340 and $4,020; and a top stratum, with 7 per cent of the families, whose incomes are above US $4,020.

The bottom stratum includes 44 per cent of agricultural, construction and industrial blue-collar workers and 30 per cent of self-employed workers. White-collar workers represent only 11 per cent of the stratum.

The middle group is composed primarily of white-collar workers (42 per cent), half of which are office employees. This middle group also includes skilled blue-collar workers, who constitute 25 per cent of the total.

The top stratum is made up of one-third employers, almost another third professionals and technicians, and the balance of rentiers and high-salary employees in executive positions.

How did the fiscal policy and the social-security system affect the relative positions of these strata? Table 47 shows the distribution of public expenditure benefits and that of the tax and social-security contributions by social groups.

The lower group appears to have been clearly benefited in net terms. For each 100 pesos spent by the State, families in this stratum received an average of 42.8 pesos. Yet of 100 pesos of domestic taxes collected by the State only 27.8 per cent is contributed by the low stratum.

[3] This indicator is based on the socio-economic position of the occupations, which combines educational and income criteria. Operationally, the index represents the arithmetical average of (i) the percentage of the economically active population in each occupational group that has completed more than 10 years of education; and (ii) the percentage of the economically active population in each occupational group earning over minimum salary. The boundaries between strata are determined through consideration of the disruptions or discontinuities in the distribution of the index and its two components (1967). See D. Raczynski *et al.*, "La estratificación ocupacional en Chile", in *Los Actores de la realidad chilena,* Santiago, Chile, Editorial del Pacífico, 1974. O. Duncan uses a similar methodology in the case of the United States. See: "A socioeconomic index for all occupations", in A. S. Reiss (ed.), *Occupations and Social Status,* The Free Press, Glencoe, New York, 1961. Also D. S. Bogne, *Principles of Demography,* J. Wiley & Sons Inc., New York, 1969.

TABLE 47

Percentages of public expenditure benefits by social groups

	Strata		
	Low	Middle	High
Total public expenditures (social + productive)	42.8	40.9	16.3
Taxes and contributions	27.8	44.1	28.1
Original income distribution	27.7	45.9	26.4
Family distribution	60.0	33.0	7.0

The middle brackets, in conjunction, obtained about 41 per cent of public expenditures, while they contributed a slightly higher percentage (44 per cent) to the financing of state activity. The middle group is basically composed of skilled workers and middle-income white-collar workers and constitutes nearly one-third of the total number of families. Its original share in income was about 45 per cent, a figure which corresponds closely to the aforementioned percentages of receipts and contributions.

It should be noted that, while a substantial percentage of public expenditure seemed to be oriented to satisfying the needs of the middle groups (a fact that is closely related to the very evolution and historical development of the state apparatus), it is no less true that the middle sectors financed their own share of those benefits, Table 47 confirms the already observed trend with respect to the net flow of resources from the higher-income groups. This stratum appears to have suffered a relative loss, whose exact magnitude cannot be defined in view of the problem of income underestimation mentioned above.

At this point, it should be pointed out that the redistributive process favouring the poorer groups that we have described was not only supported by income transfers from the rich but also by the inflow of external resources during the period, as a result of high copper prices and important foreign-aid programmes.

Financing through inflationary fiscal deficits was another way the redistributive process was partially financed. Inflation may have operated as a tax payable by the various social groups. The inflation rate during the period remained around 30 per cent per annum. It is probable that inflationary financing functioned as a regressive tax, since its effects most likely were heavier on those groups least able to defend themselves against inflation. Such groups correspond precisely to the poorer sectors of the population.[4]

Table 48 summarises the structure, orientation (percentage distribution) and the distributive sign characterising each of the income and public expenditure items, with respect to the three social groups or strata as already defined.

With regard to the financing of benefits provided at public expense, Table 48 shows that indeed the State obtained from the external sector a considerable margin for financing a redistributive process. The taxation of foreign-owned copper companies captured resources that allowed the financing of 11 per cent of the total of public expenditures. In this way the State was able to provide a net benefit to each Chilean family which amounted to 5 per cent of family income without the necessity of burdening one group in order to benefit another. If foreign loans are added to this,[5] the amount of resources obtained from abroad is raised to 18 per cent of family incomes.

The redistributive margin available through this channel was substantial. Resources obtained through taxation of foreign property alone were equivalent to about 56 per cent of the net benefits[6] received by families with incomes under US $1,340. If funds obtained through foreign credits were added, the amount of total foreign resources in the public sector would be equivalent to 90 per cent of the net benefits received by the poorer group.[7]

[4] There are two factors not considered in this study which would have to be explored in order to obtain more precise estimates of benefits. First, it is necessary to determine the inflationary impact generated by a given amount of indebtedness through the monetary system, and second, to determine the incidence of the inflation tax. Since these factors have not been taken into account, the net benefits should be considered to be overestimated.

[5] Strictly speaking, foreign indebtedness constitutes a redistribution of income from one period of time to another. Nevertheless there is a subsidy from abroad to the extent the State obtains favourable repayment conditions.

[6] The concept of the net benefits is defined as the amount of benefits received less financial contributions by the beneficiaries.

[7] The figures are by way of illustration. The results vary according to the criteria used to distribute general expenditures. The estimate given here is based on alternative I (i.e. distribution of general expenditures according to the pattern of family income). The use of alternative II increases the benefits received by the poor sector and thus reduces the

TABLE 48

The public sector budget: its structure, destination and distributive sign[a]
(Millions of escudos: percentages)

	Public revenues				Public expenditure					
								Distributive effect compared to		
Social strata (1)	Distributive effect as compared to family incomes (2)	Amount involved (000 escudos) (3)	%	Destination of tax receipts by strata (4)	Amount (5)	%	Destination of expenditure by strata (6)	Distribution of family income (7)	Numerical distribution of families (8)	Social strata (9)
1. *Direct taxes*		2,817.5	13		4,462.9	21	1. *Productive expenditures*			
Low	(+)			13.0			33.4	(+)	(−)	Low
Middle	(+)			37.0			40.8	(−)	(+)	Middle
High	(−)			49.0			25.8	(0)	(+)	High
2. *Indirect taxes*		5,728.0	27		2,149.2		1.1. *Transportation*			
Low	(−)			31.8			24.6	(−)	(−)	Low
Middle	(+)			43.9			43.9	(0)	(+)	Middle
High	(+)			24.9			31.5	(+)	(+)	High
3. *Customs duties*		1,451	7		351		1.2. *Industry*			
Low	(0)			27.7			23.1	(−)	(−)	Low
Middle	(0)			45.9			43.9	(0)	(+)	Middle
High	(0)			26.4			31.5	(+)	(+)	High
4. *Social-security taxes*		5,184.3	24		1,013.9	5	1.3. *Agriculture*			
Low	(−)			31.3			50.1	(+)	(−)	Low
Middle	(0)			48.1			33.6	(−)	(0)	middle
High	(+)			20.6			16.3	(−)	(+)	High
5. *Other receipts*[b]		1,314.5	6		355.5	2	1.4. *Mining and energy*			
Low	(0)			27.8			35.8	(+)	(−)	Low
Middle	(0)			44.1			44.4	(0)	(+)	Middle
High	(−)			28.1			19.8	(−)	(+)	High
6. *Subtotal 1*		16,495.8	77		944.3		1.5. *Other productive expenditures*			

Low	(0)			27.8	11,342.8	54	2. *Social expenditures*			
Middle	(0)			44.1			46.5	(+)	(−)	Low
High	(−)			28.1			40.8	(−)	(+)	Middle
							12.7	(−)	(+)	High
7. *Internal borrowing*		1,069.5	5		1,750.7	8	2.1. *Health*			
8. *Resources obtained from abroad*		3,747.8	18				68.3	(+)	(+)	Low
Copper		2,015.9	10				27.3	(−)	(−)	Middle
Surcharges		310.0	2				2.2	(−)	(−)	High
Foreign loans		1,421.9	6				2.2. *Education*			
							44.4	(+)	(−)	Low
							39.0	(−)	(+)	Middle
							16.6	(−)	(+)	High
					1,486.1	7	2.3. *Housing*			
							44.2	(+)	(−)	Low
							45.3	(0)	(+)	Middle
							8.5	(−)	(+)	High
					537.5	25	2.4. *Social security*			
							40.8	(+)	(−)	Low
							45.1	(0)	(+)	Middle
							14.1	(−)	(+)	High
					88.6		2.5. *Other social expenditures*			
					5,307.3	25	3. *General expenditures*			
Total		21,313.0	100		21,313.0	100				

(a) Symbols: (+) benefits higher than initial income share (or higher than proportion of families in the stratum); burdens lower than income share; (−) benefits lower than the group's share of income or population; burdens higher than initial income share; (0) benefits and burdens similar to group's share of income or population (neutral effect of the programme).

In comparing the distribution of benefits and burdens with income (columns 2 and 7) an effect was considered to be neutral when it fell within the following range of the initial income or population:

	Income		Families	
	Relative share	"O" range	Relative share	"O" range
Low group	27.7	26.3–29.1	60	57.0–63.0
Middle group	45.9	43.6–48.2	33	31.5–34.7
High group	26.4	25.1–27.7	7	6.7–7.4

(b) More than half of these receipts are tax revenues. For that reason we assumed distribution was the same as that of the other receipts.

Source: The incidence estimates for each item were obtained from previous chapters.

Another source of resources that benefit the poor was the income extracted from the well-to-do sectors. Finally, the remainder of net benefits to the lower stratum was obtained through internal borrowing. At least part of this must have resulted in an increase in inflationary pressures and in this way constituted a burden for various social groups.

Summing up, the State extracted from the foreign companies a good part of the resources devoted to benefit the poorest stratum and thereby alleviated the burden that would have been borne by the families of the highest stratum. Moreover, because of the political and economic difficulties to increasing the contributions of the richer families by means of taxes and social security, internal indebtedness was resorted to, with its resulting inflationary effect whose distributive impact is unknown.

Another aspect that deserves attention in Table 48 is the comparison between the distribution of revenues and expenditures by social strata and the relative income share by strata. This allows us to distinguish whether the programmes and levies are progressive (+), regressive (−) or neutral (0).

It is important to recall with regard to the effects of the budget on low-income groups that these groups were the principal beneficiaries of the budget. Social expenditures were the main source of benefits for these sectors. The effect of programmes in the productive sphere was mixed. Public transportation and industry expenditures had a regressive effect on income distribution whereas the programmes oriented to agriculture showed a strong redistributive effect. This is the result both of the agrarian reform process and of programmes of assistance to small farmers.

From the point of view of government revenues, the effect of indirect taxes and social security on the income of the poor was negative. All other levels had a neutral or progressive effect.

With regard to the middle-income group, the disaggregated data of Table 49 confirm what was observed at the aggregate level. The

importance of external financing to 46 and 74 per cent, depending on whether foreign borrowing is included in the estimate.

Some public programmes maintain a close relationship with the proportion of families in each social group since by their nature they are intended to serve equally the needs of the entire population. Social expenditures such as education and health are examples of programmes that ought to provide similar benefits *per capita*. That is why in many cases it is useful to compare the distribution of benefits with the proportion of families in each stratum (column 8, Table 48).

government drew resources preferentially from the middle strata of the population. (At least 46 per cent of the levies were borne by families of the middle group.) On the other hand, social expenditures – which represent 54 per cent of total public expenditure – were oriented in such a manner that nearly 41 per cent of them benefited the middle groups. Although this share is somewhat less than proportional to this group's relative income, it exceeds the corresponding proportion of the population included in the middle stratum. In other words, as compared with the family distribution by strata, public expenditures in housing, education, social security and other similar items were directed towards the middle groups in significant proportions. These results are consistent with the prevailing idea that the development of the Chilean public sector has been closely linked to the emergence and evolution of the middle classes.

Social demands generating mainly in sectors of skilled workers and public service employees were brought to bear on Chile's political and economical system for several decades. These groups increasingly pressured the government in order to augment their participation in the benefits of government programmes. This is at least a partial explanation for the quantitative importance (40 per cent) of public expenditure programmes oriented toward these groups. On the other hand, however, in view of the chronic scarcity of budgetary resources in a country with high social demands and rising overall public expenditure levels, the government appears to have concurrently chosen to finance an important part of its programmes on the basis of the middle sectors' own taxation effort.

From this point of view, one could not say that the middle groups benefit through the budget at the cost of other groups in the population. Moreover, neither do they receive a significant proportion of the resources obtained from abroad.[8]

In the case of the small group of families in the higher stratum their relative income share seems to have decreased by the effect of the public budget, although the benefits per family were higher for this stratum than for the other social groups (see column 8 once again). Programmes in the

[8] This explains why the middle groups reduce their relative share of income even though they receive positive net benefits.

productive sector were neutral with respect to this group except the transportation which improve their share of national income.

To sum up, from the point of view of income distribution, there is no doubt that fiscal and social-security policies managed to redistribute in favour of the poorer families.

The following four elements of Chile's fiscal policy in 1969 were not redistributive: (i) the negative incidence of indirect levies and social security contributions; (ii) the high rate of tax evasion; (iii) the relatively high percentage of the public budget that is devoted to general expenses (administration, defence and the like); (iv) the regressive character of some public programmes in the productive area, such as transportation expenditures.

We will discuss in sections to come some of the elements which explain these obstacles, as well as fiscal policy measures that would contribute to improve the redistributive quality of public programmes.

On the taxation side the Chilean government was able during the 1960s to implement a body of adequate direct taxes which stand out as highly progressive and of broad coverage, such as the global income tax. However, it has been unable to overcome its dependence on indirect levies as a revenue source. Such indirect levies yield more than double the proceeds from direct taxation. The high rates of indirect taxes on mass consumer goods bear heavily on lower strata. This indicates a clear priority target for fiscal reform.

The incidence of government general expenditures was at best neutral. The magnitude of general expenditures in Chile was comparable with the total volume of funds handled by social-security programmes. Since general expenditures cannot be reckoned as direct inputs in the process of growth of productive activity, it must be clear that the more effective the limits on its expansion are, the more will public funds be available for redistribution and development goals.

Government action in the field of industry, agriculture, transportation, communications, mining and energy, that is, the so-called expenditures on economic services, had reached a substantial proportion in the case of Chile. An amount similar to the total public expenditures in health and education was committed to programmes in support of private productive activity. Agencies such as CORFO (Corporation for Promotion of Production), LAN (National Airlines), ENAMI (National

Mining Enterprise) and others performed functions required by the private sector and which, furthermore, have been historically demanded by the latter. Although many of these productive expenditures bear a regressive sign and ultimately had a negative effect on the State's redistribution action, nevertheless their purpose was in line with the objective of maximising economic growth. Therefore, this is an area where there seemed to be a trade off between growth and redistribution objectives, at least in a static sense.

Finally, our study has shown that, in spite of the progressive character of public programmes, benefits *per capita* were still higher for high-income groups.

A comparison of the previous results with studies for other countries suggest that the Chilean budgetary process included programmes of wider coverage than those observed in comparable countries. Also, public programmes showed a stronger redistributive character than in other Latin American countries.

To illustrate the above, it could be pointed out that in Chile the poorest 60 per cent of the population received 43 per cent of benefits derived from social and productive expenditures, as compared to only 37 per cent in Colombia and slightly more than 24 per cent in Ecuador.[9]

Furthermore, in Chile the State seemed to be more decidedly oriented toward the middle sectors than was the case in Colombia.[10]

In brief, all these elements should be taken into account when evaluating the role of the State in the process of increasing social welfare in Chile.

Suggested policies to augment the redistributive effects of public expenditures

The net incidence findings analysed above provide an appropriate starting-point to summarise several lines of action that, from an

[9]See Miguel Urrutia and Clara Sandoval, "Política fiscal y distribución del ingreso en Colombia", in A. Foxley (ed.), *Distribución del ingreso,* Mexico, 1974, and PREALC, *Situación y perspectivas del empleo en Ecuador,* 1976.

[10]In Chile, 33 per cent of the population within the middle stratum appropriates 41 per cent of public expenditures, whereas in Colombia, 30 per cent of the population with middle income appropriates 35 per cent of public expenditures.

economic policy point of view, would allow the redistributive aspects of fiscal instruments and of the social-security system to be accentuated.

Obviously, no one should be so naîve as to think that the redistributive margin of public policies have only been narrowed by deficiencies of implementation. Doubtless, this has been an important factor, but another key element has been the scarcity of fresh resources for redistribution. This factor is a function both of the economic growth rate and of the power of the higher-income groups and their capacity to exert pressure on the State in opposing a more accelerated redistribution process.

However, we will abstract from political requisites for redistribution in our discussion in this section. These factors which have played a fundamental role in the Chilean scene in the past 20 years deserve a fully fledged study on their own. Let us at least stress here that progress toward a more egalitarian state action undoubtedly assumes that the groups to be benefited (poor and middle groups) at least are not excluded from active and permanent participation in government decision-making. For this participation to be effective, the lower- and middle-income groups must hold an important quota of political power of their own.

Having stated this qualification, it is now possible to point out the direction which fiscal policy should take if the redistributive objective is to have high priority for the community as a whole. Here we will comment on policies tending to reorient public expenditures.

An important initial point is that if the overall level of expenditures can be raised without undue inflationary effects, the fresh expenditures could at least theoretically be oriented predominantly toward the low and middle groups. Conversely, if expenditure expansion takes place through inflationary financing, the originally projected direction and magnitude of the redistributive impact could be significantly altered. The possible effect of fresh expenditures on the lower-income groups could be offset by the probable regressiveness of the inflation tax. If, instead, fresh expenditures are financed through a greater tax effort or by means of a compulsory savings scheme for the higher-income groups, or by recurring to external resources obtained through taxation levied on foreign enterprises or foreign aid, the redistributive process could have a more selective and positive effect on the middle- and low-income strata.

Once the overall level of expenditures has been defined, the basic problems to be taken up would be the following: first, how to reallocate public expenditure among sectors and within a certain sector, shifting the relative emphasis of the many programmes administered by various public agencies; and secondly, how to increase the selectivity of such programmes, diminishing the leakage of benefits to high-income groups.

It is not easy to set guidelines for the reallocation of expenditures among areas of activity. For example, does the national budget show excessive expenditures in education, or housing, or health, or industry, or mining?

International patterns are of no help on this point. Comparative studies among countries show no uniformity with regard to the proportion of expenditures that the respective countries earmark for different sectors.

If the experience of other countries is not particularly useful as a guideline to define an optimum expenditure pattern by sectors, another one could be that of allocating expenditures according to the magnitude of the relative deficits of the poorer groups in satisfying their needs for food, health, housing and job-training. Studies under way with regard to the Chilean case, take this approach.[11] The results of these studies were not available at the time of writing this chapter, however.

As has been observed, the two important components of public expenditures are those devoted to the productive sectors and those directed to the social sectors. Redistributive action in the productive sphere should make increases in productivity of the poorer groups and increases in employment opportunities for the unemployed and the underemployed the two main objectives. Action within this field should be oriented towards training programmes for the unskilled labour force and towards providing small enterprises and marginal producers with scarce complementary inputs, to which they do not have access under normal market conditions.

The redistributive objectives in the social sectors, on the other hand, should aim at supplementing the more important welfare and consumption deficiencies of the poorer groups, with direct reference to their basic needs.

As was noted in the chapter on public expenditures, the Chilean government carried out a vigorous action in both fields in the late sixties.

[11] R. Cortázar, "Pobreza y necesidades básicas", mimeo, CIEPLAN, 1976.

The programmes in the productive sectors were principally aimed at promotion of economic growth. Indeed, practically half of the outlays were for capital expenditures. Only a minor part of these investments were allocated with the goal of increasing the stock of physical capital of small producers and independent workers.

Of the latter, the most important programmes were carried out in the agricultural sector. Lines of credit and technical assistance programmes were made available to peasants in the reformed sector, and other resources – although in lesser amounts – were channelled to smallholders who were left out of the agrarian reform process. In the industrial and copper-mining sectors the small producers competed with medium-sized enterprises for the rather scarce public resources available for programmes in these sectors.[12]

The bulk of public investment in the productive sectors was directed to modern, private and public enterprises and to public works construction (communications, irrigation and energy infrastructure, etc.). Because of the nature of the techniques and scale of production and the kinds of goods produced, the distributive impact of these programmes was neutral or regressive.

This was reinforced by the preferential availability of subsidised credit to large producers and the existence of numerous tax shelters of a sectoral and regional nature, most of which benefit also large producers.

It appears obvious that an increase in the efficiency of the redistributive programmes in the productive sectors should contemplate the elimination of indiscriminate and unchecked credit subsidies in the form of low interest rates. Interest rates should reflect the opportunity cost of capital and should be paid by all producers. Subsidies for small producers would be best made in the form of direct transfers and explicit price subsidies for some key inputs in the productive process (fertilizers, for instance) or in the form of price supports for the final product. The latter is particularly important for those small producers facing very unstable prices for their product.[13] On the other hand, when a subsidised credit policy is warranted, credit should be directed exclusively to the

[12] See the chapter on public expenditure. The four programmes aimed to increase physical capital of small producers.

[13] For instance, small copper-mining operations.

small-producers sector and even so, should not be maintained indefinitely.

Part of the leakage observed in programmes in productive sectors was in the form of the government-financing contributions to offset operational deficits of public enterprises. This policy may have been justified in specific cases, but in no instance as a general rule. The trend should be toward setting up efficiency norms for state agencies that would require them to pay for the actual cost of capital and deprive them of taking advantages of special exemptions (viz. import exemptions), except in very special cases. The reduced fiscal contributions to public agencies would thus release funds that could be devoted to give direct support to low-income producers.

If it is desired that capital expenditures that increase the assets of modern enterprises and create basic infrastructure have the effect of expanding productive capacity without worsening income distribution, the evaluation of such public investment projects must contain explicit reference to the distributive effects they will produce. In this way, the decision to construct an irrigation system or a highway would take into consideration not only the productivity increases generated by these investments but also identify which strata of producers will benefit from these increases.[14]

As shown in a previous chapter, expenditures in social programmes are more redistributive in nature. This greater degree of progressivity is not only observed in Chile but also in the majority of countries for which incidence studies have been made. In the Latin American context, Chile was in the vanguard in the implementation of such programmes. For a period of 50 years, with few interruptions, the State continually created new social programmes and increased their coverage. This trend is reflected in the level of resources expended in social programmes and in the relatively favourable indicators of living standards. Table 49 shows data concerning access to the educational system, availability of housing infrastructure, health conditions and the coverage of the social-security system.

[14] For a methodology usable in these evaluations, see B. Weisbrod, ''Income redistribution effects and benefit-cost analysis'', in Samuel B. Chase (ed.), *Problems in Public Expenditure Analysis,* Brookings, 1968; and UNIDO, *Guidelines for Project Evaluation,* United Nations, New York, 1972.

TABLE 49

Latin America: social indicators

Country	Primary school enrolment as percentage of population 7–13 years of age	Infant mortality in children 1–4 years (per 1,000 inhabitants)	Availability of potable water (percentage of total population)	Elimination of sewage in urban zones (percentage of total population)	Social security (percentage of economically active population paying into systems that cover the principal risks)
Argentina	95.0[a]	2.7	56	32	67.6
Bolivia	84.6	27.6	24	19	8.4
Brazil	76.2	15.0	52	30	31.4
Colombia	62.7	11.7	61	67	14.4
Costa Rica	101.6	4.0	78	24	37.4
Cuba	103.8	1.2	74	38	–
Chile	96.9[b]	3.3	66	36	67.5
Ecuador	86.7	16.6	34	47	16.1
El Salvador	76.1	14.5	43	56	10.2
Guatemala	49.9	30.0	38	45	29.4
Haiti	31.0	33.0	10	8	1.0
Honduras	76.6	20.0	36	54	4.8
Mexico	94.4	10.6	57	50	20.9
Nicaragua	74.0	18.4	50	42	14.9
Panama	93.5	8.0	74	65	34.3
Paraguay	92.6	6.9	16	14	9.6
Peru	104.1	7.9	39	55	27.8
Dominican Republic	89.3	7.9	38	16	9.7
Uruguay	95.8	1.7	77	52	–
Venezuela	83.4	4.9	80	42	22.9

[a] 6–13 years of age.
[b] 6–14 years of age.
Source: ECLA, *Economic Survey of Latin America,* 1973.

Despite the relatively privileged situation enjoyed by Chile in comparison with other countries of the region, vast sectors of the population suffered and obviously still suffer from unsatisfied basic needs. For state action to fulfil the goal of giving priority attention to these families, its pattern of expenditure must undergo certain modifications and the nature of its social programmes must be adapted.

Our analysis of incidence of social programmes provides certain criteria that can be used as a guideline for improving policy design.

First, given resource scarcity, social programmes cannot attempt to provide free social goods to all of the population. The programmes should, to the greatest possible extent, limit beneficiaries to those households in which lack of economic means prevents the satisfaction of basic needs. This criterion is intended to counteract two common tendencies in the design of social programmes: the formulation of goals out of proportion to the availability of budgetary resources[15] and the belief that equality of opportunity means equal benefits for the entire population.[16]

In the case of programmes such as health and education, it would probably be sufficient to allocate a level of resources similar to those spent in the year of this study (1969) in order to achieve minimum consumption levels for the poor.[17] In programmes such as nutrition, the achievement of the proposed goal would require the destination of substantially increased resources.

Whichever is the case, it is necessary to identify the social groups that are to benefit from the public resources. This identification should be carried out using categories that are relevant and useful in an operational sense. In the case of medical-care programmes, for example, the need to reallocate resources towards the rural area and, in the cities, to workers not covered by the social-security system must again be emphasised.

Likewise, the price and subsidies policies for basic goods and services provided by the State should be modified. Subsidies should be channelled to the demand side (in this case families with unsatisfied basic needs) rather than to the supply side (i.e. to producers and intermediaries) in order to assure greater selectivity and less leakage. A system of discriminatory pricing might also be useful to graduate the subsidy according to the degree of need.

The quality and kind of services offered is a third important factor to be considered. Health programmes should stress preventive medicine and out-patient care; education programmes should be oriented to pre-school education, rural primary education and middle-level technical training.

[15] Examples of this tendency are the high standards set for some kinds of public housing, the excessive specialisation of certain medical programmes, and the undue over-expansion of free university education.

[16] For example, the free supply of milk to all mothers and children irrespective of income, the universality of family allotments, etc.

[17] See estimates in the chapter on public expenditure.

Notable advances can be made in the design of the programmes, if due consideration is given to the specific nature of consumption deficiencies of the poor, to their cultural patterns and to their consumption habits. Effective community participation can be of great help to orient the programmes in this direction.

The foregoing suggestions are made on the assumption that the public sector is endowed with certain flexibility to revise its programmes and improve their efficiency. However, the system's inelasticity in the allocation of expenditures for the implementation of programmes cannot be ignored. These hindrances, an outgrowth of ingrained bureaucratic habits, cause the system to be sluggish and lacking in dynamism.

Another case of inelasticity in reallocating expenditures, eliminating some programmes and creating others, is the existence of vested interests thriving in the shadow of existing programmes. Beneficiary groups pressure for the perpetuation of such programmes, regardless of their priority, advisability or efficiency. Pressure for fresh programmes does not always take the direction indicated by redistributive goals. These are obstacles which must be taken into account. The task of overcoming them has ramifications not only on the technical and administrative level but it also has clear political implications in terms of the need to organise the new target groups in support of the government's redistributive effort.

Revision of the tax system

Another way to improve net benefits of the public budget in favour of the low and low-middle strata is that of increasing the progressiveness of the tax system.

A previous chapter showed that tax incidence in Chile was practically proportional by the end of the sixties. This proportionality was explained by the combination of progressiveness of direct taxes – families within the first income strata paid only 1.5 per cent of their family income, while those in the highest income group paid 15.5 per cent and regressiveness in indirect taxes. The indirect tax payment from the first stratum reached 17 per cent of their income, it meant 11 per cent of family incomes in the upper stratum.

On the other hand, international comparisons on total tax burden, discussed in the chapter on taxation, show that in the Chilean case the total tax burden is not low. Hence the revisions that might be suggested should be aimed at sensitive nerve centres in the tax system that enable the system's redistributive efficiency to be improved, without substantially increasing the total tax burden.

The questions that will be taken up here involve changes in indirect taxes, property taxes, tax exemptions and shelters and, finally, in measures to combat tax evasion.

Indirect taxes

The relative importance of indirect taxes with respect to total taxation has been constantly increasing in Chile. The proportion was 43.3 per cent in 1960, and climbed to 47 per cent in 1970 and to 60 per cent in 1973.

On the other hand, international comparisons show that in countries with *per capita* incomes ranging from \$500 to \$850 (1968) there is a negative correlation between collection rates for indirect taxes and *per capita* gross national product. The data for Chile not only reverse this correlation, but also contradict what would be expected of a normal indirect tax level as a whole. As can be observed in Table 50, which summarises these comparisons, only Argentina and Uruguay show a higher ratio of indirect taxes to total taxation. As a point of comparison, it can be added that in industrialised countries such as Japan, Sweden and the United States, the proportion of indirect taxes to total taxes lies between 20 and 30 per cent.

The growing trend in indirect taxes is related to the rapid expansion in public expenditures that has taken place during recent decades in Chile, as a response to the increasing social demands posed by the middle- and low-income groups. Financing of the high level of expenditures was often accomplished, using the easy expedient of inflationary financing or raising various indirect taxes, particularly the sales tax.[18] Summing up, the greater redistributive selectivity on the expenditures side was not accompanied by an equal concern for the distributive effects of tax

[18] For instance, the general sales tax rate went up from 6 per cent in 1965 to 7 per cent in 1967, to 8 per cent in 1968 and to an all-time high of 20 per cent in the value added tax rate imposed in 1975.

TABLE 50
Composition of tax revenues in several countries

Countries with GNP between $501 and $850	Estimated *per capita* GNP 1968	Percentage of total tax revenues deriving from: Indirect taxes	Customs duties	Selective taxes	Selective & various indirect taxes	Sales tax
Chile	510	(60)	(11.5)	(7)	11	(27)
South Africa	550	38	15	21	23	0
Singapore	570	65	36	24	29	0
Uruguay	570	83	–	–	–	–
Trinidad Tobago	630	51	29	13	22	0
Spain	640	45	14	13	13	18
Greece	660	35	10	17	19	7
Argentina	780	65	21	20	26	19
Venezuela	850	15	6	8	9	0
Average		50	18	15	20	9 (19)

Source: DUE and OECD (1968); Figures in parentheses are our own estimates of the Consolidated Balance. Figures for Greece are stated in 1965 dollars and those for Argentina in 1966 dollars.

increases. The question of who would ultimately bear the burden was not a predominant concern; the main criterion seems to have been the political and administrative expediency in imposing certain kinds of taxes *vis-à-vis* others.

The foregoing analysis undoubtedly points to one of the key areas of tax reform, and this is how to diminish the regressive characteristics of indirect taxation. Two routes are feasible and complementary to this end; one, reduction of rates bearing on mass consumption goods, such as food staples, home fuels, etc. At the same time, the rates applied to goods consumed preferentially by the higher income brackets, such as gasoline, car sales, bank interest, service taxes, and other, should be raised. A third way of diminishing the regressiveness of these taxes would be to extend the tax coverage to infrastructure and certain durable goods, the demand for which tends to be concentrated in the high-income strata. What we have in mind are the British type of "usercharge taxes", such as the "road tax" and the like.

Property taxes

A second goal for tax reform should concentrate on property taxation. Although property is much more concentrated than income, it was subject to very low tax rates in the period under study. Table 51 shows the pattern of property distribution by social groups in Chile, as registered in property tax forms filed with the Internal Revenue Service. The data have been made compatible with the income brackets in the Family Income National Survey. It can be observed that according to the Revenue

TABLE 51

Property distribution

Social class	Proportion of families in each stratum (%)	Distribution of family income (%)	Relative distribution of net property valuation (%)
Low	60	27.7	10.8
Middle	33	45.9	35.7
High	7	26.4	53.5
Total	100.0	100.0	100.0

Source: National Survey of Family Income, National Institute of Statistics, 1968, and Property Tax returns, Internal Revenue Service.

Service official valuation, 54 per cent of property was owned by 7 per cent of households.

On the other hand, property was not only subjected to low taxation rates but, furthermore, the effective revenue has been decreasing over the years, representing only 3.1 per cent of total tax revenue in 1973, a drop from 13.1 per cent in 1965.

The decrease in the property tax revenue has been caused by several factors. First the erosion in the tax base due to the lag in the property assessments in the face of high inflation rates.[19]

A second factor in the deterioration of the property tax revenue, and possibly the most important one from the point of view of long-term effect, was the elimination in 1974 of a tax on personal wealth that was established after much political controversy in 1968. The tax, which

[19] Agrarian property assessments were devalued by almost 30 per cent between 1965 and 1972; urban real-estate assessments lost about 20 per cent of their value in the same period.

yielded 10 per cent of total direct taxes on property in 1969, and reached 31.2 per cent in 1974 through a rate increase valid only for that year, was abolished in 1975.

A third factor that explains the slight importance of revenue yield from property and capital is to be found in the low rates of inheritance and gift tax. This tax yielded barely 1.8 per cent of revenue on property in 1965, and 0.5 per cent in 1974.

The elimination of the wealth tax, plus the deterioration of the property tax base, coincided with an increase in tax levies on labour, as a result of increases in the wage-earners' income tax and other taxes affecting workers income in recent years. Both mutually reinforcing factors cause a substantial reduction of the tax burden on the capital factor and an increase in the tax incidence on labour. This trend becomes even more dramatic because it is accompanied by an increase in the participation of capital and other factors in national income at the expense of the workers' share. The picture shown in Table 52 would look even worse had indirect-tax incidence been considered.

Table 52 depicts one of the central aspects of inequity in Chile's tax system (and probably, in that of quite a number of other Latin American

TABLE 52

Factoral incidence of direct taxes

Year	Worker's share in national income	Tax burden on labour	Capital share in national income	Tax burden on capital
1969	51.2	44	48.8	56
1972	62.8	62	37.2	38
1974	43.2	73	56.8	27

countries). The bias against labour and in favour of capital should be corrected through simultaneous action on several fronts. The first one would be to institute an automatic yearly adjustment on the assessed value of rural, urban and other property. This automatic adjustment has to be supplemented with periodic reassessments at market prices of the property value.

Even more important is the establishment on a permanent basis of a tax on personal wealth or of a tax on imputed income generated by the total patrimony of every person, whether a natural or legal entity. No wealth category would be excluded, although there should no doubt be an exemption for families in the low-income group.

The two modifications above are *sine qua non* conditions to correct the strong element of regressiveness in the Chilean tax system.

Tax shelters and horizontal equity

The Chilean tax system has been characterised by an extremely high number of tax shelters and exemptions that favour regions or specific activities.

Tax shelters have not been a mechanism to increase the equity of the system. Rarely have they been granted to provinces with a relatively large needy population nor applied to productive activities in such a way as to encourage more intensive labour use. Furthermore, they have been established on a permanent basis. They are insufficiently selective and often they represent a disguised way of subsidising activities operating in oligopolistic or monopolistic markets. In the latter instance, tax exemptions merely serve the purpose of increasing capital profits.

In the Chilean case, shelters granted to enterprises generally have had an "asymmetric" effect, for, unlike what happens with the tax levies that are passed on to consumers or to labour, exemption benefits tend to remain in the hands of capital and, more so, to accumulate in the sector or enterprise directly benefited.

Revision of the amount and type of shelters in the direction of achieving greater redistributive impact and efficiency would entail drastic reduction of those existent at present, and the limitation of the use of tax-exemption mechanisms only to those selected cases that carry with them a clear benefit for the more destitute groups or regions, or for groups or regions that clearly generate an important number of jobs in the economy.

Transitoriness of shelters is a basic condition for insuring not only equity but also efficiency. In any case, in accordance with an already accepted principle with regard to the government control and knowledge of the direction and volume of its distributive policy, tax exemption will always be a less efficient policy instrument than the alternative of granting an explicit temporary subsidy in a fixed amount to the sector, social stratum or region whose needy situation relative to other sectors, social strata or regions, justifies it.

Tax evasion

Another extremely vulnerable aspect in the Chilean tax system – and a common trait among developing countries – is the lack of administrative capacity to control the system's high evasion rate.

Besides evasion, there is the loss of resources as a result of the multiplicity of loopholes and legal exemptions. These devices not only legalise the erosion of the tax base, but complicate verification of returns and thus facilitate evasion. Legal erosion plus evasion affect nearly 70 per cent of the real income of professionals and more than 60 per cent of business profits from the tax base. This means that these sectors pay taxes on barely one-third of their earnings. This is in great contrast to the situation of wage earners, for whom controls are much easier to enforce and erosion of revenues is much lower. The concentration of tax evasion among the high-income groups is an important source of regressivity in the system.

The other tax whose evasion rate was high toward the end of the sixties was the sales tax. This benefited mainly the small industry and commerce. The introduction of the value added tax should significantly reduce sales tax evasion.[20]

Curtailment of tax evasion is every government's goal. The difficulty lies in adapting the income-tax administrative apparatus to attain efficient control of payments or, alternatively, to apply harsh penalties to evaders. This should be a policy objective to which considerable human and physical resources should be devoted, for improvement in the efficiency of administrative control and collection mechanisms will necessarily have a high social rate of return.

Other actions in this field are directed to eliminate understatement of incomes from property. To achieve this, introduction of devices such as a tax on imputed income, upheld by a system of better controls and stiffer penalties, might cause tax evasion to diminish significantly.

[20] However, due to its high legal rate and the elimination of exemptions for products such as bread, milk and books, this tax appears to be negative from a redistributive point of view.

The social security system

Previous findings show that the social security system as a whole has a net progressive effect on income distribution, although its financing is clearly regressive. Twenty-two per cent of the expenditures benefit the 60 per cent of families whose incomes are below US $670 whereas only 4.5 per cent accrue to the higher 7 per cent of the families earning $6,700 or more.

From the point of view of the previously defined social groups, Chilean social security is a programme oriented to the middle classes, for this group receives about 45 per cent of the system's total benefits and contributes 48 per cent to its financing.

In net terms the social-security system manages to redistribute in favour of the low stratum, a condition which contrasts with international patterns. Studies have concluded that in developing countries the social-security redistribution process basically represents "a movement from the top and from the base toward the center".[21]

The financing structure of the Chilean social security is shown in Table 53.

TABLE 53

Financial sources of social security

Type of financing	Relative importance (%)
(a) Employers' contributions	37
(b) Government contributions and special taxes	30
(c) Workers' contributions	23
(d) Goods and services sales and other	6
(e) Capital incomes	4

At variance with the great majority of underdeveloped countries, where employers' contributions represent a high percentage of total financing (percentages between 40 and 60 are frequent);[22] the Chilean case is nearer the position of intermediate developed countries (over US $500 *per capita* GNP), where the workers' direct contributions have a greater relative weight. These contributions constitute 10 per cent of total

[21] F. Paukert, "Social security and income redistribution: A comparative study", *International Labour Review,* ILO, 1968.

[22] F. Paukert, *op. cit.*

financing in underdeveloped countries and 20 per cent or more in intermediate countries. Furthermore, it should be noted that the Chilean government contributes one-third of the system's funds, which allows for sustained ample coverage in terms of benefits provided and number of persons eligible. The Chilean Social Security System's 50 years of experience has accentuated its "share" or "common fund" character.[23]

Another potential area where social security may be of importance for underdeveloped countries is that of being a possible source of public savings.

What must be clear, though, is that savings may be realized regardless of whether the system is of a "common fund" or "individual capitalisation" nature. In the former (the scheme in effect at present in Chile) it would suffice that an important proportion of revenues plus other of the system's own income, instead of being distributed as greater current benefits, be invested directly or turned into budgetary funds available to the public sector as a whole.

These remarks are important from the point of view of reform policies. Of the two alternatives of shifting to private hands and improving the present system's efficiency, the latter obviously offers undisputed advantages from a redistributive point of view.

In regard to financing, one of the features that most urgently needs revision is the negative effect on employment caused by employers' contributions. The present system's negative effect on employment fluctuates between 8 and 25 per cent of total man-years of labour in the economy. For other countries, such as Venezuela, it has been estimated that this effect is around 2.1 per cent, as a result of the lower rates of employer contributions in the country.[24]

Although the employment effect is a once-and-for-all effect, what should be plain is that until substitute financing for social-security contributions from other direct sources (income tax or value added tax) is not implemented, the economy will experience the yearly loss of the

[23] This is clearly at odds with currently proposed policies oriented to "private capitalisation régimes". It should be kept in mind that the reform of the pension and indemnisation programmes alone in the direction of a private savings capitalisation system would mean a transfer of at least US $150 million (1974) in savings from the Chilean public sector to the private sector.

[24] PREALC, "Acción de los Ministerios de Trabajo en la política del empleo del Grupo Andino", PREALC/87, Santiago, Chile (1975).

productive contribution of all those workers displaced by the tax disincentive.

The substitute financing for social security is feasible in view of the larger margins of taxable profits that would become available as employers' contributions are eliminated and salaries and wages are correspondingly increased. The base for direct tax assessment would be expanded accordingly. Financing of the system could be achieved through pooling of potential sources, namely, taxes on profits, value added, real estate and personal income.

On the expenditures side, three new action schemes could bring about the improvement of the system's redistributive effect: an all-encompassing unemployment subsidy covering both members of social-security plans and non-members; the incorporation into social security of previously non-affiliated families such as those of independent workers; and the implementation of a guaranteed minimum pension for all persons above 65 years of age.

The introduction of an all-encompassing unemployment subsidy would have a maximum cost of US $8 million dollars per year. This figure is arrived at by assuming a monthly *per capita* payment of one minimum income (approximately 33 dollars) and also by assuming that the total number of persons eligible for payments is equivalent to a monthly unemployment rate of 10 per cent.

Another course of action is the expansion of the system's coverage. Although coverage is not low (incorporates 75 per cent of the labour force), it excludes independent workers.

This is one of the policy areas where there is a clear option between the "vertical efficiency" criterion (insuring that the programmes are selective, covering only the needy) and the "horizontal efficiency" criterion (insuring coverage of all groups). Under the latter criterion, high programme costs may result from extending benefits to persons who, from the point of view of income, should not be eligible.

One of the institutional mechanisms to assist in determining "selectivity" and "reach" in the case of independent workers would be the opening of a "self-employed workers' registry" wherein up-to-date information would be recorded on occupational categories, economic activity, family size, and average income levels of independent workers. Reasonable incentives (professional identity cards, information services, minimum legal, or medical assistance, etc.) to encourage registration could be devised.

A third line of action, already mentioned, refers to a guaranteed minimum pension policy available to all adults over 65 years of age, regardless of non-affiliation to pension plans. This is a typical example of a redistributive policy devised to insure reaching needy sectors.

CONCLUDING REMARKS

As can be seen from the preceding analysis, the Chilean experience in state intervention has been rich in the variety of mechanisms utilised.

Although the intervention of the State in economic life is a topic of permanent controversy, our exercise has advanced criteria for judging Chilean state action in a more thorough way than it has traditionally been done.

At this stage, it should be clear that government performance should be evaluated in the light of the real objectives expressed by the socio-political system. The strongly redistributive orientation of public action in Chile during the period 1965–70 surely reflects social demands exerted through a democratic political process, the final objective of which was to achieve greater equality in income and opportunities.

Therefore, the measurement of state performance should not only be done in terms of such traditional goals as growth of output, economic efficiency and the attainment of price stability, but should also take into account the achievement of greater social equality. In terms of this last goal, it is certain that government action in Chile had a positive sign in the period that we have studied.

True, looking in perspective there was a wide scope for increasing the redistributive efficiency and the reach of public action along the lines suggested throughout the previous chapters in this book.

We have seen that there were four critical elements in the Chilean case which directly limited vertical efficiency: first, the magnitude of net resources available for redistribution at a given moment of time (the "redistributive margin" obtained from transfers of resources away from the rich, from reducing tax evasion, from taxation on copper, taxation on foreigners, and from foreign loans and aid); secondly, the limit imposed by the regressive character of indirect levies and social-security contributions; thirdly, the high per cent of the Budget devoted to General Government Expenses; and fourthly, the regressive character of some public programmes in the productive sphere.

Also, we have pointed out that a crucial factor for better redistribution is the adequate identification of the social groups to be benefited by public action. This should be tied with mechanisms which reduce or eliminate existing leaks going to well-to-do groups. Both the selectiveness in social expenditure programmes, as well as the preferable utilisation of explicit subsidies or of direct transfers rather than tax franchises, cheap-loans and other fiscal incentives which tend to hide the real amount of resources transferred by the government are significant ways of getting closer to the redistributive target.

A problem to which we have not devoted much attention is that state action must continually confront pressures from vested interests and powerful groups in society, which frequently exert influences in an opposite direction to that of redistribution. Redistributive policies, just like any other type of economic policy, are not applied in an institutional vacuum. The issue is to determine which is the real degree of freedom enjoyed in a given political-institutional context, and in a particular historical situation, to implement these policies.

The fact that this problem is not thoroughly analysed by the authors does not mean that its importance is underestimated. We hope that the empirical material we have presented and that the analysis we have performed may prove helpful for attempting this second task.

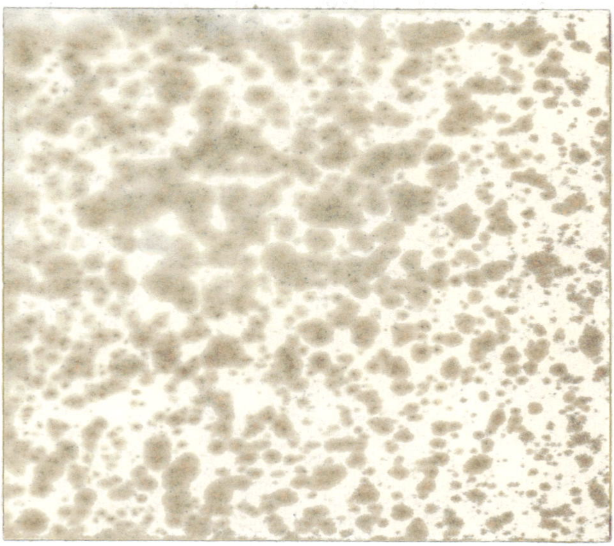

CHAPTER 7

The Role of Asset Redistribution in Poverty-focused Development Strategies

INTRODUCTION

A critical factor explaining differences in personal incomes is the distribution of assets among individuals and families. It is the ownership of land, of physical and human capital plus the access to services rendered by public capital that determines to a large extent income differentials.

On the other hand, it is an empirical fact that assets tend to be more concentrated than income.[1] Thus, redistributing assets can be an effective and rapid way of reducing disparities in personal incomes. Asset redistribution may take the form of transferring existing capital from high- to low-income families; or reorienting new investment towards the poorer groups in society, and changing the composition of public services such as health and education so that low-income groups have more access to those services.

Although in recent years the literature in the economic development field has rediscovered the importance of the subject of income distribution, not much has been done in terms of systematically exploring the policy alternatives faced by policy makers responsible for implementing redistributive-oriented development strategies.[2] Particularly little has been done in the examination of the potential of asset redistribution as a

[1] J. E. Meade, *Efficiency, Equality and the Ownership of Property,* Allen & Unwin, London, 1969.

[2] One notable exception is H. Chenery *et al., Redistribution with Growth,* Oxford University Press, 1974. Another is J. E. Meade, *op. cit.*

"non-traditional" means of income redistribution (being fiscal transfers and taxes, the more "traditional" instruments). Even less attention has been paid to the empirical examination of asset redistribution schemes in contemporary development processes. This chapter will attempt to deal with these issues. Sections 2, 3 and 4 of the chapter will be devoted to examining critically the alternatives available in asset redistribution, with particular emphasis on nationalisation schemes in the corporate sector of the economy and land-reform programmes in the rural sector. The following sections will consist of an empirical analysis of the results obtained in the implementation of such redistributive schemes in a country which has experimented with both kinds of programmes in the last decade. The country is Chile and the programmes are land reform as carried out in the period 1965–72, and the more recent experience with expropriation of industrial enterprises to constitute the so-called "Area of Social Property" (ASP) during the period 1970–73.

7.1. ALTERNATIVES FOR ASSET REDISTRIBUTION

The economic objective of asset redistribution is the deconcentration of private ownership of capital, transferring assets, directly to low-income groups or to the government. The assumption in the latter case is that in appropriating redistributed assets, the government can generate a surplus that it can use to finance investment or consumption expenditures directed to the poorer groups.

The political objective is to break up the power structure, so that the government gains degrees of freedom to redistribute income.

The most effective mechanism to redistribute ownership of assets will depend on the sectors in which poorer groups are and on the characteristics of such groups in each sector. It is now generally agreed that poverty groups are constituted by landless peasants, part-time workers and minifundia owners in the rural sector, and by the chronically unemployed in small industry and commerce, and the self-employed in urban areas.

An examination of the alternatives available for redistributing assets will have to start by recognising the basic difference between the problem as it exists in rural and urban areas. The most concentrated asset in the rural sector is usually land.[3] This is a productive factor which is divisible and in the exploitation of which economies of scale are not important. Land redistribution can take the form of a transfer from big private landowners to individual peasants' families or to a collective of agricultural workers.

On the other hand, the redistribution of existing assets in the corporate sector of the economy will not generally lead to an individual distribution of property due to indivisibilities in the accumulated capital in the industrial sector. Thus the transfer must almost necessarily be made to the State or to a collective of workers, who gradually participate on a co-operative basis in the property of the enterprise. Examples of the first type of transfer can be found in most socialist countries (with the exception of Yugoslavia). And examples of the latter can be found in Peru.[4]

If a more direct transfer to poverty groups is to be achieved, the government can allocate new investment so that it directly benefits small producers (credit, machinery, infrastructure, marketing facilities), self-employed workers (co-operative production, training, technical assistance) and deficitary consumers (new housing, expanded health and education services, nutrition programmes, etc.).[5]

We shall now examine the options of asset redistribution in the urban and rural sectors in more detail.

7.2. ASSET REDISTRIBUTION IN THE URBAN SECTOR

One of the more frequent patterns of asset redistribution in the urban sector consists of the nationalisation of modern industrial enterprises that in some sense are considered strategic or monopolistic and incorporate them to the public sector.

The rationale for such a transfer is to break up the power base of industry owners, source of high income disparities, and by this means

[3]Sometimes water is the scarce key resource and the more concentrated one.

[4]See A. Figueroa, "The impact of current reforms on income distribution in Peru", in A. Foxley (ed.), *Income Distribution in Latin America,* Cambridge University Press, 1976.

[5]See C. L. G. Bell and J. Duloy, "Rural target groups", and D. C. Rae, "Urban target group", in H. Chenery *et al., op. cit.*

also decrease their influence in policy-making. This is believed to be a necessary although not sufficient condition for the State to be able to implement effective and permanent income redistribution policies. Nationalisation would also allow the government to induce rapid changes in the composition of production, changes that are required to meet the new structure of consumption resulting from the income-redistribution policies. Finally, if the nationalisation of industrial enterprises includes, as in some cases it does, the more modern, capital-intensive and at least potentially highly productive units, an important surplus could be extracted from them by the government which can be used either to reinvest in high-priority industrial projects, fostering the rate of economic growth, thus incrementing the redistributive margin; or to transfer to low income groups in the form of selective income-supporting programmes. If this were the case, the nationalised sector would provide an additional means besides taxation to sustain a redistributive programme that could benefit directly those groups more in need.[6]

Can nationalised industries perform this redistributive role? The issue, which at first sight looks simple, is in fact a very complicated one. It is often obscured or confused by the fact that the performance of government-owned corporations in the context of mixed economies does not always seem to be satisfactory according to empirical evidence available. A study of sixty-four public enterprises in twenty-six countries, which includes twenty-four government-owned corporations in Latin America, shows that although the enterprises, on the average, do cover current operating costs they are not able to finance depreciation expenditures let alone new investment programmes.[7] The average deficit excluding net investment measured as a percentage of the firm's "activity" is 24 per cent for the sample as a whole and 21 per cent for Latin America. When new investment expenditures are taken into

[6]Quite often, though, nationalisation takes place only when large private enterprises cannot make a profit, as the recent UK experience shows. This has also been the case in many instances in Latin America. See L. Whitehead, "Public sector activities" in K. Griffin (ed.), *Financing Development in Latin America,* MacMillan, 1971, See also W. Baer, A. Villiela and I. Kerstenezky, "The changing role of the state in the Brazilian economy", *World Development,* November 1973.

[7]A. H. Gantt and G. Dutto, "Financial performance of government-owned corporations in less developed countries", *IMF Staff Papers,* Vol. XV, 1968.

account the deficit goes up as high as 66 per cent for the whole sample and 56 per cent for the Latin American public corporations.

In order to interpret these results correctly, some comments have to be made. The first one concerns the deficit when current expenditures plus depreciation allowances are considered. One thing that must be pointed out is that the average deficit is explained by an extremely poor performance of basically two types of public enterprises, those in the transport sector including the railways and those in "declining industries" such as coal. Public enterprises in other sectors like petroleum, energy and communications do provide a positive surplus before reinvestment (as high as 22 per cent for enterprises in the petroleum sector in Latin America).[8]

The high deficit when expenditures for expansions in productive capacity are taken into account is at least partly explained by the fact that public enterprises tend to expand at a much faster rate than the average in the economy. The enterprises investment in the sample grew at 15 per cent a year on the average. The level of investment expenditures of public enterprises is often a function of social needs, independent of performance. This explains that investment expenditures in such highly deficitary sectors as public transport were equivalent to 30 per cent of activity in the data collected by Gantt and Dutto. This behaviour only added to the financial difficulties of those types of government corporations.

What on a more general level the previous figures are suggesting is something that has been stressed in the studies on public enterprise performance for some time now.[9] This is that the role of the public corporation in a mixed economy has often been that of undertaking those activities which the private sector will not take either because they are not profitable but perform a social function or because they require huge investments with long gestation lags and low rates of return, like investments in infrastructure.

Once these investment programmes are undertaken by the government, pressure will mount for a below-cost pricing of the goods or services

[8]Includes Argentina, Bolivia, Colombia and Mexico, data for the late fifties and early sixties. See A. H. Gantt and G. Dutto, *op. cit.*

[9]See L. Whitehead, *op. cit.*, and A. Nove, *Efficiency Criteria for Nationalized Industries*, Allen & Unwin, London, 1973.

produced by the public corporation. The pressure will be stronger the more the publicly produced output is used as an input by the private sector. Thus, the government enterprise is used as a means of generating a hidden subsidy for the private sector. The government ''pays the bill'' by means of transfers of funds from the fiscal budget to cover the nationalised corporation deficit.[10]

The previous argument does not mean to say that there is no problem as far as the efficiency of public enterprises is concerned. The figures given and their rather high order of magnitude do suggest that inefficiency must be involved. We do not know how important it is. But obviously performance as such is negatively affected by the fact that the government has to run non-profit-yielding productive activities that the private sector will not undertake; or even if profitable, the firms will probably tend to underprice their product particularly when these are used as inputs by private firms, or for distributive reasons when the products are mostly consumed by low-income groups (for example, public transport in Latin America).

What we can conclude so far is that when the nationalised sector covers only the ''traditional'' areas of infrastructure, transport and communications, and declining non-profitable industries, the flow of resources will very likely be from the Central Government to the public corporations and not the other way around. The redistributive potential of the sector will not consist in what the government does with the (non-existent) surplus extracted from the nationalised enterprises, but in who ends up receiving the subsidies transferred by the government to the enterprises and who finances them.

The situation might be quite different when the nationalisation process goes beyond the traditional areas and actually includes a whole number of highly profitable, modern industrial firms. Then it is not clear that the result has to be similar to that reported by Gantt and Dutto. In fact it might just be the opposite and, as has been stated, this is the assumption beyond the socialist strategy of massive expropriation of industrial enterprises.

Whether a positive surplus will exist as a result of extended nationalisation of modern enterprises will now depend on factors such as

[10]Then private interest groups build a ''strong'' case against the efficiency of public enterprises.

the wages and employment policies followed by the enterprises (will they overpay and overemploy workers?), the pricing policies (will they subsidise consumers by underpricing their products?), the organisation of production (what does the public firm maximise and what decisions are centralised and which ones decentralised?). Depending on the specific form these policies take the outcome might be in one or the other direction. It is one of the purposes of this paper to shed some light on these issues through the study of recent Chilean experience.

7.3. ASSET REDISTRIBUTION IN THE RURAL SECTOR

The scarcest asset in the rural sector is quite often land. The control of land implies a control of agricultural production. If public policies are designed to stimulate output and productivity in agriculture, be it through cheap credit, better prices, public investment in roads, irrigation, etc., the benefits of these policies will inevitably accrue to those who own a larger share of agricultural land and thus control most of agricultural production. It is in this context that land reform (LR) is not only egalitarian *per se* but becomes a prerequisite for a more egalitarian effect of public policies in the sector as well.

A more equal distribution of income and wealth within the rural sector is an objective of high priority in any poverty-oriented development strategy. It is in the rural sector that a larger proportion of the poor are and, conversely, of what is said of nationalisation schemes in the urban sector, land reform tends to be more feasible in political terms and can benefit more directly a large number of the poor.

Land can be segmented and distributed directly among low-income peasant families. This direct transfer of land to poor peasants is sometimes called a "distributivist" land reform.[11] Another alternative in LR programmes consists of transferring the land to the State or to workers' collectives. Between both pure models, it is quite possible to find a hybrid combination of the two. The Chilean experiment in LR that will be explored later on in this paper provides an example of a mixed system of individual and collective exploitation within a single farm. The

[11] See M. Lipton, "Towards a theory of land reform", in D. Lehmann (ed.), *Agrarian Reform and Agrarian Reformism,* Faber & Faber, London, 1974. The discussion in this section has been enriched by valuable comments made by E. Klein.

property of such a farm is in the hands of an Agricultural Society with State and peasants' participation. After a transition period of up to 5 years, property would be transferred to individual families or to peasants' co-operatives.

Land redistribution may have quite diverse effects in terms of income distribution according to which is the tenancy system that develops after the expropriation of land has taken place. We shall examine the probable effects of both distributivist and collectivist LR programmes in what follows.

Who are the main beneficiaries of a "distributivist" LR programme? Empirical evidence seems to suggest that if land is directly distributed in individual plots, it will most probably benefit tenant farmers, sharecroppers and to some extent minifundia procedures. These groups will most likely have access to redistributed land and will thus be able to increase their productivity and incomes.

Given that land is not an unlimited resource, and the very large number of poor peasants in most developing countries, it is quite likely that such a programme will not be able to benefit all low-income families in the rural areas. One group that might not benefit at all from land redistribution due to the unfavourable rural population to land ratio is that of landless peasants. They might even be worse off temporarily if, as a result of the uncertainty brought about by LR on private producers, the demand for temporary labour force declines.

The indirect redistributive effects via employment creation of a distributivist LR seem to be on the whole positive. There is in fact almost general agreement now that small farms tend to be a highly labour-absorptive system.[12] Existing data for India, Sri Lanka, Thailand, Taiwan, the US, Chile, Peru, Bolivia and Mexico confirm that labour intensity is higher in small farms than in larger ones. The evidence also points to the fact that output per unit of land is greater in smaller than in larger farms.[13]

[12] P. Dorner, *Land Reform and Economic Development,* Penguin, 1972, chapter 4. See also ILO, *Matching Employment Opportunity and Expectations: a Report on Ceylon,* Geneva, 1971. See also K. Griffin, *The Political Economy of Agrarian Change,* Macmillan, 1974.

[13] See M. Lipton, *op. cit.* and P. Dorner, *op. cit.*

Labour absorption takes the form of a reduction in the underemployment of family labour rather than that of large decreases in open unemployment. The beneficiaries of the new employment creation will then be the families of the new owners of redistributed land in the first place, and secondly, the families of landless peasants only to the extent that the small producers' sector proves to be dynamic enough to demand more labour than is available in their own families.

What are the likely distributive effects of collectivist LR programmes?

The transfer of land to the State allows it to extract a surplus from agriculture. This surplus has been historically directed to finance state industrial investments and to some extent to subsidise the prices of food products consumed by the urban population. The beneficiaries of the policy are, then, this part of the population and the State.

In terms of indirect redistributive effects via employment creation, the scarce empirical information available seems to suggest that workers' collectives and state farms, in spite of the fact that they tend to be capital-intensive, in fact absorb more labour than the latifundia, although not nearly as much per unit of land as the small farm.[14]

Labour absorption in workers' collectives is as much dependent on government decisions as on the power of peasants. If the former predominates, labour absorption could in theory be high. Not only underemployment of family labour could be reduced but open rural unemployment as well. On the other hand, if peasants do have a strong say in the labour-absorption problem as they might when co-operatives are organised, then labour absorption could be lower given a tendency by peasants to maximise income per head. In the practice of socialist countries, the government's ability to expand employment in collective farms has found some constraints due to the difficulties and eventual inefficiencies accompanying the organisation and supervision of a very large labour force within the collective farm.[15]

Summing up, it seems that a distributivist LR would tend to create more employment than a collectivist or co-operative one. The employment effect in the former would consist in a fuller utilisation of the family labour of those peasants having access to the subdivided land. Since land would normally be insufficient to incorporate all labour force

[14] See P. Dorner, *op. cit.*, chapter 4.

[15] See A. Nove.

in agriculture, a mass of agricultural workers would be left out of the benefits of LR. A distributivist LR would produce fuller employment of fewer workers. The income of these workers would increase substantially.

As a contrast, a collectivist LR would probably imply a lower over-all employment effect, in terms of men-hours demanded per hectare. But, instead of a fully utilised smaller labour force, it would employ more workers at a lower level of utilisation. Average labour productivity would be lower and consequently the employed workers' income would not be as high as in the distributivist LR case. But the benefits of an albeit partial employment expansion would spread to a larger number of workers.

A government pursuing LR as an objective is not totally free to choose between one scheme or the other. The choice is constrained by a multitude of factors. One is the tenure system under which the peasants were working before LR.[16] If it were predominantly a system of very small proprietors, share-croppers and tenant farmers, that is, peasants with a strong attachment to a certain plot of land as in many parts of Asia, the resistance of the farmers to any collectivisation may be such that the collective or even co-operative option would be of only theoretical interest, but impossible of implementing in practice. The security in individual tenure may be the critical prerequisite for higher productivity and employment absorption in this case. On the other hand, when the peasants were typically salaried workers before LR, collective or co-operative LR may not only be feasible but also more socially efficient. Agricultural workers would not demand land in this case, but better income and working conditions.[17]

Another critical factor is the type of infrastructure available before LR (field layouts, buildings, irrigation channels, type of machinery, etc.). If these are available in a form appropriate for large-scale production, the cost of a distributivist LR may increase well beyond its probable benefits. It would imply transforming roads, field layouts, building new houses, storage facilities, buying a different type of machinery (like lighter tractors, etc.). It would also mean that distribution networks,

[16]See E. Klein, "Conflicts between rural workers and landowners in Central Chile", D.Phil. Thesis, University of Sussex, 1973.

[17]E. Klein, *op. cit.* R. Urzúa, *La Demanda Campesina,* Ediciones Nueva Universidad, Santiago. P. Brevis and C. Pizarro, "Los sindicatos agrícolas y el proceso de Reforma Agraria en la década del sesenta", CEPLAN. *Estudios de Planificación,* No. 47, 1975.

government extension services and credit channels would have to be modified.

The problem might be particularly acute for the efficient working of state farm support programmes, when having to deal with a much larger number of very small productive units. Training programmes to develop basic technical and managerial capacities would have to be multiplied, since the new individual peasant-owners would have very low levels of education, rudimentary technical knowledge and would tend to be agents resisting rather than promoting the diffusion of the new technologies required to achieve increases in productivity. All these factors would certainly influence the type of tenure to be promoted by the government in its LR programme.

Finally, the form that the reformed sector takes is not independent of the kind of structure existent or being promoted by the government in other sectors of the economy. This is a factor related to ideology and the image of future society that the groups in power have in mind. If the government is primarily interested for ideological and political reasons in creating a rural middle class of small proprietors, it is obvious that the distributivist option will be chosen, whatever its cost.

A balance of all these factors in Chile during the mid 1960s seems to have pushed the government towards a co-operative-collectivist type of LR, at least during a transition period of 5 years. What its distributive and employment effects were in practice we shall analyse in a subsequent section.

7.4. A GENERAL FRAMEWORK FOR THE EMPIRICAL ANALYSIS OF ASSET REDISTRIBUTION

After describing the general issues involved in asset redistribution both in the corporate sector of the economy and in rural areas, and the probable distributive effects of such changes given alternative organisation schemes in the now nationalised sectors, we must presently proceed to analyse the case studies that we have chosen, that is nationalisation in the industrial sector in Chile during the period 1970–73; and the land-reform programme carried out between 1965 and 1972.

Since both programmes implied the use of asset redistribution as an explicit instrument to achieve both a higher income equality and growth objectives, they constitute an interesting case study of the kind of policies discussed in a generally abstract level in the first part of this paper.

In order to proceed with the empirical study, we must provide some general framework which will allow us to analyse consistently the actual redistributive effects of both programmes.

When analysing asset redistribution it is convenient to separate two sequential effects. One is the net transfer of resources away from the owners of large industrial enterprises or latifundia towards the State. It deconcentrates wealth and reduces the "economic muscle" of the old owners. The second is the distribution of the surplus by the government among the various socio-economic groups in the population. Actually this way of looking at the problem is better suited for the study of nationalisation in the industrial sector where state enterprises were created than for the study of the effects of LR. The latter programme had, as a basic objective, the redistribution of wealth from big landowners to peasants (organised in co-operatives). The State was only an intermediary during a 5-year transitory period. Since this is the period we study, we can actually look at the government role as one of an intermediary disposing of a certain surplus produced by the land-expropriation process, just as in the case of nationalisation of industries. We can call both processes "nationalisation".

The surplus that the government gets from nationalisation is a function of profit levels, reinvestment rates and of the amount and conditions established for the compensation of the expropriated owner. Profit levels determine the gross volume of resources that are being transferred by the policy. Reinvestment rates, although by definition are not part of a freely disposable surplus by the government, determine the future growth rate of the nationalised sector, and thus are influential in conditioning future income streams and profits within the expropriated sector. The conditions under which compensation payments are made, such as period established for paying back to the original owners, assessment of the value of the assets being transferred (e.g. book or market value) and the fraction of the original value which is paid back, are all factors influencing the volume of resources that are going to be recycled back to the expropriated property owners.[18]

[18] A formal model using this kind of framework has been developed by J. Cauas and M. Selowsky, "Potential distributive effects of nationalization policies", mimeo, IBRD Development Research Center, 1973.

Not all the surplus obtained by the government through nationalisation are new resources, though to the extent that the expropriated enterprises paid some taxes before nationalisation. That means that the net value of resources freely available to the government are profits net of compensation payments, minus taxes previously paid by the old owners of the transferred assets. On the other hand, if the nationalisation policy affects the behaviour of the private sector in general, say due to the uncertainty it creates on producers, then it is conceivable that reinvestment by the non-nationalised sector will decrease somewhat. One consequence of such behaviour under the assumption that profit levels are a function of reinvestment rates will be that taxes paid will be lower. This may be an additional cost of nationalisation policies, at least in the transition period when the policy is being implemented.[19] But on the other hand, non-nationalised firms may increase their productivity and output levels in the short run, as an attempt to avoid being subjected to nationalisation on grounds of poor performance, and also to maximise short-term profits given an uncertain future. Also the government can compensate this effect by forcing enterprises to reinvest a larger share of their profits.[20]

The other aspects of the problem consists of determining how the net surplus is distributed by the government. This is obviously greatly dependent on the organisation schemes and property relationship in the expropriated sector. But on a general level, the beneficiaries of the policy will be the following:

- Workers (or peasants) that formed part of the original labour force in the nationalised enterprise; they would benefit from the policy if wages rise faster after the transfer; or if they become owners of part or total of the transferred assets. In the latter case they will benefit if the price paid for the purchase of the assets is subsidised. Also afterwards a part of the total profits will accrue to the workers, thus increasing their income beyond pre-nationalisation levels.
- The unemployed will benefit to the extent that the expropriated sector demands more labour, either because of changes in production techniques, or simply due to a deliberate employment creation policy on the part of the government. If the new labour demanded

[19] These points have been made by J. Cauas and M. Selowsky, *op. cit.*

[20] These aspects were not considered in Cauas and Selowsky's model. They prove to be of significant validity in the empirical findings reported in the second part of this paper.

is unskilled, the beneficiaries of the policy will be low-income workers. If the additional demand consists of highly skilled labour force, then the income effect is going to favour middle-class income groups.

– Consumers in general are going to benefit from the policy if goods and services produced by the expropriated sectors are sold at below equilibrium prices. This is equivalent to using the potential (but not realised) surplus to directly subsidised consumption of certain goods in the economy. The beneficiaries of such a policy will be consumers in different income brackets, depending on their propensities to consume the various products, whose prices are subsidised. If the enterprise produces intermediate inputs used by private firms, as it is often the case, the subsidy benefits these enterprises and not necessarily the consumers.[21]

– If the government is able, after all payments have been made, to retain a proportion of the surplus, the new resources can be used to increase government expenditures. Who the beneficiaries of such an increase will be depends on the sectors in which expenditures are made and the particular programmes that are financed by the new resources available. We deal in detail with this subject elsewhere.[22]

– Thus far we have assumed that the nationalised sector in fact generates a positive surplus after compensation payments, reinvestment, wage increases and new employment are financed. If this were not the case, that is if the enterprise runs a deficit, then the flow of resources goes in the opposite direction. The government must finance the deficit, drawing on its own scarce resources. If taxes are increased to provide a non-inflationary financing of the deficitary enterprises, then the beneficiaries of the policy are the workers (old and new) in the nationalised sector, and consumers in general, at the expense of taxpayers. A more probable behaviour on the part of the government will be to increase the transfers to the expropriated sectors financed out of the fiscal budget. This action will very likely tend to generate inflationary pressures in the economy, to the extent that the expanded fiscal deficit has to be financed by increasing the money supply. Who pays the "inflation tax"? It depends on who

[21] See L. Whitehead, *op. cit.*

[22] See Chapters 3 and 4.

the holders of cash balances are (wealth effect) and on whether the price-indexation mechanisms for inflationary correction discriminate in favour or against particular groups in society (income effect). But the general direction of the resource transfers would now be from expropriated owners, holders of cash balances and "losers" on the income adjustment for inflation towards the nationalised enterprise workers (and consumers in general, if prices are subsidised).

The previous characterisation of the types of effects and likely beneficiaries of the asset redistribution policies will be used as a general framework to study in the next sections, the Area of Social Property and the Land Reform Programmes in Chile.

7.5. NATIONALISATION IN THE INDUSTRIAL SECTOR: THE AREA OF SOCIAL PROPERTY[23]

The creation of the "Area of Social Property" in Chilean industry undertaken in the last part of 1970 was a keystone in the redistributive strategy of the Allende Government. By November 1970, before the policy was implemented, sixty-one industrial enterprises were in the public sector. By the end of 1971 the number had risen to 173. In September 1973, 300 enterprises had been transferred from the private to the public sector in industry, making a total of 362 firms that constituted the so-called Area of Social Property (ASP).

The general aims of this policy was to redistribute wealth and power from the high-income monopolistic sector, to change social relationships in production; to generate and extract a large surplus from the nationalised enterprise in order to finance a redistributive process elsewhere in the economy; and to control a large share of industrial production so that rapid changes in the structure of the production could be promoted by the government to meet the rapidly increasing demand of

[23] This section is based on Roberto Zahler, "Significación y aspectos distributivos del área de propiedad social y mixta en la industria chilena: 1970–73", mimeo, CEPLAN-Departamento de Economía Universidad de Chile, Santiago, Marzo 1975, 154 pp. It has also benefited from S. Bitar and A. Mackenna, "Impacto de las áreas social y mixta en la industria chilena", *El Trimestre Económico,* Mexico, 1974.

wage-goods. The latter would, of course, be the consequence of a policy of rapid income redistribution.

The creation of ASP was carried out in a context of a deep power struggle for the political control of institutions in the country. The process of nationalisation was accelerated in some areas, delayed in others, according to the nature and intensity of the political conflict in each particular sector of activity. In many instances nationalisation was forced by the workers themselves who took *de facto* control of the enterprise. Thus, the functioning of ASP was necessarily conditioned by the high degree of conflict in Chilean society at the time. Our analysis will not make this explicit in each step of the argument, but it must be borne in mind as an important constraint on the performance of the sector.

The relative importance of ASP is shown by the following indicators. Between 1970 and 1973 the share of industrial capital belonging to the private sector decreased dramatically from 71.6 to 30.6 per cent, while the ASP participation in total industrial assets increased from 28.4 to 69.4 per cent respectively. The share of ASP employment in industry increased from 9.1 per cent in 1970 to 23.7 per cent in 1973. The gross value of production from 11 to 32.0 per cent. On the other hand, the ASP was generally a sector highly intensive in the use of capital. The capital-labour ratio in ASP was 7 times that of the area of private property (APP) in 1973, but it was only 4 times larger in 1970.

The value of the capital-labour coefficients reflects the fact that the expropriation process was selective in that it included the more modern, capital-intensive industries. As has been shown by Bitar and Mackenna,[24] the latter were in turn often the largest industries and the ones controlling a larger share of production within each particular sub-branch.

Before discussing the results of ASP as a redistributive instrument, let us give an idea of the volume of resources that could potentially be transferred to the government through a nationalisation of industry of the magnitude implied by the previous figures. The National Planning Office (ODEPLAN) estimated that the share of profits over GDP for the state enterprises should increase from 4.9 per cent in 1970 to 10.1 per cent of GDP in 1976, as a result of the rapid expansion in the nationalised

[24] S. Bitar and A. Mackenna, *op. cit.* Figures for 1970 are from the Industrial Census. Figures for 1973 are hypothetical in the sense that they represent an *ex-ante* projection of the desired coverage for ASP, which in fact was exceeded.

sector. These figures include not only the industrial sector, but mining (copper), transport, etc.[25] Since nationalisation was concentrated in the industrial sector, the marginal increase would be mostly generated in that sector. On the other hand, Cauas and Selowsky estimated by means of a simulation model the *net* surplus (after compensation payments, tax receipts foregone, etc.) that the government might get as a result of nationalisation in the industrial sector alone. Under particularly pessimistic assumptions about the negative effects of nationalisation over the rest of the economic activities, their results show that the present value of the net transfer to the government (profits minus reinvestment minus compensation payments and forgone taxes) could reach a 1.4 per cent of GNP.[26]

Both figures are not comparable because they measure different things. On the other hand, just as one estimate is probably on the low side due to particularly pessimistic assumptions, the other one might be too optimistic. The true figures both for "gross profits" and "net surplus to the government" must lie somewhere between the values reported here. What interests us is to point out that the volume of the potential ASP surplus was large. We shall study next to what extent the government was actually able to generate such a surplus and who benefited from the results of the nationalisation policy. The analysis is necessarily short-run, it covers a period of only 3 years and one where political turmoil was an omnipresent factor. Results must be interpreted within this context.

ASP and wages policy

We shall study the course taken by the following economic variables in ASP: wages policy, employment, prices, investment and credit policies. We shall particularly look at the distributive consequences of each policy.

The wages policy was a basic instrument in the income-redistribution programme of the Allende Government. The extent to which

[25] ODEPLAN, *Plan de la Economía Chilena 1971–1976,* Santiago, 1971.

[26] This maximum value could be lower, in fact even negative if no reinvestment takes place in nationalised industries and if compensation is equal to the market value of the transferred assets, rather than a fraction of it. On the other hand, if the maximum potential surplus were realised, government expenditures could be expanded by 10 per cent without causing additional inflationary pressures in the economy. See Cauas and Selowsky, *op. cit.*

redistribution was pursued through wage and salary increases is better understood by looking at functional income shares. The proportion of wages and salaries in National Income increased from 52.3 per cent in 1970 to 61.7 per cent in 1971, the first year of the Allende Administration.[27] This means that when wage changes within ASP are examined, one must bear in mind that those changes were part of a general policy of substantial expansion in wages and salaries throughout the economy.

Within this context it could be hypothesised that wage expansion in ASP could well exceed that in APP. The reasons for this behaviour would lie first in the fact that the power of labour unions in the modern, high-productivity enterprises incorporated to ASP was extremely strong; and secondly that the government, looking for political support from the workers towards nationalisation plans, would be more than willing to concede wage increases even beyond the average increases for the economy as a whole. If that were the case and depending on the relative importance of wage increases *vis-à-vis* the potential surplus that ASP firms could generate, a case could be built in favour of the hypothesis that ASP workers would be the main beneficiaries of the nationalisation policies. Given that the labour force in the modern industrial enterprises comprising ASP consists basically of skilled labour belonging to the middle-income strata rather than to low-income groups, assets redistribution through ASP would be benefiting not the poor groups in the labour force but those relatively well off. This type of distributive effect would be consistent with that experienced in other countries.[28]

What do the figures actually show? In Table 54 we can see the evolution of ASP workers' income *vis-à-vis* that of wages and salaries in the industrial sector and in the economy as a whole.

Table 54 shows that ASP wage and salary increases were way below the average wage and salary increases in the economy as a whole. The figures must be taken with care because coverage is not complete and non-monetary income is excluded.[29] On the other hand, the increase in *per*

[27]ODEPLAN, *Cuentas Nacionales 1960–1971,* Santiago, 1973.

[28]See A. Figueroa, *op. cit.* and P. K. Bardhan, "Country experience: India", in H. Chenery *et al., op. cit.*

[29]The latter was particularly important as part as ASP workers income. It consisted of payments in kind. When the black market was booming (late 1972) it could add substantially to a worker's income. No estimates are available for this component.

TABLE 54

Annual growth rates in wages and salaries, 1970–73

	1971	1972	1973 (first semester)
Wages and salaries	52.1	84.0	113.2
Salaries	52.6	77.4	102.3
Wages	51.5	90.9	123.8
Industrial wages and salaries	53.1	100.9	127.5
ASP wages and salaries[(a)]	28.6	86.0	n.a.
"Old" ASP, wages and salaries[(b)]	51.1	87.9	n.a.
Consumer Price Index[(c)]	20.1	77.8	125.6
Consumer Price Index[(d)]	29.9	107.4	154.8

[(a)] Includes all industrial firms in the ASP sector in the respective year.

[(b)] Includes a sample of twenty-eight firms who were in the public sector before 1970 and formed part of ASP afterwards.

[(c)] The basis is the Consumer Price Index computed by the National Statistics Office, INE (figures for 1973 are those corresponding to the first semester).

[(d)] Consumer Price Index computer by the Institute of Economics of the Universidad de Chile.

Source: Roberto Zahler, *op. cit,* p. 85, and Departamento de Economía Universidad de Chile, Indice de precios al consumidor.

capita income of ASP workers was also lower than the increase in average wages *per capita* in the economy.

The figures, although tentative, do not seem to support the hypothesis of privileged wage and salary increases in ASP. In fact in 1971 ASP workers' income lagged behind other wage and salary increases by a substantial amount. Wages and salaries in the industrial sector as a whole increased by 27.4 per cent in real terms, whereas the increase in ASP was 7.1 per cent.[30] These results seem to indicate some degree of self-restraint on the part of ASP workers at least during 1971, a year in which inflation was a reasonable 20.1 per cent and was pretty much under control. It must be noticed that the 7.1 per cent increase is not far from the raise in productivity which was 6.4 per cent for the ASP in 1971.

Wage increases in the private sector in the order of 26 per cent in 1971 are way out of line with productivity increase, which was not higher than 8.1 per cent in 1971. So that in fact there was a stampede in wages in the

[30] The real wages and salaries have been estimated with the official consumer price index which underestimates the effective increase in prices. The problem is especially important after July 1972.

private sector. The reason for this may well have been that a management, frightened by the prospect of nationalisation, was willing to give in to almost any pressure for higher wages and salaries. The workers, aware of the shift in power in the political sphere, rushed to increase their income share as fast as possible, disregarding other factors altogether.

The direction of changes in workers' income, if not the magnitude involved, do not seem to necessarily contradict redistributive objectives in a statistic sense. For example, it can be noticed that wages grow more than enterprises tended to be even more capital-intensive, on the *average*, than faster than the income of the relatively privileged ASP workers. The time trend of these changes, though, indicates that the initial income gains of both white- and blue-collar workers were particularly lost in subsequent years, particularly in 1973, where the inflation process was of an explosive nature and workers' income could not keep pace with changes in the price level.

It is also interesting to note from Table 54 that "old" ASP firms, that is, those which were in the public sector before 1970, raised workers' income faster than ASP as a whole. In fact the behaviour of those firms in terms of wage increases was not too different from the average including the private sector. The figures indicate that the government was to some extent able to control wage increases in firms recently expropriated, but it could not do so with the traditional public enterprises. The latter, having drifted away from close government control well before 1970 and having very strong labour unions, followed a policy close to that of the private sector at least in terms of wages and salaries.

Summing up, the partial evidence available does not seem to sustain the hypothesis that the main beneficiaries of asset redistribution in the industrial sector were ASP workers, except in the general sense that they shared (for some time) the benefits of an across-the-board policy of workers' income expansion, which was an important element in the overall redistribution strategy.

Another aspect which deserves some attention is that related to intersectoral comparison of average wages and salaries within the ASP.

We can see in Table 55 and the accompanying note that dispersion between maximum and minimum average wages decreases through time.

TABLE 55

Average wages and salaries dispersion between sectors in ASP

	1970	1971	1972	1973
Maximum W & S	125.8	133.8	124.2	130.7
Average W & S	100.0	100.0	100.0	100.0
Minimum W & S	46.8	55.8	54.3	59.2

Note: Figures are index numbers representing the maximum W & S average by sector, the "average" W & S average by sector and the lowest W & S average by sector. In the period 1970–72 the highest W & S average is paid by the energy sector and the lowest by the wood and furniture sector. In 1973 the highest is steel, the lowest fisheries.

Source: Robert Zahler, *op. cit.*, p. 81.

Also that it does have a correspondence with capital-intensity. It is worth noticing, for example, that the energy sector is the one with highest capital-labour ratio whereas wood and furniture has the lowest.

It is also interesting to note that a larger number of sectors have higher than average wages in 1973 (seven sectors) than in 1970 (two sectors). This fact also reinforces the notion that intrasectoral wage disparities within ASP tended to decrease throughout the period, a result consistent with an objective of income redistribution from higher to lower income groups.[31] This change was probably caused partly by a deliberate redistributive policy, but also by the fact that the new nationalised enterprises tended to be even more capital-intensive, on the *average*, than traditional public sector firms.

Employment policy in ASP

Another aspect worth considering here is the employment policy in ASP. The economic policy in the period 1970–73 was an expansionary one. The government applied an economic policy of expanding government expenditures particularly in public works and housing; at the same time private consumption received a boost due to the rapid increase in the purchasing power of workers in general, a result of substantial increases in money wages and price controls. Total employment grew at 5.3 per cent in 1971, as can be seen in Table 56.

[31] No information is available about maximum and minimum wages within each production branch in the ASP. The previous figures refer to a comparison of average wages between sectors.

TABLE 56

Employment: yearly growth rate

	1970–71	1971–72	1972–73
Total employment	5.3	3.4	0.2
Industrial employment	6.6	6.0	4.4
ASP employment[(a)]	12.2	7.1	7.3
"Old" ASP employment[(b)]	14.2	7.2	10.3

[(a)]Sample of ninety-seven firms incorporated to ASP in the period 1970–72.

[(b)]Thirty-nine firms that were in the public sector before 1970 and were later incorporated in ASP.

Source: Roberto Zahler, *op. cit.*, p. 47.

The expansion of total employment was shared by the industrial sector and by ASP. But as Table 56 indicates, the growth rate of employment in ASP was significantly higher than that in industry as a whole. The accumulated growth rate for the 3-year period is 30 per cent in ASP *vis-à-vis* an increase of 18 per cent in the industrial sector.

The marginal increase of ASP employment above the average labour-absorption rate in industry represents the creation of 15,000 new jobs in 1971, that is, a reduction of 8 per cent on total unemployment in the economy. This would be the magnitude of the employment effect attributable to ASP as such, independent of the general trend for higher demand for labour in industry that ASP did not escape. In this sense the figure is rather significant from a redistributive point of view, particularly because most of the new labour force hired by ASP was largely unskilled. Total job creation in ASP compared to the 1970 employment level for the same universe of firms was 37,000, which represents a reduction of 16 per cent on total unemployment.

It is also worthwhile noticing in Table 56 that employment in firms belonging to ASP before 1970 expanded at a faster rate than that in new ASP enterprises (35 per cent *vis-à-vis* 30 per cent). That is, the "old" ASP firms increased both wages and employment beyond the ASP average, with clear consequences in the financial position of the firms as we shall see later.

Another way of looking at the question of the nature of the employment policies in ASP is to explore what happened with labour productivity. Some figures are given in Table 57 although the lack of production figures for ASP after 1971 do not allow us to make a comparison beyond 1971.

Productivity increases in ASP are not significantly different from the average increase in the industrial sector in 1971. On the other hand, the production increase in ASP was very high in 1971. This means that

TABLE 57

Production and labour productivity, growth rates

	1970–71	1971–72	1972–73
Industrial production	14.7	2.8	−5.4
ASP production	14.9		
AVG industrial productivity	8.1	−3.2	−8.9
ASP productivity	6.4		

Note: The figures of production in this table and employment in Table 56 are not comparable because the latter covers only a sample of ninety-seven firms.

Source: R. Zahler, *op. cit.*, pp. 59–61.

probably a large part of the expansion in employment was the result of additional labour demand derived from expansion in output, rather than an autonomous phenomenon.

After 1971 the situation changes. Industrial employment grew again at 6 per cent in 1972 *vis-à-vis* a rate of growth in production of only 2.8 per cent. The situation was even more imbalanced in 1973. Employment grew at 3.5 per cent and production fell 5.4 per cent. Since we know that ASP employment grew at a faster rate than industrial employment and given that the fall in output was very probably of a similar magnitude for ASP and APP, it is possible that productivity fell even more in ASP than the average. The employment policy in 1972 and 1973 was induced by the government in spite of lower output, in order to maintain a positive redistributive impact in low-income groups. Thus, a conclusion in this section is that employment policy in ASP played an important role as a redistributive instrument and that it very probably benefited mainly unskilled low-income workers. The cost of such a policy will be better understood when we examine the financial position of ASP enterprises.

Price policy in ASP

Another variable affecting ASP income distribution is price policy. Prices were in fact used as a redistributive instrument in the period 1970–73 and particularly ASP prices. The idea was to control the general price level while at the same time expanding money wages, thus increasing real purchasing power of workers. On the other hand, a discretionary policy of price controls was established affecting differently wage goods and luxury goods. The prices of the former were rigidly controlled and lagged behind the general price level. The prices of the latter were either free or more loosely controlled so that they tended to move together with the average price index.

Given that the government had an easier control of ASP prices, most of the price discrimination tended to affect ASP firms, as the figures in Table 58 seem to confirm. The figures in Table 58 consist of price increases affecting goods produced by ASP as compared to the price increase in similar products produced by APP. While the former were more closely controlled, the latter were free in most cases.

The figures in Table 58 clearly indicate that prices of ASP products were consistently fixed at a lower level than the general price level and than the prices of goods produced by the private sector. The objective of this manipulation of relative prices was to provide cheap goods for low-

TABLE 58

Price increases for selected products between October 1970 and August 1973

	ASP	APP
Fruit preserves	409	
Powered milk		824
Threads	446	
Wool		1,116
Tyres	62	
Other rubber products		456
Cement	148	
Tiles		1,767
Steel products	302	
Bronze ingots		1,420
Wholesale Price Index: 575		

Source: Roberto Zahler, *op. cit.*, pp. 99–101.

income groups, while at the same time trying to control inflation. Given that many ASP industries produced intermediary inputs purchased by private firms, instead of final consumption goods bought by the poor, probably part of the redistributive effects of price controls were of "perverse" nature: they subsidised high-income private firms' owners.

Large disparities were created in relative prices. The demand for price-controlled products rose beyond the expansion in production, giving rise to rationing through black markets. On the other hand, free prices of goods produced by APP rose beyond the average rate of inflation. Once this disruption in the price system was present, it was very difficult to control who the beneficiaries would be of the price-controls policy. It obviously depended on who had the access to the ASP products and on the extent to which the government succeeded in establishing mechanisms to distribute ASP-produced wage-goods directly to low-income groups. Given the government efforts in this direction, some redistributive effect was achieved, one which is quite impossible to measure, though, given the lack of data. To what extent this effect was wiped off by the need to pay extremely high speculative prices for goods not distributed through official channels is a critical question if the net effect of the price-controls policy over low-income groups is to be verified.

What will be clear in the next section is that this policy had a negative effect on the performance of ASP firms, as measured by the size of the surplus (or deficit) they generated. On the other hand, from a resource allocation point of view, price controls prevented ASP enterprises (or government officials trying to evaluate their performance) from having a yardstick against which relative efficiency could be measured. As a matter of fact the effect of price controls were not symmetrical, even for firms within ASP, let alone in the rest of the economy. To the extent that some firms used cheap subsidised imported or ASP-produced inputs, and others used APP inputs that had to be bought at higher relative "free" prices, it was not possible any more to know which enterprise was deficitary due to "wrong" prices or to lack of efficiency in production. No consistent planning could function under these conditions. Neither could the market perform a role as an instrument for efficient resource allocation. The output loss due to this factor has to be weighted against the transitory gains in income for those low-income consumers that were able to have access to ASP produced goods at highly subsidised prices.

The financial position of ASP firms

We have so far established that the principal redistributive effects of ASP were achieved through the employment and pricing policies of ASP products. It has also been stated that after a good year (1971) when both industrial and ASP output grew at a high rate, the scarcity of raw materials and inputs plus a lack of new investment made it impossible to maintain the rate of industrial expansion in subsequent years, until in 1973 there was in fact a reduction in industrial output of 5.4 per cent. A fixed exchange rate in the face of rapid inflation helped deteriorate the balance of payments, until it became a bottle-neck for industrial production.

What was the combined effect of higher employment, undervalued prices and stagnation or fall in production? As might be expected, the financial position of ASP firms became extremely difficult. In fact ASP firms in all branches of industrial production except the electronics industry were running huge deficits by 1972. As we can see from Table 59, the deficit of ASP enterprises was equivalent to 33 per cent of their total expenditures. The figure rose to 44 per cent in 1973.

Sectoral data given in Table 59 show that the ASP deficit is highly concentrated in three branches: Energy, Steel and Agricultural industries. These three sectors account for 60 per cent of the total deficit. It must be noticed that the first two (Energy and Steel) are the largest of the "old" traditional public enterprises. They were created by the government in the 1940s and 1950s. As we have seen previously, it was in these "old" enterprises where wages rose faster, employment expanded more rapidly and prices (or rates) were tightly controlled. The third sector (Agricultural Industry) is also constituted by "old" ASP firms, although these are more diversified and not so large as the previous ones. Sugar beet, milk products and food imports are the main lines of production here. All these have been traditionally affected by the policy of cheap food prices followed by most governments in Chile during the last two decades. They have been the first in the row of firms applying for government subsidies needed to cover their operations' deficit.

The fact that wage and employment expansion were largest in "old" ASP firms and that these firms were able to finance the increased costs through government subsidies indicates both the degree of autonomy and

TABLE 59

Deficit, expenditures and investments programmes in ASP industries by sector, 1972

Sectors	Deficit	Deficit/ Expend.	Investment	Invest./ Deficit	Invest./ Expend.
Agriculture	1,061	16.6	382	36	6.0
Fisheries	540	47.1	46	8	3.9
Forestry	1,346	51.7	891	66	34.2
Textiles	947	19.0	76	8	1.5
Construction	390	25.1	48	12	3.1
Copper Inds.	436	29.1	18	4	1.2
Chemical	2,117	42.5	168	8	3.4
Steel	3,686	36.6	936	25	9.3
Electrical (-)	66		43	66	7.1
Transport Equip.	184	28.8	32	17	5.1
Agriculture Equip.	279	52.2	17	6	3.4
Energy	4,586	37.7	441	10	3.6
Total ASP	15,597	32.8	3,104		6.5

Source: R. Zahler, *op. cit.*, p. 132.

the power over the Central Government that these enterprises were able to gain through the years. This was the "wrong" kind of autonomy. It did not consist of decentralisation of current economic decisions, like import policies where in most cases the market could have been let free to operate. Decentralisation was in the field of total expenditures, including the use of the surplus. Decentralisation also existed for the enterprise to determine the size of its deficit to be financed by the Central Government!

The autonomous power of the large traditional public firms also showed itself in their ability to maintain a high rate of reinvestment in spite of more than occasional lapses into the "red". To what extent was this an additional cost pressure "explaining" the large deficits observed in 1972 and 1973?

Investment programmes were not a large proportion of total expenditure except in the forestry sector (34 per cent), as can be seen in Table 59. It is thus difficult to "explain" the deficit in terms of excessive expansions in productive capacity by "old" ASP firms during the period we are considering.

The previous analysis suggests the following from the distributive point of view: the creation of ASP implied a transfer of resources away from private shareholders, probably high-income groups, towards ASP enterprises, which were owned by the government.

The resources transferred were mainly used to finance employment expansion in ASP and to cover the difference between rising costs and fixed controlled prices. The beneficiaries of the price subsidisation scheme were consumers in general, with some more than proportional effect on low-income groups due to direct, out-of-the-market distribution of ASP goods by the government to low-income consumers and black market speculators.

The size of the previous transfers exceeded the amount of resources available as a consequence of the asset redistribution scheme (potential profits net of reinvestment and compensation payments). Thus the government could not obtain new resources from ASP to finance redistributive programmes elsewhere in the economy. On the contrary, it was forced to pump resources away from other sectors in the economy to finance the large ASP deficits. In order to do this, it incurred in inflationary financing. Credit to ASP as a fraction of money supply rose from 13 per cent in 1970 to 60 per cent in March 1973; and as a fraction of total credit from 12 per cent to 42 per cent. Again the largest expansion occurred in "old" ASP firms, where credit for the "average" firm increased 3 times as fast as it did in ASP as a whole.

On the other hand, almost 90 per cent of the expansion in money supply was devoted to finance the public sector deficits in 1973, of which ASP deficits were a large part. The fast expansion in the supply of money (1790 per cent between December 1970 and August 1973) forced by the financial disequilibrium in the public sector was largely responsible for the acceleration of inflation. The resulting "inflation tax" was partly a responsibility of ASP. The "inflationary tax" was in fact the main source for financing the deficits in the ASP.

It is very difficult to assess who ended up paying the inflation tax and who benefited from it once inflation accelerates. There is a welfare loss in the economy as a whole. The relative position of income groups will change according to the various defence mechanisms that they are able to develop. But once inflation takes the leading role as a distributive instrument, the relative importance of ASP as a means of extracting a surplus from high income groups and redressing it to the poorer groups decreases in importance. The selectivity and irreversibility of the redistribution process are no longer guaranteed.

7.6. THE LAND REFORM PROGRAMME

A second interesting case in the study of asset redistribution is given by the Land Reform Programme initiated in Chile in 1965 and carried on both by the Frei and Allende Administrations.

Since different aspects of this programme have been described elsewhere,[32] we shall concentrate here in the distributive effects of LR. As was mentioned in the first part of this paper the distributive effects of LR depend not only on the amount of land to be transferred and the form of compensation payments, but also very critically on the pattern of ownership and economic organisation arising from the expropriation process. We discussed the various alternatives grouped under distributivist and collectivist LR programmes.

The Chilean LR programme cannot be firmly classified under any of the preceding headings. The aim of the programme was to create a new form of tenure where individual property rights were combined with collective exploitation.[33] The reasons for this were of various nature, from ideological (a preference for communal or collective mode of production) to economic. The latter consisted in recognising the high cost that might be implied by individual redistribution of land, given the expropriated farms' layout, the availability of infrastructure and machinery, the scarcity of administrative capacity, etc. It is within this institutional context that we must analyse the results of the LR programme.

The importance of the Programme can be better judged by looking at Table 60. Total land expropriated 7 years after the initiation of the Programme amounted to 35.5 per cent of total standard irrigated hectares existing in the country.[34] The expropriation process practically

[32]S. Barraclough and J. A. Fernandez, *Diagnóstico de la Reforma Agraria, Chilena.* Siglo XXI Editores, Mexico, 1974; W. Thiesenhusen, "Agrarian Reform in Chile", in P. Dorner (ed.), *Land Reform in Latin America,* Land Economics Monograph No. 3, University of Wisconsin Press, and several other publications by the Land Tenure Center of the University of Wisconsin. This section has benefited substantially from R. Cortázar and R. Downey, "Efectos redistributivos de la Reforma Agraria", *Estudios de Planificación,* CEPLAN, 1975.

[33]Thirteen per cent of expropriated land was cultivated as individual family plots in 1972. These plots were a part of larger collective farms. Property of the collectives would be transferred after 3 to 5 years to the peasants, associated in co-operatives.

[34]S. Barraclough and J. A. Fernandez, *op. cit.*

TABLE 60

Farm-size distribution before and after Land Reform, in per cent

	No. of farms		Standard irrigated hectares	
Size	1965	1972	1965	1972
Less than 5	81.4	79.3	9.7	9.7
5 to 20	11.5	11.3	12.7	13.0
20 to 40	3.0	3.3	9.5	11.6
40 to 60	1.3	2.5	7.1	14.5
60 to 80	0.8	1.6	5.7	12.8
More than 80	2.0	0.1	55.3	2.9
Reformed sector	0.0	1.9	0.0	35.5
	100.0	100.0	100.0	100.0

Source: S. Barraclough and J. A. Fernández, *op. cit.*

eliminated all private farms larger than 80 hectares. Farms larger than 80 irrigated hectares accounted for 55.3 per cent of irrigated land in 1965, the proportion was reduced to 2.9 per cent in 1972.[35]

As can also be seen in Table 60, LR did not change at all the tenure situation of small producers. Both the number of minifundia and family holdings and the percentage of land owned by small producers remains the same after LR. Some subdivision of land took place but it consisted of very large farms being subdivided into middle-sized farms. This was due to the fact that in most cases the old owner had a right to a "reserve" of land for himself. Thus only a fraction of the old farm was actually transferred to the reformed sector of agriculture.

The fact that the minifundia sector (that below 5 hectares of land) and the small producers (below 20 hectares) were excluded from the benefits of the redistribution of land has immediate distributive consequences. A characterisation of the sector is given in Table 61. Income per person is the lowest for small producers, between 12 and 25 per cent of that of the income per workers in medium-sized farms and a much smaller proportion of large producers' income.[36] Another way of describing it

[35]The concept of "standard irrigated hectares" corresponds to a conversion method established as an attempt to equalize the production possibilities of different kinds of land. A conversion table of equivalents for each zone and type of land was established.

[36]PREALC, *El Empleo y el Proceso de Desarrollo en Chile 1960–1970,* mimeo, Santiago, 1973.

TABLE 61

Characterisation of the agricultural sector, 1965 (Percentage)

	(1) Minifundia	(2) Family holdings	(3) = (1) + (2) Small producers	(4) Medium producers	(5) Large producers
Hectares	0.8	12.2	13.0	13.2	73.8
Employment	21.4	36.3	57.7	16.1	26.2
Gross value of production	13.0	22.2	35.2	22.4	42.4
Capital	6.6	17.7	24.6	23.0	52.7
Index of value added per worker	1	2		8	26

Source: PREALC, *op. cit.*

would be that 80 per cent of self-employed workers in agriculture earned incomes below what would be required to satisfy "basic consumption" needs.[37]

Labour used per unit of land is 12 times as large in smallholdings as in the largest land holdings. This figure must be taken with care though, because labour use is measured here as number employed regardless of the degree of utilisation which is lower in smallholdings than in large ones. Capital per hectare is also higher in smallholdings (2.5 times that of large farms), although the labour capital ratio is 6 times higher for small than for large producers.

Given the previous figures, it is not surprising that output per unit of capital and output per hectare turns out to be higher in smaller than larger farms. But labour productivity is only 0.38 in the former relative to the latter.

These results should be expected. They conform to the type of technological relations predicted in the first section of this paper for small farms. At the same time they confirm that the small producers sector has a low income; that it is highly labour absorptive; and that for equal amounts of land and capital (the same resources) it produces more output, given that it uses more labour. On all accounts it should then be a "target" group for an LR programme: low incomes, high employment,

[37]See A. Foxley, "Redistribution of consumption: effects on production and employment", *Journal of Development Studies,* forthcoming. Also A. Foxley and O. Munoz, "Income redistribution, economic growth and social structure", *Oxford Bulletin of Economics and Statistics,* February 1974.

high output potential. But as we have seen in Table 60, the Chilean LR programme did not alter the position of these groups with respect to the key factor in explaining their poverty status; access to land.[38] This is an important consideration regarding the redistributive effects of LR. We shall now analyse the others.

The sources of redistributive effects will be the following: redistribution away from landowners to the extent that compensation payments do not cover the value of the assets being transferred; redistribution in favour of peasant incorporated to the reformed sector through increases in personal income due to participation in profits and eventually as owners of the expropriated land; redistribution in favour of the unemployed or underemployed if LR expands employment above the average in the agricultural sector; transfers to consumers in general, if prices for reformed sector output lag behind other prices in the economy; or transfers from other producing sectors if prices of inputs lag behind those of agricultural output. Finally, there might be some additional redistributive effects in favour of peasant incorporated to the LR sector if subsidised credit is available to them at favourable conditions relative to other sectors in the economy.

The period for which better empirical information exists is that comprised between 1965 and 1970. Of particular importance for selecting that period instead of the total 1965–73 period was the fact that a survey of farms, representing the largest 1067 farms in Central Chile, was available. The survey had been taken by the Land Tenure Center of the University of Wisconsin before LR in 1965, and repeated again in 1970 after 37 of the 105 farms included in the original sample had been totally or partially expropriated, 27 had been subdivided by private owners and 41 remained as large private farms. The survey, which had not been previously processed, provided a good opportunity to compare the performance of the reformed sector *vis-à-vis* the private sector with respect to variables such as income and employment. Other data, such as compensation payments, assessed value of land, etc., were also available up to 1970 but not for later years. Thus it was decided that 1965–70 would be the basic period for the empirical study of the LR programme.

[38]Although large amounts of public resources were devoted to expand credit, technical assistance, seeds and fertilizer use by the small producers.

The effect of LR on landowners can be measured by calculating the proportion of the value of the expropriated assets that goes back to landowners as compensation payments.[39] Compensation is determined as a function of the assessed value of land. Thirty yearly instalments are paid by the government. Interest rate is about 3 per cent a year, and payments are indexed to inflation but in such a way that only 70 per cent of the payment was readjusted with inflation. This was true for 63 per cent of the farms, that is, those expropriated under the Frei Administration LR law; 37 per cent were expropriated by the same administration under the older Alessandri Law (pending Congress approval of the new Law) where compensation payment was equal to the assessed value of land, with full indexation for annual payments. Interest rate in this case is about 4 per cent a year.

Calculations carried out under alternative assumption about the proportion of land value paid in cash (from 1 to 10 per cent), about the rate of inflation (between 20 and 40 per cent) and about the opportunity cost of capital (between 5 and 15 per cent), show that landowners received a payment in the order of 20–50 per cent of the assessed value of land, the average being 35 per cent. Given that the latter underestimates the real value of land (due to lagged adjustments in land assessments with respect to inflation in a proportion variable from year to year) our figure should be considered as a maximum value,[40] and could in fact be considerably lower.

Once these resources were transferred to the government, who benefited from their use?

Agricultural workers' income

Let us examine first the changes in personal income of workers in the reformed sector of agriculture *vis-à-vis* that of workers in non-expropriated farms. The data originate in the same survey of farms

[39]See R. Downey and R. Cortázar, "Impacto Distributivo del Proceso de Reforma Agraria", CEPLAN, 1975.

[40]To have a more precise idea of the net yearly transfer to the government due to expropriation, we would need to know the market value of land (net present value of future income streams) and its difference with assessed value. Unfortunately lack of data prevents us from doing a calculation similar to that illustrated for ASP.

before and after LR. Individual surveys were conducted to determine personal income. The latter includes not only money income (wages and share in profits) but payments in kind as well.[41]

However, the income figures refer to annual averages for permanent workers only. No information was available about temporary worker's income.

We can see in Table 62 the cumulative growth rates of workers' income between 1965 and 1970 as well as the ratio between this income and the minimum wage in agriculture and the percentage of workers whose income is below a predefined "acceptable" level.

TABLE 62

Land Reform and personal income, 1965–70

	Personal income growth rates accum. 1965–70	Income/min. wage agric.		% of workers below "acceptable" income level[(a)]	
		1965	1970	1965	1970
Non-expropriated farms	0.30	2.7	2.8	78.7	58.0
Expropriated farms	0.45	2.5	2.9	85.7	51.8
Subdivided farms (private)	0.54	2.8	3.4	71.4	29.3
Minimum agricultural wage	0.26				
Minimum industrial wage	0.16				
Minimum salary	−0.07				

[(a)] Acceptable income level is defined as being equal to 2 times the minimum salary. For an explanation of the basis for using this yardstick, see A. Foxley "Redistribution of consumption, effects on production and employment.", in A. Foxley (ed.), *Income Distribution in Latin America,* Cambridge University Press, 1976.

Source: R. Cortázar and R. Downey, *op. cit.*, p. 32.

The figures show an increase in income of permanent workers irrespective of the type of land tenure under which they work. The rate of growth in income is higher than that of average salaries in the economy; personal incomes tend to grow at a higher rate than the minimum agricultural wage.

Income increases reflect to a large extent a government policy at the time, of redistributing income in favour of agriculture *vis-à-vis* the urban

[41] Figures are from R. Downey and R. Cortázar.

sector, by using both the wages structure and relative prices. This redistribution process can be shown not only by the very existence of the LR programme, but also by the fact that the rate of increase in the personal incomes of permanent workers in agriculture exceeded by far the rate of growth of minimum industrial wages or salaries.

Looking at the ratio of income to minimum wage in 1970 as compared to 1965, it is observed that permanent workers of expropriated farms and of subdivided private farms are those who obtain the higher welfare gains. The rapid increment in this ratio is not surprising in the case of workers of expropriated farms who were the main intended beneficiaries of the LR programme, and the even higher increase shown for subdivided farms (from 2.8 to 3.4 times the minimum agricultural wage) may be explained in terms of the "demonstration effect"[42] that the LR programme induced over private producers in general, and the higher efficiency levels brought forth by subdivision.

The distribution of income within all classes of farms seems to have improved substantially, as can be seen from the figures showing a decrease in proportion of workers below what we have called an "acceptable" income level. In the case of expropriated farms, there is a dramatic shift in this ratio from 85.7 per cent in 1965 to 51.8 per cent in 1970 – a fact which shows that a more egalitarian income distribution existed after LR.

The direct measurement of income changes reported in Table 62 does not allow us to say much about the probable trend of income for other groups in the agricultural population who happen to be the poorest. We refer to landless labourers and minifundia owners. Both are the recruiting source for temporary workers. This we can do by looking more generally to the indirect distributive effects of LR, mainly employment creation.

Changes in employment under Land Reform

Employment changes are depicted in Tables 63, 64 and 65.[43]

Table 63 describes changes in the number of persons employed

[42] It must not be forgotten that expanding wages above the average may be used as a deterrent to labour disputes, which may bring expropriation along when a massive LR programme is under way.

[43] More detail on these figures can be found on H. Ortega, "Efectos de la Reforma Agraria en Aspectos de Técnicas de Producción y Emplea", CEPLAN, 1975.

TABLE 63

Employment 1965–70 (no. of workers)

	Permanent workers		Employees		Temporary workers		Total	
	1965	1970	1965	1970	1965	1970	1965	1970
I. Non-expropriated	1,347	1,316	168	167	2,344	1,541	3,859	3,024
II. Expropriated	1,209	1,487	151	5	917	1,643	2,277	3,135
III. Partially expropriated	782	1,049	82	39	1,156	793	2,020	1,881
IV. Subdivided	933	826	120	85	1,425	2,442	2,478	3,353
Total	4,271	4,678	521	296	5,842	6,419	10,634	11,393

Source: R. Cortázar and R. Downey, *op. cit.*, p. 26.

TABLE 64

Working days per year (in thousands)

	Permanent workers		Temporary workers		Total	
	1965	1970	1965	1970	1965	1970
I. Non-expropriated	298	361	82	114	379	475
II. Expropriated	270	432	33	17	304	449
III. Partially expropriated	185	307	63	26	248	332
IV. Subdivided (private)	181	226	63	58	244	283

Source: R. Cortázar and R. Downey, *op. cit.*, p. 26.

according to the various tenure systems between 1965 and 1970. Table 64 describes changes in the number of work-days per year for the categories of permanent and temporary workers.

Total employment in the area affected (directly or indirectly) by LR seems to have increased by 7 per cent, according to our figures. On the other hand, the total work-days increased by 31 per cent, thus indicating that a higher total labour utilisation was possible in 1970 as compared to 1965. Finally, a higher labour-to-land ratio was observed, as can be seen in Table 65.

Before attempting an explanation of these employment effects, it might be worth noticing that they occur in a period in which there is a displacement of labour away from agriculture. Active population in agriculture in fact decreased at a rate of 0.9 per cent a year between 1965 and 1970. The net effect of both changes, that is, higher labour utilisation due to LR and smaller labour force, are the factors behind the reduction in rural underemployment from 17.3 per cent in 1965 to 15.6 per cent in 1970.[44]

A further look at Tables 63, 64 and 65 show some interesting trends in the composition of employment. Permanent-workers' employment rises very significantly, 9.5 per cent in the number of workers employed and 42 per cent in total work-days. At the same time administrative personnel decreases by some 30 per cent (see 'employees' in Table 63).[45]

In the case of temporary workers it does not appear a definite trend. Though Table 64 shows a decrease in working-days per year, figures are not statistically significative with 95 per cent of confidence.

A closer look to disaggregated figures for each type of land tenure will give us a better understanding of these changes.

Changes in the non-expropriated farms take the following form: the number of all types of workers employed decreases between 1965 and 1970, but yearly work-days figures show an increase during the same period. This clearly means that labour utilisation has increased from an average of 98 to 157 days per worker per year.

The lower general level of employment (no. of workers) may have an explanation in the higher cost of labour due to the fast increase in the obligatory minimum wage and the uncertainty created by the expropriation process.[46] Given that the organisation of labour in the rural sector was directly stimulated by the government (a new law was passed to that effect) non-expropriated landowners, fearing that labour disputes might bring expropriation as a consequence, chose to have a smaller, better utilised, higher-paid permanent labour force than a large mass of

[44]See A. Corbalán, "Algunos conceptos ocupacionales en el sector agrícola", CEPLAN, 1975.

[45]Some of the administrative tasks in the expropriated farms were taken over by government officials of the Land Reform Corporation. They are not included in the present figures.

[46]There might be a bias, however, due to the actual timing in the legislation on minimum wages, an effect which might have been already included in the 1965 figures of the survey. The law which equalised minimum wages in agriculture with those in industry was passed in April 1965.

TABLE 65

Labour intensity per hectare of irrigated land

	No. of irrigated hectares		Working days per hectare	
	1965	1970	1965	1970
I. Non-expropriated	15,328	15,328	24.8	31.0
II. Expropriated	15,656	15,656	19.7	28.7
III. Partially expropriated	9,762	9,762	25.4	34.1
IV. Subdivided (private)	10,209	10,209	23.9	27.8

Source: H. Ortega, *op. cit.*, p. 30, and R. Cortázar and R. Downey, *op. cit.*, p. 26.

occasional workers, whose low income and lack of housing, educational facilities, etc., made them specially prone to social conflict.

The net (overall) result of such behaviour on the part of landowners resulted in a slight change in labour-intensity as measured by the number of men-days per hectare (see Table 65).

The situation was quite different in the expropriated farms. Here, the total number of workers increased by 38 per cent and working days per year rose by 45 per cent. The average number of days worked during the year per worker remained virtually constant (it changed from 136 to 143 work-days per worker).

The expansion in permanent employment reflects the government policy, whose goal was to incorporate to the labour force in expropriated farms not only the heads of families permanently living in the farms, but also members of the family which were over 18 years old, as well as many outside workers (*afuerinos*) as possible. The latter objective encountered some resistance from peasants who had always lived in the farm (*inquilinos*) and who feared that too large a number of workers would mean a lower average income per worker. But the net result of these conflicting forces was that in fact the labour-to-land ratio increased from 20 to 29 men-days per hectare between 1965 and 1970. Therefore, expropriated farms had a positive general contribution towards employment levels in the Agricultural sector.

Employment in subdivided private farms grew at a more moderate rate. The land-to-labour ratio does not change substantially.

This is consistent with the fact that a rapid mechanisation seemed to occur in these farms.[47] Let us note that these are small- to medium-sized

[47]See H. Ortega, *op. cit.*

farms, thus not subject to expropriation and subdivided by private owners precisely to it. A preference for mechanisation, and for as small a labour force as possible is apparent. This seems to result basically from the higher cost of labour.

What are the distributive consequences of the employment changes described above? Some have already been dealt with when analysing income changes. But let us sum up some of them.

In general, total figures in the numbers employed, in total working days and in working days per hectare, show that either directly or indirectly the process had a positive contribution to labour utilisation in agriculture.

The main beneficiaries of higher employment were the permanent workers, whose income is 2.5 to 3.4 times the legal minimum, who live in the farms, have a house there and normally a small private plot. Temporary workers on the contrary did not enjoy from this labour absorption. These workers are both landless labourers and minifundia producers. They are both in the lower income scale. Their incomes would typically be around the minimum agricultural wage.[48]

Agricultural policy in the period tried to compensate for the exclusion of minifundia from the benefits of LR by developing special programmes of direct credit and technical assistance to small farmers as well as through improvement in the relative prices of their produce. The results of these policies are analysed elsewhere.[49] But it seems that no policies were designed to deal with the problems of displaced landless labourers. Although such labour-intensive programmes as forestry were carried out, it is none the less true that no massive rural works programme was implemented. Temporary workers in agriculture were the main sources of migration to urban areas, where they joined the ranks of the permanently unemployed in the city.[50] Of course, this is a process non-attributable to LR only, but one which began much earlier and which reflects a historical trend.

Let us also note that the fact that the expansion in permanent employment favoured family members of already reasonably well-paid

[48]Calculated from figures given by ICIRA, ''Relaciones de poder en una localidad rural'', Santiago.

[49]See Chapter 4.

[50]D. Raczynski, ''Oibreza y Movilidad Social'', in CEPLAN, *Bienestar y Pobreza,* Ediciones Nueva Universidad, Santiago, 1974.

workers probably had the effect of increasing the income differential between families of permanent workers *vis-à-vis* that of temporary workers or minifundia producers.

The distributive effect of agricultural prices

The changes in personal income that we have previously observed in the LR sector are explained not only by the general wage policy of the government but also the concomitant employment effects. Given that the expropriated sector was organised as some sort of profit-sharing co-operative, it is obvious that price policies must have played a role in explaining income changes for the sector. This is the case also with large and small private producers. We just saw that the latter were not favourably affected by LR as such, but it might be that if the relative prices of their produce improved as part of the LR policies, small producers might have been better off and in this very indirect sense be beneficiaries from the LR process. At the same time it is interesting to see whether the manipulation of agricultural prices implied some transfer from the LR sector to consumers in general, thus extending the redistributive effects of the new agricultural policies to non-agricultural workers.

In order to consistently examine this problem we have used an existing study of redistribution effects of relative prices in Chilean agriculture by Echeverría.[51] This study incorporates in a comprehensive model all relative prices (including wages) that affect either positively or negatively real relative income in agriculture. Results for the period 1964–67 indicate that the net result of movements in relative prices implied a loss of relative income for large agricultural producers (−7.8 per cent), for small agricultural producers (−1.23 per cent), and for non-agricultural producers (−11.6 per cent). The gains in income were obtained by agricultural and non-agricultural workers.[52]

[51] R. Echeverría, "The effect on agricultural price policies on intersectoral income transfers", Cornell University Dissertation Series, 1969.

[52] See R. Echeverria, *op. cit.* In order to understand better these results it must be established that it was an explicit government policy in the period to improve prices of agricultural products with respect to industrial prices. This was achieved for a short time (1965 and 1966) but the relative gains could no longer be maintained after 1967. On the other hand, prices of imported inputs tended to lag behind agricultural prices all through the period. The consumer price index rose at a rate similar to that of agricultural products.

This result reflects the very rapid expansion in both rural and urban wages and salaries, with a negative cost effect on producers in general. The negative result for large producers in particular is partly compensated by the relatively lower price they paid for imported and domestically produced inputs, a consequence of lagging industrial products prices and undervalued foreign exchange.

If we try to infer what was the net effect of these changes on the reformed sector in agriculture we must take into account that workers' income in the sector is not distinguishable with respect to source (wage and profit-sharing). The workers in expropriated farms perform both the role of entrepreneur and worker alike. What is the net effect of relative price changes in them as producers and workers? If we take Echeverría's results and make the assumption that the relative weights given to entrepreneurial income *vis-à-vis* workers' income is equal for the LR sector as for agriculture as a whole, we arrive at the very tentative conclusion that the net income effect of relative price changes was probably neutral for the reformed sector.

A different picture emerges if price-induced income changes for small producers are examined. Echeverría's results point that there was a relative loss in income for the small producers equal to 1.2 per cent. The loss is explained almost entirely by a deterioration of their produce prices, given that the higher cost of labour has no important influence in this sector. It must be noted that the prices of products typically produced by small farmers increased at a slower rate than agricultural prices as a whole.[53] Thus, again we find that this low-income sector did not particularly benefit from the agricultural policies designed in the context of the LR programme.

The trend after 1967 turned probably against both the reformed sector and small farmers alike. Agricultural prices lost ground to industrial prices and to the cost of imported inputs, although they increased slightly faster than the Consumer Price Index.[54] It is quite likely that the combined effect of these price changes deteriorated the relative position of small producers. The result is not so clear for the LR workers.

[53]The products are cereals (73 per cent), tubercles (19 per cent) and legumes (8 per cent). A price-index with these weights is built. This is the small producers price index. See R. Echeverría, *op. cit.*, p. 361.

[54]R. Echeverría, *op. cit.*, Statistical Appendix.

Although profits in the sector certainly declined, this reduction was at least partly compensated for by the increase in the minimum guaranteed wage paid to workers in the reformed sector of agriculture. If the surplus in the sector would not cover the minimum wages paid, subsidised government credit was readily available as we shall see next.

Credit policy for the LR sector

Expropriated farms had to cope simultaneously with a rapid increase in wages for their labour force, a relative deterioration in their surplus as producers due to lagging agricultural prices and financing vast amounts of investment required to replace tools and machinery taken away by the old owners as a by-product of the way the LR law was passed. To maintain the redistributive effect in favour of the peasants incorporated to LR and succeed in increasing investment, the government resorted to subsidised credit expansion.

The credit policy in favour of the LR sector implied a credit expansion of 180 per cent in real terms between 1967 and 1970. Credits were provided to finance working capital and investments. The first were given for one year, with interest rates of 12.5 per cent as an average and no readjustment for inflation. Loans for investment purposes were fully readjustable with inflation and the interest rate was 4 per cent a year. On the other hand, only 50 per cent of the total volume of loans was paid back. If all these considerations are taken into account, the implicit transfer of resources from the government to the LR sector can be calculated. It was roughly equivalent to 44 per cent of Agricultural Value Added and approximately in the order of 20 per cent of Value Added in the reformed sector. These are considerable resources. The beneficiaries of this subsidy were, again, workers in the LR sector.

7.7. CONCLUSIONS

What general conclusions, if any, can be drawn from the experience with asset redistribution in the Chilean case? Is there a systematic pattern as far as redistributive and employment effects are concerned?

We must first make explicit that neither of the schemes represented direct asset redistribution to poverty groups. In both cases, the State acted as an intermediary and thus maintained the potential control in the use of the resources being transferred. Their use was clearly influenced by the general economic policies pursued by the government, be it the Frei or the Allende Administrations.

Were the redistribution objectives achieved? We saw that moderate income gains for workers in the expropriated enterprises and farms were obtained and that these increases were accompanied by a lesser degree of inequality in incomes within the reformed sectors themselves. The income gains in the ASP sector were smaller than the increase in minimum and average wages in industry. The reverse is true of the Land Reform sector. Given that the initial income of workers in the nationalised sectors was well above the average, the trend seemed to be towards greater income equality for wage and salary earners in the industrial sector. In the Land Reform sector there was a move towards greater income equality *within* the universe of those affected by the LR process.

Another point which is important is that personal incomes in the private non-nationalised enterprises increased at a faster rate than in ASP. For LR personal incomes in subdivided private farms grew faster than in expropriated farms, and in general personal incomes in all types of farms (non-expropriated, expropriated, subdivided) grew at very fast rates. This is apparently caused by a "fear of nationalisation effect" on the part of non-expropriated production units. This factor made them prone to giving in to labour pressures, agreeing to wage increases, irrespective of their effect on short-term profits and general performance of the enterprise.

Who are the groups left outside the benefits of these income increases? It is clear that workers in small industry and commerce as well as the self-employed did not particularly benefit from ASP in terms of income, except through the higher demand for unskilled labour generated by ASP firms. On the other hand, we have already stressed that Land Reform did not affect the tenure situation of minifundia producers and was not able to give productive employment to many of the landless labourers. The groups left relatively outside the benefits of asset redistribution were generally among the poverty groups.

The previous statement does not mean that no effort was made by the

Frei and Allende Administrations to improve the economic opportunities for the poor. In fact, very many programmes were designed to improve education, health and housing facilities for the lower-income groups, as well as to extend subsidised credit, better marketing facilities, inputs and new machinery for small producers. The argument here is that asset redistribution schemes as such did not particularly benefit those groups.

But looking at workers' income is only one aspect of the redistributive process. Another one concerns the changes in employment that occurred in the nationalised sectors. It is now clear that there was a higher employment absorption in the reformed sectors as compared with private. Both in the case of ASP and of LR, the higher employment consisted – basically – of unskilled workers, who also happen to be low-income groups. However, whereas in ASP the new workers were previously unemployed, in the LR area labour absorption took the form of higher utilisation of family labour. The distributive effect in terms of family income of the former could be more progressive than the latter.

The bias in labour-absorption in expropriated farms was strongly in favour of permanent workers recruited from the family ranks, *vis-à-vis* temporary workers, workers which were not directly benefited by the LR process, and presumably would belong to the lowest income strata.

Another set of conclusions refers to the use of prices of goods produced by nationalised enterprises as a redistributive instrument. We saw that relative prices probably played a neutral role in the Land Reform programme (1965–70) and a very active one in ASP. It is interesting to note that the former was able to sustain a good production response, and when there was a deficit it was of manageable proportions. In the case of the period for which LR was studied (1965–70) instruments other than prices were used for selective redistribution. In the ASP experience, on the other hand, ASP nominal prices were fixed so as to benefit consumers, hoping that they would belong to low-income groups. We suggested that although some short-term benefit was probably obtained by some in the poorer social strata, it was short-lived due to the indirect effects of the policy, mainly huge deficits in ASP firms and inefficient resource allocation. Both factors made for a lack of selectivity in the redistribution effects.

With respect to the potential surplus that can be extracted from a nationalised sector, we saw that this effect is not necessarily automatic and does not have to be taken for granted. It is true that the two "negative" hypotheses usually found in the literature, that which states that the surplus will leak entirely to wage increases in the nationalised sector and the other that productivity must necessarily fall, are not sustained by the data, except under special circumstances. Wage increases were relatively moderate. And productivity did not fall in LR firms, nor in ASP firms as long as no major macroeconomic disruptions were present. When these occurred under the form of galloping inflation, balance-of-payment crises, etc., falls in ASP productivity were unavoidable.

Yet, there is a rather consistent behaviour of expropriated enterprises, both in the rural and urban sectors. They tend to overextend expenditure, as a result of simultaneous increases in wages, employment and investment. Firms do not seem to operate under any real budget constraint. The access to cheap, subsidised government credit was apparently an open, unrestricted possibility.[55] As a result of this, both ASP and LR enterprises tended to show deficits although of very different relative magnitudes.

The relative size of the deficit is important if one wishes to know who bears the burden of this particular way of redistributing incomes. If the deficit is not too large it may be financed without resorting to the "inflation tax". To the extent that credit is subsidised and that a larger proportion of the subsidised credit is not used by the deficitary nationalised enterprises, a shift of resources away from private firms towards the nationalised sector is likely.

Quite a different distributive effect takes place if the deficit implies inflationary financing. Here holders of cash balances and "losers" in the struggle for money-income-shares pay the inflation tax. Is this a progressive or a regressive tax? It depends on income levels (money demanded for transactions purposes) and on the financial alternatives offered by the capital markets and the interest rates being offered there as

[55] This is a situation which can be easily improved if the opportunity cost of the use of capital is charged to nationalised firms, as it should indeed be for any firm in the economy. And if some decisions, mainly those referring to the use of the surplus (reinvestment schemes and the like), are subjected to the scrutiny and approval of the Central Government, at least for those investment decisions implying a use of funds beyond a predetermined level.

a hedge against inflation. It is probable that an inflation tax which would be slightly progressive in the beginning would become more regressive as high income groups develop defence mechanisms through the capital markets. The outcome of the policy is highly uncertain anyway,[56] and to a large extent it escapes the control of the government.

What can be learned from the point of view of economic organisation from these experiences? Many points could be raised about this. Let us just briefly mention a few which seem to be particularly relevant. One important issue is whether other alternatives were in fact possible. The main one would be that of direct asset redistribution to the poor. Certainly, that was possible in the case of LR. It was theoretically feasible to subdivide land and give it to individual peasant families. However, the cost of such a scheme (when all infrastructure has developed in the past as a function of a system of large farms) may be too high.

Some argument can also be made in favour of direct asset redistribution to poor groups in the urban sector. The difficulties here are on the implementation side of these programmes and particularly on the question of where do the resources come from to expand poverty-oriented investment programmes. If the tax structure is too rigid, nationalisation of highly productive activities might provide a source of new funds to the government.

The problem with the latter, of course, is how can it be guaranteed that a nationalised enterprise will be run as an efficient productive unit generating a positive surplus and if that is not the case how can its performance be improved. There is a problem of incentives here, which is particularly obvious under mixed property schemes such as the LR programme we have examined, where private and collective exploitation of land coexist in each expropriated farm, simultaneously. The problem is how to design a system of incentives that does not divert most of the productive effort away from collective exploitation. A fixed guaranteed wage on collective work is perhaps the best way to make incentives work in the wrong direction. The same can be said to some extent of

[56]A more complete picture could be drawn if an analysis was done on the relative importance of different types of income-sources (wages, salaries, rent, dividends, independent income, etc.) for the various income-brackets, on the lags that these sources experiment in terms of "keeping-up" with inflation, and on the effects of changes in relative-prices induced by the inflationary process.

nationalised industries. The choice here is probably between collective work and leisure. In order to maximise the former, personal incomes must be closely tied to performance.

Another aspect of interest to improve the performance of nationalised enterprises refers to the role of the market and that of government controls. It seems that the answer is that one should have more of both although on different spheres. A greater role of the market is necessary to guide current economic decisions by the enterprise. A positive role of the price system is very important as the ASP case study suggests. The point has been repeatedly stressed throughout this paper that price controls, when widely used with no co-ordination and consistency with the other policy instruments, do not seem to be an effective instrument either for redistribution or to efficiently guide enterprise decisions.

At the same time, though, a greater role for the government is also needed. We saw that the older public enterprises tended to become more and more autonomous from the government in decisions affecting all groups in society. We referred to their tendency to overspend, charging the bill to the general public through government deficit financing. It is clear that public enterprises should operate under a budget constraint. Paying for the cost of capital is one step in the right direction. The other would be that of imposing Central Government supervision to the use of the surplus, particularly investment programmes by public enterprises.

Under clearly predefined rules of the game, with the right combination of incentives, use of the price mechanism and selective government controls, there is no reason why nationalised enterprises could not as well fulfil their role as other forms of economic organisation. Perhaps the most important role for a public enterprise on a poverty-oriented development strategy would be that of providing net new resources to the government that can be used to sustain redistributive efforts in those other sectors of the economy where the poor are located. For this to be possible, productive efficiency and public control of public enterprises are requisites of paramount importance. These are some of the areas where the attention of economists and policy-makers should concentrate if the redistributive strategy is to be successful.

Index